Chāndogya
and
Brihadāranyaka Upanishads

Two large and difficult Upanishads are presented (without original Sanskrit verses) in simple modern English for those **advanced students** who have read Bhagavad-Gita and other **9 Principal Upanishads**. Simpler important verses are printed in **underlined-bold**; commentaries from translators, references & Glossary.

By

Swami Swahananda
and
Swami Madhavananda et al.

Editor: Ramananda Prasad

INTERNATIONAL GITA SOCIETY

"… Dr. Pr ... difficult to ... gives acces ... ancient sage ... ... book gives us a view of the information which was divulged by those teachers. It is easy to read and understand and will encourage you to delve deeper into the subject matter."

CONTENTS

1. **Chāndogya Upanishad..................** 3
    1. The big famine…………………………….. 6
    2. The cart-man……………………….………13
    3. Satyakama Jabala and Sevā………………… 14
    4. Fire teaches Upakosala…………………. 15
    5. Svetaketu: five questions…………………. 18
    6. Svetaketu: nature of sleep…………….. 22
    7. That thou art, O Svetaketu………………23
    8. Indra and virochana……………………. 29

    Commentary……………………………….. 31

    End of Commenrary…………………………. 55

2. **Brihadāranyaka Upanishad ………..56**
    9. Dialogue: Ajtsatru-Gargya……………..….. 61
    10. Yajnavalkya and maitreyi ……………….…63
    11. Meditation taught through horse's head.. 65
    12. Yajnavalkya: The best Vedic Scholar…… 66
    13. Three 'Da' ………………………………………78

    Commentary………………………………….. 84

    14. Each soul is dear to the other……………..90
    15. The Wisdom of the Wise (Yagnavalkya)… 91
    16. Gargi and the Imperishable ………………94
    17. Janaka and Yajnavalkya 1 ………………….95
    18. Janaka and Yajnavalkya 2 ………………….97
    19. The Process of Reincarnation…… …..… 100

    End of Commenrary …………………………105

A Brief Sanskrit Glossary
On page 844 of 908 of the pdf:

www.gita-society.com/108Upanishads.pdf

*****

Editor's note: Most of the materials in this book are taken from the above webpage which does not have a Copyright mark. We have put in a book format as a service to our readers. Readers may use the materials in this book as they wish.

1. Chāndogya Upanishad

This forms the last eight chapters of Chandogya Brahman of the SamVeda. It is the second biggest of the major Upanishads, next only to the Brihadaranyaka Upanishad.

Translated by Swami Swahananda Published by Sri Ramakrishna Math, Chennai

Om! Let my limbs and speech, Prāna, eyes, ears, vitality and all the senses grow in strength. All existence is the Brahman of the Upanishads. May I never deny Brahman, nor Brahman deny me. Let there be no denial at all: Let there be no denial at least from me. May the virtues that are proclaimed in the Upanishads be in me, who am devoted to the Atman; may they reside in me.

Om! Shantih! Shantih! Shantih!!

1.1.1: One should meditate on the syllable Om which is called the Udgītha. The explanation of Om follows. 1.1.2: The essence of all these beings is the earth. The essence of the earth is water. The essence of water is vegetation. The essence of vegetation is man. The essence of man is speech. The essence of speech is Rik. The essence of Rik is Saman. The essence of Saman is Udgītha. 1.1.3: The syllable Om which is called Udgītha, is the quintessence (heart) of the essences, the supreme, deserving of the highest place and the eighth. 1.1.4: Which one is Rik? Which one is Saman? Which one is Udgītha? This is being considered now. 1.1.5: Speech alone is Rik. Prāna is Saman. The syllable Om is Udgītha. Speech and Prāna, (the sources of) Rik and Saman, taken together form a couple. 1.1.6: This couple is joined together in the syllable Om. Whenever a couple come together, they, indeed, fulfill each other's desire. 1.1.7: He who meditates upon this syllable as Udgītha knowing it thus (as the fulfiller), verily becomes a fulfiller of all the desirable ends. 1.1.8: That verily is the syllable of assent, for whenever one assents to a thing, one says only 'Om'. Assent alone is prosperity. He who meditates upon this syllable as Udgītha, knowing it thus (as endowed with the quality of prosperity), verily becomes one who increases all the desirable ends. 1.1.9: With this does the threefold knowledge proceed; (because) with Om does one cause to listen; with Om does one recite; with Om does one sing aloud. For the worship of this syllable, with its own greatness and essence (the Vedic rites are performed). **1.1.10: He who knows it thus and he who does not know— both perform actions with it. For knowledge and ignorance are different (in their results). Whatever is performed with knowledge, faith and meditation becomes more effective. Up to this truly is the explanation of (the greatness of) this syllable Om.**

1.2.1: Once upon a time the gods and the demons, both descendants of Prajapati, were engaged in a fight. In that fight, the gods performed the rites of the Udgatir priests resolving, 'With this we shall defeat them'. 1.2.2: Then they meditated on (the deity of) Prāna connected with the nose, as Udgītha; the demons pierced it with evil. Therefore with it, the nose, one smells both the fragrant and the foul, for it has been pierced with evil. 1.2.3: Then they meditated on (the deity of) speech as Udgītha; the demons pierced it with evil. Therefore with it one speaks both truth and untruth, for it has been pierced with evil. 1.2.4: Then they meditated on (the deity of) eye as Udgītha; the demons pierced it with evil. Therefore with the eye one sees both the sightly and the unsightly, for it has been pierced with evil. 1.2.5: Then they meditated on (the deity of) ear as Udgītha; the demons pierced it with evil. Therefore with the ear one hears both the pleasant and the unpleasant, for it has been pierced with evil. 1.2.6: Then they meditated on (the deity of) mind as Udgītha; the demons pierced it with evil. Therefore with the mind one thinks both good and evil thoughts, for it has been pierced with evil. 1.2.7: Then they meditated on the Prāna in the mouth as Udgītha. The demons came in clash with it and were destroyed, just as a lump of clay is destroyed, striking against a hard rock. 1.2.8: Thus it is that the Prāna in the mouth has not been destroyed and is pure. Even as a lump of clay striking against a hard rock is destroyed, so will he be destroyed who wishes to do evil to one who knows this (the purity of Prāna) or who (actually) injures that knower, for he is like a hard rock. 1.2.9: With this Prāna in the mouth one discerns neither sweet smell nor foul, for it is free from sin. What one eats or drinks through this, even with that he maintains the other Prānas. And not finding this at the time of death, the Prāna in the mouth and its dependents depart; and thus indeed one opens the mouth at the time of death. 1.2.10: Angiras meditated on that Prāna as Udgītha. The sages consider this alone as Angirasa which is the essence of the limbs. 1.2.11: So Brihaspati meditated on Prāna as Udgītha. The sages consider this alone as Brihaspati, for speech is great and this Prāna is its lord. 1.2.12: So Ayasya meditated on Prāna as Udgītha (identifying it with himself). The sages consider this alone as Ayasya for it goes out of the mouth. 1.2.13: Baka, the son of Dalbha, knew it thus. So he became the Udgatir-singer of the sacrificers dwelling in Naimisa. For their sake he sang to fulfill their desires. 1.2.14: He who knows it thus and meditates on the Udgītha as the syllable Om, looking upon it as Prāna, certainly becomes the singer (and procurer) of the desired objects. This is the meditation with reference to the body.

1.3.1: Now the meditation (on the Udgītha) with reference to the gods is described. One should meditate on him who gives heat (i.e. the sun) as

Udgītha. Verily, when he rises, he sings aloud for the sake of all creatures. When he rises, he dispels darkness and fear. Verily, he who knows the sun as being endowed with these qualities, becomes the dispeller of darkness and (the consequent) fear. 1.3.2: This Prāna in the mouth and that sun are the same. This is warm and that is warm. People call this as Svara (that is going) and that as Svara and Pratyasvara (that is going and coming). Therefore one should meditate on this Prāna and that sun as Udgītha.

1.3.3: Now, verily one should meditate on Vyana as Udgītha. That which one breathes out is Prāna and that which one breathes in is Apana. The junction of Prāna and Apana is Vyana. That which is vyana, even that is speech. Therefore, one utters speech while one neither breathes out nor breathes in. 1.3.4: That which is speech, even that is Rik. Therefore while one neither breathes out nor breathes in, one pronounces the Rik. That which is Rik, even that is Saman. Therefore, while one neither breathes out nor breathes in, one sings the Saman. That which is Saman, even that is Udgītha. Therefore, while one neither breathes out nor breathes in, one sings the Udgītha. 1.3.5: Therefore whatever other actions require strength, such as the kindling of fire by friction, running a race towards a goal, the bending of a strong bow, are all performed, while one neither breathes out nor breathes in. For this reason one should meditate on Vyana as Udgītha. 1.3.6: Now, one should meditate on the syllables of 'Udgītha'—namely, the syllables 'ut', 'gi' and 'tha'. Prāna is 'ut', because through Prāna one arises (ut-tisthati). Speech is 'gi', because speech is called word (girah). Food is 'tha', because upon food all this is established (sthitam). 1.3.7: Heaven is ut, the sky is gi, the earth is tha. The sun is ut, the air gi, the fire, tha. The Sama-Veda is ut, the Yajur-Veda gi, the Rig-Veda tha. For him, speech yields the milk which is the benefit of speech. And he becomes rich in food; and an eater of food, who knows thus and meditates on the syllables of 'Udgītha', namely, ut, gi and tha. 1.3.8: Now follows the fulfillment of wishes: One should meditate on the objects contemplated. One should reflect upon Saman by means of which one proceeds to sing the Stotra. 1.3.9: One should reflect upon the Rik in which that Saman occurs, upon the sage by whom it is intuited and upon the deity to whom he proceeds to pray. 1.3.10: One should reflect upon the meter in which he proceeds to sing a Stotra; and he should reflect upon the hymn with which he proceeds to sing it. 1.3.11: He should reflect upon the quarter (of heaven) towards which he proceeds to sing a Stotra. 1.3.12: Lastly, having thought about himself, he should sing a Stotra reflecting upon his desired object avoiding all faults. Very quickly will be fulfilled for him the desire, desiring which he may sing the Stotra yes, desiring which he may sing the Stotra.

1.4.1: One should meditate on the syllable Om, the Udgītha, for one sings the Udgītha beginning with Om. Of this the explanation follows. 1.4.2: Verily, the gods, being afraid of death, took refuge in the three Vedas. They covered themselves with the metrical hymns. Because they covered themselves with these, the metrical hymns are called Chandas. 1.4.3: Just as a fisherman would see a fish in water, so did Death observe the gods in the (rites connected with) Rik, Saman and Yajus. They, too, knowing this, arose from the Rik, Saman and Yajus, and entered the Svara (the syllable Om). 1.4.4: Verily, when one learns the Rik, he loudly pronounces 'Om'. It is the same with Saman and with Yajus. This syllable Om is indeed Svara; it again is immortality and fearlessness. Having entered into Svara (i.e. having meditated) the gods became immortal and fearless. 1.4.5: He who worships this syllable knowing it thus, enters this syllable, the Svara, which is immortality and fearlessness. And having entered it, he becomes immortal by that nectar, by which the gods became immortal.

1.5.1: Now, that which is Udgītha is verily Pranava and that which is Pranava is Udgītha. The yonder sun is Udgītha and also Pranava, for he moves along pronouncing 'Om'. 1.5.2: 'To him (the sun itself) I sung; therefore you are my only son' thus said Kausitaki to his son. 'Reflect upon the Udgītha as the rays of the sun, then surely, you will have many sons. This is the meditation with reference to the gods. 1.5.3: Now (is the meditation) with reference to the body: One should meditate on him who is this Prāna in the mouth, as Udgītha, for he moves along pronouncing 'Om'. 1.5.4: 'To him (the Prāna itself) did I sing; therefore you are my only son', thus said Kausitaki to his son. "I shall get many sons", thinking thus, sing praise to the Udgītha as the manifold Prānas.' 1.5.5: 'Now, that which is Udgītha, is verily Pranava; and that which is Pranava, is Udgītha', so one should think. As a result of it, even if he chants wrongly, he rectifies it by the act done from the seat of the Hotr priest.

1.6.1: The earth is Rik, the fire is Saman. This Saman rests upon that Rik. Therefore the Saman is sung as resting upon the Rik. The earth is 'sa', the fire is 'ama', and that makes 'Sama'. 1.6.2: The sky is Rik, the air is Sama. This Saman rests upon that Rik. Therefore the Saman is sung as resting upon the Rik. The sky is 'sa', the air is 'ama', and that makes 'Sama'. 1.6.3: Heaven is Rik, the sun is Saman. This Saman rests upon that Rik. Therefore the Saman is sung as resting upon the Rik. Heaven is 'sa', the sun is 'ama', and that makes 'Sama'. 1.6.4: The stars are Rik, the moon is Saman. This Saman rests upon that Rik. Therefore the Saman is sung as resting upon the Rik. The stars are 'sa', the moon is 'ama', and that makes 'Sama'. 1.6.5: Now, the while light of the sun is Rik, the blue (light) that is extremely dark is Saman. This Saman rests upon that Rik. Therefore the Saman is sung as resting upon the Rik. 1.6.6: Again, the white light of the sun is 'sa', the blue (light) that is extremely dark is 'ama', and that makes 'Sama'. Now, that Person, effulgent as gold, who is seen within the sun, who is with golden beard and golden hair, is exceedingly effulgent even to the very tips of his nails. 1.6.7: His eyes are bright like a red lotus. His name is 'ut'. He has risen above all evils. Verily, he who knows thus rises above all evils. 1.6.8: Rik and Saman are his two joints. Therefore he is Udgītha. Because the priest is the singer of this 'ut', he is the Udgītha. Moreover, he (this Person called 'ut') controls the worlds which are above that sun, as also the desires of the gods. This is with reference to the gods.

1.7.1: Now (is the meditation) with reference to the body: Speech is Rik, Prāna is Sama. This Saman rests upon that Rik. Therefore the Saman is sung as resting upon the Rik. Speech is 'sa', Prāna is 'ama' and that makes 'Sama'. 1.7.2: The eye is Rik, the self (reflected in the eye) is Saman. This Saman rests upon that Rik. Therefore the Saman is sung as resting upon the Rik. The eye is 'sa', the self is 'ama', and that makes 'Sama'. 1.7.3: The ear is Rik, the mind is Saman. This Saman rests upon that Rik. Therefore the Saman is sung as resting upon the Rik. The ear is 'sa', the mind is 'ama', and that makes "Sama". 1.7.4: Now, the white light of the eye is Rik, the blue (light) that is extremely dark is Saman. This Saman rests upon that Rik. Therefore the Saman is sung as resting upon the Rik. The white light of the eye is 'sa', the blue (light) that is extremely dark is 'ama' and that makes 'Sama'. 1.7.5: Now, this person who is seen within the eye—he indeed is Rik, he is Saman, he is Uktha, he is Yajus, he is the Vedas. The form of this (person seen in the eye) is the same as the form of that (person seen in the sun). His joints are the same as those of the other; his name is the same as that of the other. 1.7.6: That (person in the eye) is the lord of all the worlds that are extended below, as also of the desired objects of men. So those who sing on the lute (an instrument), sing of him alone and thereby become endowed with wealth. 1.7.7: Now he who sings the Saman after knowing the deity Udgītha thus, sings to both. Through that (person in the sun), he (that singer) gets the worlds beyond that sun and also the desired objects of gods. 1.7.8-9: Similarly, through this person in the eye, one gets the worlds that are extended below this person, and Udgatir priest who knows thus should ask (the sacrificer): 'What desire shall I obtain for you by singing the Saman?' For he alone becomes capable of obtaining also the desired objects of men. For this reason, the desires by singing, who knowing thus sings the Saman—yes, sings the Saman.

1.8.1: In ancient times there were three proficient in Udgītha: Silaka the son of Salavat, Caikitayana of the Dalbhya family and Pravahana the son of Jivala. They said, 'We are proficient in Udgītha. If you agree, let us enter on a discussion of Udgītha'. 1.8.2: 'Let it be so', saying this they sat down. Then Pravahana Jaivali said, 'You two, revered sirs, speak first; and I shall listen to the words of two Brāhmanas conversing'. 1.8.3: Then Silaka Salavatya said to Caikitayana Dalbhya, 'If you permit, I shall question you'. 'Question', said he. 1.8.4: (Silaka asked), 'What is the essence of Saman?' 'The tune', said (Dalbhya). 'What is the essence of the tune?' 'Prāna', said (Dalbhya). 'What is the essence of Prāna?' 'Food', said (Dalbhya). 'What is the essence of food?' 'Water', said (Dalbhya). 1.8.5: 'What is the essence of water?' 'That (heavenly world)', said (Dalbhya). 'What is the essence of the world?' 'One cannot carry (the Saman) beyond the heavenly world', said Dalbhya; 'we locate the Saman in the world of heaven, for Saman is praised as heaven'. 1.8.6: Then Silaka Salavatya said to Caikitayana Dalbhya: 'O Dalbhya, your Saman is not indeed established. If someone one were to say, "Your head shall fall down", surely your head would fall down'. 1.8.7: (Dalbhya) 'Will you permit me, sir, to learn this of you?' 'Learn', said (Silaka). 'What is the essence of that (heavenly) world?' 'This earth', said (Silaka), 'What is the essence of this earth?' 'One cannot carry the Saman beyond this world as its support', said Silaka; 'we locate the Saman in this world as its support, for Saman is extolled as the earth'. 1.8.8: Pravahana Jaivali said to him, 'O Salavatya, your Sama, really, has a further end. If someone now were to say, "Your head shall fall down", surely your head would fall down. (Salavatya) 'Will you permit me, sir, to learn (this of you?) 'Learn', said (Jaivali).

1.9.1: (Salavatya) 'What is the essence of this world?' 'Ākāsha' said (Pravahana); 'All these beings arise from Ākāsha alone and are finally dissolved into Ākāsha; because Ākāsha alone is greater than all these and Ākāsha is the support at all times.' 1.9.2: It is this Udgītha which is progressively higher and better. This again is endless. He who, knowing thus, meditates upon the progressively higher and better Udgītha, obtains progressively higher and better lives and wins progressively higher and better worlds. 1.9.3: Atidhanvan, the son of Sunaka, having taught this to Udarasandilya, said, 'As long as among your descendants, this knowledge of the Udgītha continues, so long their life in this world will be progressively higher and better than ordinary lives.' 1.9.4: 'And in that other world also their state will be similar'. He who knows and meditates thus—his life in this world surely becomes progressively higher and better, and so also his state in that other world—yes, in that other world.

1. The big famine

1.10.1: When the crops in the Kuru country had been destroyed by hailstorms, there lived Usasti, the son of Cakra with his young wife in a deplorable condition in the village of elephant-drivers. 1.10.2: He begged food of an elephant-driver, while he was eating beans of an inferior quality. The driver said to him, 'There is no other food than what is set before me'. 1.10.3: 'Give me some of them', said Usasti. The driver gave them to him and said, 'Here is drink at hand, if you please' 'Then I shall be drinking what is defiled', said Usasti. 1.10.4: 'Are not these beans also defiled?' 'Unless I ate them, I would surely not have survived', said Usasti, 'but drinking is at my option'. 1.10.5: Usasti, after he had eaten, brought the remainder to his wife. She had already obtained her food by alms; so after receiving it she kept it by. 1.10.6: Next morning while leaving the bed he said, 'Alas, if I could get a little of food, I could earn a little wealth. There a king is going to institute a sacrifice; he would appoint me to all the priestly offices'. 1.10.7: His wife said to him, 'Well, lord, here are the beans (given by you).' Having eaten them he went off to that sacrifice which was being performed. 1.10.8: Seeing the singing priests seated there, he sat down near the singers in the place for singing the Stotras. And then he addressed the Prastotir priest. 1.10.9: 'O Prastotir, if you sing the Prastava without knowing the deity that belongs to the Prastava, your head will fall down'. 1.10.10: In the same manner he addressed the Udgatir priest, O Udgatir, if you sing the Udgītha without knowing the deity that belongs to the Udgītha, your head will fall down'. 1.10.11: In the same manner he addressed the Pratihartir priest, 'O Pratihartir, if you sing the Pratihara without knowing the deity that belongs to the Pratihara, your head will fall down'. Then they all sat down silently suspending their duties.

1.11.1: Then the principal of the sacrifice said to him, I should like to know you, revered sir, 'I am Chakrayana Usasti', said he. 1.11.2: He said, 'I searched for you, revered sir, for all these priestly offices, but not finding you, sir, I have chosen others.' 1.11.3: 'Revered sir, you yourself take up all the priestly offices for me'. 'Be it so; then, let these same priests sing the hymns, being permitted by me. But you should give me as much wealth as you give them.' 'Very well', said the sacrificer. 1.11.4: Then the Prastotir priest approached him and said, 'Revered sir, you said to me: 'O Prastotir, if you sing the Prastava without knowing the deity that belongs to the Prastava, your head will fall down". Which is that deity?' 1.11.5: 'Prāna', said Usasti, 'all these movable and immovable beings merge in Prāna (during dissolution) and rise out of Prāna (during creation). This is the deity that belongs to the Prastava. If you sang the Prastava without knowing him, after your having been warned thus by me, your head would have fallen down.' 1.11.6: Then the Udgatir priest approached him and said, 'Revered sir, you said to me: 'O Udgatir, if you sing the Udgītha without knowing the deity that belongs to the Udgītha, your head will fall down". Which is that deity?' 1.11.7: 'The sun', said Usasti, 'all these movable and immovable sing the praise of the sun when he has come up. This is the deity that belongs to the Udgītha. If you sang the Udgītha without knowing him, after your having been warned thus by me, your head would have fallen down.' 1.11.8: Then the Pratihartir priest approached him and said, 'Revered sir, you said to me: 'O Pratihartir, if you sing the Pratihara without knowing the deity that belongs to the Pratihara, your head will fall down". Which is that deity?' 1.11.9: 'Food', said Usasti, 'all these movable and immovable beings live by partaking of food only. This is the deity that belongs to the Pratihara. If you sang the Pratihara without knowing him, after your having been warned thus by me, your head would have fallen down.'

1.12.1: Therefore next begins the Udgītha seen by the dogs. Once Dalbhya Baka, called also Maitreya Glava, went out (of the village) for the study of the Vedas. 1.12.2: Before him a white dog appeared and other dogs gathered around it and said, 'Revered sir, please obtain food for us by singing; we are hungry.' 1.12.3: The white dog said to them, 'Come to me over here tomorrow morning.' (The sage named) Dalbhya Baka and Maitreya Glava kept watch there for them. 1.12.4: Just as those who recite the Stotras singing the Bahispavamana hymn move along clasping one another's hand, even so did the dogs move along. Then they sat down and began to pronounce 'him'.

1.12.5: 'Om, let us eat! Om, let us drink! Om, may the (sun who is) god, Varuna, Prajapati and Savitir bring us food here. O Lord of food, bring food here, yes bring it, Om!'

1.13.1: Verily, this world is the syllable 'hau' (which is a Stobha), the air is the syllable 'hai', the moon is the syllable 'atha', the self is the syllable 'iha' and the fire is the syllable 'I'. 1.13.2: The sun is the syllable 'u' (which is a Stobha), invocation is the syllable 'e' the Visvadevas are the syllable 'auhoyi', Prajapati is the syllable 'him', Prāna is the Stobha 'svara', food is the Stobha 'ya' and Virat is the Stobha 'vak'. 1.13.3: The undefinable and variable thirteenth Stobha is the syllable 'hum'. 1.13.4: For him, speech yields the milk, which is the benefit of speech; and he becomes rich in food and an eater of food, who thus knows this sacred doctrine of the Samans—yes, knows the sacred doctrine of the Samans.

2.1.1: Om. Surely, the meditation on the whole Saman is good. Anything that is good, people call as Saman, anything that is not good, as Asaman. 2.1.2: Thus, when people say, 'He approached him with Saman', then they say only this: 'He approached him with a good motive'. And when they say, 'He approached him with Asaman', then they say only this" 'He approached him with an evil motive.' 2.1.3: Again, people say: 'Oh, this is Saman for us', when it is something good; then they say only this: 'Oh, this is good for us'. Again, they say, 'Oh, this is Asaman for us', when it is not good; then they say only this: 'Oh, this is evil.' 2.1.4: When one who knows it thus meditates on the Saman as good, all good qualities hasten towards him and serve him.

2.2.1: Among the worlds one should meditate upon the Saman as fivefold. The earth is the syllable him, the fire is Prasrava, the sky is Udgītha, the sun is Pratihara, and heaven is Nidhana. Thus this meditation pertains to the higher worlds. 2.2.2: Now, among the lower worlds. Heaven is the syllable him, the sun is Prastava, the sky is Udgītha the fire is Pratihara, and the earth is Nidhana. 2.2.3: The worlds in the ascending and descending lines belong to him. Who, knowing it thus (endowed with the quality of 'good') meditates on the fivefold Saman in the worlds.

2.3.1-2: One should meditate on the fivefold Saman as rain. The wind that precedes is the syllable Om, the cloud that is formed is Prastava, the shower is Udgītha, lightning and thunder are Pratihara, and the ceasing is Nidhana. It rains for him—indeed, he causes rain—who, knowing it thus, meditates on the fivefold Saman as rain.

2.4.1: One should meditate on the fivefold Saman in all the waters. When a cloud gathers, it is the syllable him. When it rains, it is Prastava. Those (waters) that flow to the east, are Udgītha. Those that flow to the west are Pratihara. The ocean is Nidhana. 2.4.2: He who, knowing it thus, meditates on the fivefold Saman in all the waters, does not drown in water and he becomes rich in water.

2.5.1: One should meditate on the fivefold Saman as the seasons: The spring is the syllable him, the summer is Prastava, the rainy season is Udgītha, the autumn is Pratihara, and the winter is Nidhana. 2.5.2: He, who knowing it thus, meditates on the fivefold Saman in the seasons, him the seasons serve and he becomes rich in seasons.

2.6.1: One should meditate on the fivefold Saman as the animals. The goats are the syllable him, the sheep are Prastava, the cows are Udgītha, the horses are Pratihara, and man is Nidhana. 2.6.2: He, who knowing it this, meditates on the fivefold Saman in animals, to him animals belong and he becomes rich in animals.

2.7.1: One should meditate on the progressively higher and better fivefold Saman as the senses; The organ of smell is the syllable him, the organ of speech is Prastava, the eye is Udgītha, the ear is Pratihara, and the mind is Nidhana. Verily, these are progressively higher and better. 2.7.2: He who knowing it thus, meditates on the fivefold Saman, progressively higher and better, in the senses, to him belong progressively higher and better lives and he wins ever higher and better worlds. So much for (the meditation on) the fivefold Saman.

2.8.1-2: Next is the meditation on the sevenfold Saman. One should meditate on the sevenfold Saman as speech. Whatsoever in speech is 'hum', that is the syllable him; whatever is 'pra', that is Prastava; whatever is 'a', that is Adi (the first); whatever is 'ut', that is Udgītha; whatever is 'prati', that is Pratihara; whatever is 'upa', that is Upadrava; and whatever is 'ni', that is Nidhana. 2.8.3: He who knowing it thus, meditates on the sevenfold (whole) Saman as speech, for him speech yields milk i.e. its appropriate benefit, and he becomes rich in food and an eater of food.

2.9.1: Next, one should meditate upon the sevenfold Saman as the yonder sun. He is the Saman because he is always the same. He is the Saman because he is the same to all, for each one thinks, 'He faces me, he faces me.' 2.9.2: One should know that all these beings are dependent on him. What he is before rising, that is Himkara. On this, the animals are dependent. As they participate in the Himkara part of this Saman, do they utter him (before sunrise). 2.9.3: Then, the form of the sun when it has just risen, that is Prastava. On this, men are dependent. As they participate in the Prastava part of this Saman, so are they desirous of praise, direct and indirect. 2.9.4: And the form of the sun as it appears at the time of the assembling of its rays, that is Adi. On this, the birds are dependent. As they participate in the Adi part of this Saman, so do they hold themselves unsupported in the sky and fly about. 2.9.5: Next, the form of the sun that appears just at midday, that is Udgītha. On this, the gods are dependent. As they participate in the Udgītha part of this Saman, so are they the best among the off springs of Prajapati. 2.9.6: Next, the form of the sun that appears just after midday and before (the latter part of) afternoon, that is Pratihara. On this, the fetuses are dependent. As they participate in the Pratihara part of this Saman, (so are they held up in the womb) and they do not fall down. 2.9.7: Next, the form of the sun that appears when it is past afternoon and before sunset, that is Upadrava. On this, the wild animals are dependent. As they participate in the Upadrava part of this Saman, so do they, when they see a man, run away to the forest, as to a place of safety. 2.9.8: Now, the form of the sun that appears just after sunset, that is Nidhana. On this, the fathers are dependent. As they participate in the Nidhana part of this Saman, so do people lay them aside.

2.10.1: Now, verily, one should meditate on the sevenfold Saman, which has all its parts similar, and which leads beyond death. 'Himkara, has three syllables; 'Prastava' has three syllables. So they are equal to each other. 2.10.2: 'Adi' has two syllables; 'Pratihara' has four syllables. We take one syllable from Pratihara to Adi. So they are equal to each other. 2.10.3: 'Udgitha' has three syllables; 'Upadrava' has four syllables. Three and three become equal. One syllable is left over; that really is tri-syllabic; so it also becomes equal. 2.10.4: 'Nidhana' has three syllables, and this too is equal (to the others). These, indeed, are the twenty two syllables (of the sevenfold Saman). 2.10.5-6: He who, knowing this Saman thus (as good), meditates on the sevenfold Saman, which has all its parts similar and which leads beyond death, reaches the sun (Death) by the number twenty-one; for, counting from this world the yonder sun is verily the twenty-first. With the remaining twenty-second syllable he conquers the world beyond the sun. That world is of the nature of bliss, and is free from misery. (That is), he obtains victory over the sun, and then a victory still higher becomes his, who meditates on the sevenfold Saman.

2.11.1: The mind is Himkara, speech is Prastava, the eye is Udgitha, the ear is Pratihara, and the Prāna is Nidhana. This is the Gayatra Saman woven in (the Prāna and) the senses. 2.11.2: He who thus knows this Gayatra Saman as woven in (the Prāna and) the senses, becomes the possessor of perfect senses, reaches the full length of life, lives gloriously, becomes great with offspring and cattle, and great also with fame. His holy vow is that he should be high-minded.

2.12.1: One rubs, that is Himkara. The smoke is produced, that is Prastava. It blazes, that is Udgitha. The embers are formed, that is Pratihara. It goes down, that is Nidhana. It is completely extinguished, that is Nidhana. This is the Rathantara Saman woven in fire. 2.12.2: He who thus knows this Rathantara Saman as woven in fire becomes radiant with the holy effulgence born of sacred wisdom, is endowed with good appetite and reaches the full length of life, lives gloriously, becomes great with offspring and cattle, and great also with fame. His holy vow is that he should neither sip nor spit facing the fire.

2.13.1-2: The Vamadevya Saman is woven in a couple. He who thus knows this Vamadevya Saman as woven in a couple becomes one of the couple and procreates. He reaches the full length of life, lives gloriously, becomes great with offspring and cattle, and great also with fame. His holy vow is that he should not despise any woman.

2.14.1: The rising sun is Himkara; the risen sun is Prastava; the midday sun is Udgitha; the sun in the afternoon is Pratihara, and the setting sun is Nidhana. This is the Brihat Saman woven in the sun. 2.14.2: He who thus knows this Brihat Saman as woven in the sun becomes refulgent and endowed with good appetite, reaches the full length of life, lives gloriously, becomes great with offspring and cattle, and great also with fame. His holy vow is that he should not find fault with the burning sun.

2.15.1: The white clouds gather, that is Himkara. The (rain-bearing) cloud is formed, that is Prastava. It rains, that is Udgitha. It flashes and thunders, that is Pratihara. It ceases, that is Nidhana. This is the Vairupa Saman woven in the rain-cloud. 2.15.2: He who thus knows this Virupa Saman as woven in the rain-cloud acquires cattle of handsome and manifold forms, reaches the full length of life, lives gloriously, becomes great with offspring and cattle, and great also with fame. His holy vow is that he should not find fault with the rain-cloud when it rains.

2.16.1: The spring is Himkara, the summer is Prastava, the rainy season is Udgitha, the autumn is Pratihara, and the winter is Nidhana. This is the Vairaja Saman woven in the seasons. 2.16.2: He who thus knows this Vairaja Saman as woven in the seasons shines with offspring, cattle and the holy effulgence born of sacred wisdom, reaches the full length of life, lives gloriously, becomes great with offspring and cattle and great also with fame. His holy vow is that he should not find fault with the seasons.

2.17.1: The earth is Himkara, the sky is Prastava, heaven is Udgitha, the quarters are Pratihara, and the ocean is Nidhana. This is the Sakvari Saman woven in the worlds. 2.17.2: He who thus knows this Sakvari Saman woven in the worlds, becomes the possessor of the worlds, reaches the full length of life, lives gloriously, becomes great with offspring and cattle and great also with fame. His holy vow is that he should not find fault with the worlds.

2.18.1: The goats are Himkara, the sheep are Prastava, the cows are Udgitha, the horses are Pratihara, and man is Nidhana. This is the Revati Saman woven in the animals. 2.18.2: He who thus knows this Revati Saman woven in the animals, becomes the possessor of animals, reaches the full length of life, lives gloriously, becomes great with offspring and cattle, great also with fame. His holy vow is that he should not find fault with animals.

2.19.1: The hair is Himkara, the skin is Prastava, the flesh is Udgitha, the bone is Pratihara, and the marrow is Nidhana. This is the Yajnayajniya Saman woven in the limbs of the body. 2.19.2: He who thus knows this Yajnayajniya Saman, woven in the limbs of the body, is endowed with all the limbs, and is not crippled in any limb; he reaches the full length of life, lives gloriously, becomes great with offspring and cattle and great also with fame. His holy vow is that he should not eat fish and meat for a year, or rather, he should not eat fish and meat at all.

2.20.1: Fire is Himkara, Air is Prastava, the Sun is Udgītha, the Stars are Pratihara, and the Moon is Nidhana. This is the Rajana Saman woven in the deities. 2.20.2: He who knows thus knows this Rajana Saman woven in the deities, abides in the same world or gets the same prosperity as these very deities or attains union with them; he reaches the full length of life, lives gloriously, becomes great with offspring and cattle and great also with fame. His holy vow is that he should not find fault with the Brāhmanas.

2.21.1: The three Vedas are Himkara; the three worlds are Prastava; Fire, Air and the Sun are Udgītha; the Stars, the birds and the rays are Pratihara; the serpents, the celestial singers and the fathers are Nidhana. This is the collection of Samans woven in all things. 2.21.2: Verily, he who thus knows this collection of Samans as woven in all things becomes the lord of all things. 2.21.3: There is this verse about it: That which is fivefold in groups of three—there is nothing else greater or other than these (fifteen). 2.21.4: He who knows that knows all. All the quarters bring offerings to him. His holy vow is that he should meditate 'I am all'—yes, that is his vow.

2.22.1: 'Of the Samans, I choose the one that bellows, as it were, and is good for cattle,' thus (some think). This is the loud singing sacred to Agni, the undefined one to Prajapati, the defined one to Soma, the soft and smooth to Vayu, the smooth and strong to Indra, the heron-like to Brihaspati, and the ill-sounding to Varuna. Verily, one may practice all these, but should avoid the one sacred to Varuna. 2.22.2: 'May I obtain immortality for the gods by singing', (thinking) thus one should sing. 'May I obtain my singing, oblation for the fathers, hope for men, grass and water for animals, the heavenly world for the sacrificer, and food for myself', -- thus reflecting in his mind on all these, he should sing the Stotra attentively. 2.22.3: All vowels are the embodiments of Indra; all sibilants are the embodiments of Prajapati; all Sparsa consonants are the embodiments of Death. If anyone should reprove him for the pronunciation of his vowels, he should tell him, 'I have taken my refuge in Indra; he will answer you.' 2.22.4: And if someone should reprove him for sibilants he should tell him, 'I have taken my refuge in Prajapati; he will crush you'. And if someone should reprove him for his Sparsa consonants, he should tell him, 'I have taken my refuge in Death; he will burn you up.' 2.22.5: All vowels should be pronounced sonant and strong, (with the thought), 'May I impart strength to Indra (Prāna)'. All sibilants should be pronounced, neither inarticulately, nor leaving out the elements of sound, but distinctly (with the thought), 'May I give myself to Prajapati (Virat).' All Sparsa consonants should be pronounced slowly, without mixing them with any other letter, (with the thought), 'May I withdraw myself from Death.'

2.23.1: Three are the branches of religious duty. Sacrifice, study and gifts—these are the first. Austerity alone is the second, and the celibate student of sacred knowledge, who lives in the house of the teacher throughout his life mortifying his body in the teacher's house, is the third. All these become possessors of meritorious worlds; but he who is established firmly in Brahman, attains immortality. 2.23.2: Prajapati brooded on the worlds. From them, thus brooded upon, issued forth the threefold Veda (as their essence). He brooded on this. From this, thus brooded upon, issued forth the syllables Bhuh, Bhuvah and Svah. 2.23.3: He brooded on them. From them, thus brooded upon, issued forth (as their essence) the syllable Om (Brahman). Just as all the parts of the leaf, are permeated by the ribs of the leaf, so are all the words permeated by the syllable Om. Verily, the syllable Om is all this—yes, the syllable Om is verily all this.

2.24.1-2: The expounders of Brahman say, 'The morning libation is of the Vasus, the midday libation is of the Rudras and the third libation is of the Adityas and of the Visvadevas. Where, the, is the world of the sacrificer?' How can he who does not know this, perform (sacrifices)? It is only after knowing this that he should perform (sacrifices). 2.24.3-4: Before the commencement of the morning chant, the sacrificer sits down behind the Garhapatya fire, facing the north and sings the Saman sacred to the Vasus: '(O Fire), open the door of this world that we may see you for obtaining the kingdom.' 2.24.5-6: Then he offers the oblation (with the Mantra)—'Salutation to Fire, who dwells in the region of the earth. Obtain the region, for me the sacrificer. This region, indeed, is to be obtained by the sacrificer. At the end of the duration of this life, I, the sacrificer, am willing to come here—Svaha.' 'Unbar the door of the region', saying this he gets up. (As a result) the Vasus grant him (the region connected with) the morning libation. 2.24.7-8: Before the starting of the midday libation, the sacrificer sits down behind the Agnidhriya fire, facing the north, and sings the Saman sacred to the Rudras: '(O Fire), open the door of the region of the sky that we may see you for obtaining the sovereignty of the sky.' 2.24.9-10: Then he offers the oblation (with the Mantra): 'Salutation to Vayu, who dwells in the region of the sky. Obtain this region for me, the sacrificer. This region, indeed, is to be obtained by the sacrificer. At the end of the duration of this life, I, the sacrificer, am willing to go there—Svaha'. 'Unbar the door of the region', saying this he gets up. (As a result) the Rudras grant him (the region of the sky connected with) the midday libation. 2.24.11-13: Before beginning the third libation, the sacrificer sits down behind the Ahavaniya fire, facing the north, and sings the Saman sacred to the Adityas and the one sacred to the Visvadevas: '(O Fire), open the door of the region of heaven that we may see you for obtaining the sovereignty of heaven'. This is the Saman sacred to the Adityas. Next is the one sacred to the Visvadevas; '(O Fire), open the door of the region of heaven that we may see you for obtaining the supreme sovereignty.' 2.24.14-15: Then the sacrificer offers the oblation (with the Mantra): 'Salutation to the Adityas and to the Visvadevas, the inhabitants of the region of heaven. Obtain the region of heaven for me, the sacrificer. This region, indeed, is to be obtained by the sacrificer. At the end of the duration of this life, I, the sacrificer, am willing to go there—Svaha'. 'Unbar the door of the region', saying this, he gets up. 2.24.16: The Adityas and the Visvadevas grant him (the region appropriate to) the third libation. He alone knows the real character of the sacrifice, who knows thus.

3.1.1: Om. The yonder sun indeed is the honey of the gods. Of this honey, heaven is the cross-beam, the sky is the honey comb, and (the water particles in) the rays are the eggs. 3.1.2-3: The eastern rays of that sun are its eastern honey-cells; the Riks are the bees, (the ritual of) the Rig-Veda is the flower and those waters are the nectar. Those very Riks (the bees) pressed this Rig- Veda. From it, thus pressed, issued forth as juice, fame, splendor (of limbs), (alertness of) the senses, virility, and food for eating. 3.1.4: That juice flowed forth; it settled by the side of the sun. Verily, this it is that appears as the red hue of the sun.

3.2.1: And its southern rays are its southern honey cells. The Yajus verses are the bees. The Yajur- Veda is the flower; and those waters are the nectar. 3.2.2: Those very Yajus verses pressed this Yajur-Veda. And from it, thus pressed, issued forth as juice, fame, splendor of limbs, alertness of the senses, virility, and food for eating. 3.2.3: It, flowed forth; it settled by the side of the sun. Verily, this it is that appears as the white hue of the sun.

3.3.1: And its western rays are its western honey cells. The Samans are the bees. The Sama-Veda is the flower; and those waters are the nectar. 3.3.2: Those very Samans pressed this Sama-Veda. From it, thus pressed, issued forth as juice, fame, splendor of limbs, alertness of the senses, virility, and food for eating. 3.3.3: It flowed forth; it settled by the side of the sun. Verily, this it is that appears as the black hue of the sun.

3.4.1: And its northern rays are its northern honey cells. The Mantras of the Atharva-Veda are the bees. The Itihasa and the Purana are the flower; and those waters are the nectar. 3.4.2: Those Mantras of the Atharva-Veda pressed this Itihasa-Purana. From it, thus pressed, issued forth as juice, fame, splendor of limbs, alertness of the senses, virility, and food for eating. 3.4.3: It flowed forth; it settled by the side of the sun. Verily, this it is that appears as the deep black hue of the sun.

3.5.1: And its upper rays are its upper honey cells. The secret teachings are the bees. Brahman (Pranava) is the flower. Those waters (the results of the meditations on the Pranava) are the nectar. 3.5.2: Those secret teachings pressed this Pranava. From it, thus pressed, issued forth as juice, fame, splendor of limbs, alertness of the senses, virility, and food for eating. 3.5.3: It flowed forth; it settled by the side of the sun. Verily, this it is that appears as the quivering in the middle of the sun. 3.5.4: Verily, these hues are the juice of the juices, for the Vedas are the essences and these are their essence. These hues indeed are the nectar of the nectars, for the Vedas are the nectar and these are their nectar.

3.6.1: That which is the first nectar (i.e. the red form), that verily Vasus enjoy with Agni as their leader. The gods, indeed, neither eat nor drink, only by seeing this nectar are they satisfied. 3.6.2: They enter into this very form (color) and out of this form they emerge. 3.6.3: He who knows thus this nectar becomes one of the Vasus, and with Agni as the leader, is satisfied only with seeing this nectar. He enters into this very form and out of this form he emerges. 3.6.4: As long as the sun rises in the east and sets in the west, so long does he retain the sovereignty and the heavenly kingdom of (or similar to that of) the Vasus.

3.7.1: And that which is the second nectar (i.e. the white form), that verily the Rudras enjoy with Indra as their leader. The gods, indeed, neither eat nor drink; only with seeing this nectar are they satisfied. 3.7.2: They enter into this very form and out of this form they emerge. 3.7.3: He who knows thus this nectar becomes one of the Rudras, and with Indra as the leader, is satisfied only with seeing this nectar. He enters into this very form and out of this form he emerges. 3.7.4: As long as the sun rises in the east and sets in the west, even twice so long does he (the Sun) rise in the south and set in the north and even so long does he retain the sovereignty and the heavenly kingdom of the Rudras.

3.8.1: And that which is the third nectar (i.e. the black form), that verily the Adityas enjoy with Varuna as their leader. The gods, indeed, neither eat nor drink; only with seeing this nectar are they satisfied. 3.8.2: They enter into this very form and out of this form they emerge. 3.8.3: He who knows thus this nectar becomes one of the Adityas, and with Varuna as the leader, is satisfied only with seeing this nectar. He enters into this very form and out of this form he emerges. 3.8.4: As long as the sun rises in the south and sets in the north, even twice so long does he (the Sun) rise in the west and set in the east and even so long does he retain the sovereignty and the heavenly kingdom of the Adityas.

3.9.1: And that which is the fourth nectar (i.e. the deep black color), that verily the Maruts enjoy with Soma as their leader. The gods, indeed, neither eat nor drink; only with seeing this nectar are they satisfied. 3.9.2: They enter into this very form and out of this form they emerge. 3.9.3: He who knows thus this nectar becomes one of the Maruts, and with Soma as the leader is satisfied only with seeing this nectar. 3.9.4: As long as the sun rises in the west and sets in the east, even twice so long does he (the Sun) rise in the north and set in the south and even so long does he retain the sovereignty and the heavenly kingdom of the Maruts.

3.10.1: And that which is the fifth nectar (i.e. the quivering form within the sun), that verily the Sadhyas enjoy with Pranava as their leader. The gods, indeed, neither eat nor drink; only with seeing this nectar are they satisfied. 3.10.2: They enter into this very form and out of this form they emerge. 3.10.3: He who knows thus this nectar becomes one of the Sadhyas, and with Pranava as the leader is satisfied only with seeing this nectar. 3.10.4: As long as the sun rises in the north and sets in the south, even twice so long does he (the Sun) rise in overhead and set below and even so long does he retain the sovereignty and the heavenly kingdom of the Sadhyas.

3.11.1: Then, rising from there upward, he will neither rise nor set. He will remain alone in the middle. There is this verse about it: 3.11.2: 'Never does this happen there. Never did the sun set there nor did it rise. O gods, by this, my assertion of the truth, may I not fall from Brahman'. 3.11.3: Verily, for him the sun neither rises nor sets. He who thus knows this secret of the Vedas, for him, there is perpetual day. 3.11.4: Hiranyagarbha imparted this Doctrine of Honey to Prajapati, Prajapati to Manu, and Manu to his progeny. And the father told his eldest son Uddalaka Aruni this very knowledge of Brahman. 3.11.5: A father may declare to his eldest son or to any other worthy disciple this very knowledge of Honey. 3.11.6: And not to any one else, even if one should offer him this sea-girt earth filled with wealth. This (doctrine) is certainly greater than that. This certainly is greater than that.

3.12.1: Gayatri indeed is all this, whatever being exists. Speech indeed is Gayatri; for speech indeed sings and removes fear of all this that exists. 3.12.2: That which is this Gayatri, even that is this earth; for on this earth are all the beings established and they do not transcend it.

3.12.3: That which is this earth (as Gayatri), even that is this, i.e. this body in respect of this person; for these senses are indeed established in this body and they do not transcend it. 3.12.4: That which is the body in respect of a person, even that is identical with) the heart within this body; for these senses are indeed established in it and they do not transcend it. 3.12.5: This well-known Gayatri is four footed and six fold. The Gayatri Brahman is thus expressed in the following Rik: 3.12.6: Such is the greatness of this (Brahman called Gayatri). The Person is even greater than this. All this world is a quarter of Him, the other three quarters of His constitute immortality in heaven. 3.12.7-9: That which is (designated as) Brahman, even that is this Ākāsha outside the body. That which is the Ākāsha outside the body, even that is the Ākāsha inside the body. That which is the Ākāsha inside the body, even that is this Ākāsha within the (lotus of the) heart. This Brahman is all-pervading and unchanging. He who knows (Brahman) thus, gets all-filling and unchanging prosperity.

3.13.1: Of the said heart, there are, indeed, five doors guarded by the gods. (He who is in) that which is the eastern door of this, is Prāna. He is the eye, he is the sun. This (Brahman called Prāna) should be meditated upon as brightness and as the source of food. He who meditates thus, becomes resplendent and an eater of food. 3.13.2: And (he who is in) that which is the southern door of this (heart), is Vyana. He is the ear, he is the moon. This (Brahman called Vyana) should be meditated upon as prosperity and fame. He who meditates thus becomes prosperous and famous. 3.13.3: And (he who is in) that which is the western door of this (heart), is Apana. He is speech, he is fire. This (Brahman called Apana) should be meditated upon as the holy effulgence born of sacred wisdom and as the source of food. He who meditates thus becomes radiant with the holy effulgence born of sacred wisdom and also an eater of food. 3.13.4: And (he who is in) that which is the northern door of this (heart), is Samana. He is the mind, he is Parjanya (the rain-god). This (Brahman called Samana) should be meditated upon as fame and grace. He who meditates thus becomes famous and graceful. 3.13.5: And (he who is in) that which is the upper door of this (heart), is Udana. He is the air, he is the Ākāsha. This (Brahman called Udana) should be meditated upon as strength and nobility. He who meditates thus becomes strong and noble. 3.13.6: These, verily, are the five persons under Brahman, the sentinels of the heavenly world. He who adores thus these five persons under Brahman, the sentinels of the heavenly world, in his family is a hero born. He who adores thus these five persons under Brahman, the sentinels of the heavenly world, reaches the heavenly world. 3.13.7: Again, the light of Brahman that shines above this heaven, above everything, above all, in the incomparably good and the highest worlds, even this is the light within the body of man. This light can be seen inasmuch as one has a perception of warmth when one touches the body. It can be heard inasmuch as, on closing the ears, one hears something like the sound of a chariot or the bellowing of a bull, or the sound of a blazing fire. One should meditate on the light as seen and heard. One who meditates on this thus, becomes beautiful and illustrious—yes, one who meditates thus.

3.14.1: Verily, all this universe is Brahman. From Him do all things originate, into Him do they dissolve and by Him are they sustained. On Him should one meditate in tranquility. For as is one's faith, such indeed one is; and as is one's faith in this world, such one becomes on departing hence. Let one, therefore, cultivate faith. 3.14.2-3: He, who is permeating the mind, who has Prāna for his body, whose nature is consciousness, whose resolve is infallible, whose own form is like Ākāsha, whose creation is all that exists, whose are all the pure desires, who possesses all the agreeable odors and all the pleasant tastes, who exists pervading all this, who is without speech (and other senses), who is free from agitation and eagerness—this my Atman, residing in (the lotus of) the heart—is smaller than a grain of paddy, than a barley corn, than a mustard seed, than a grain of millet or than the kernel of a grain of millet. This my Atman residing in (the lotus of) the heart is greater than the earth, greater than the sky, greater than heaven, greater than all these worlds. 3.14.4: He, whose creation is all that exists, whose are all the pure desires, who possesses all the agreeable odors and all the pleasant tastes, who exists pervading all this, who is without speech (and other senses), who is free from agitation and eagerness, He is my Atman residing in (the lotus of) the heart; He is Brahman. On departing hence I shall attain to His being. He alone who possesses this faith and has no doubt about it (will obtain the result). Thus declared Sandilya — yes, Sandilya.

3.15.1: The chest (i.e. the universe), having the sky as its hollow and the earth for its (curved) bottom, does not decay. The quarters are indeed its corners and heaven its upper lid. This well-known chest is the container of wealth. All things rest in it. 3.15.2: Of that chest, the eastern quarter is named Juhu, the southern is named Sahamana, the western is named Rajni and the northern is named Subhuta. The air is their calf. He who knows this air, the calf of the quarters, thus (as immortal), never weeps in mourning for his son. I, wishing my son's, longevity, worship thus this air, the calf of the quarters. May I never weep to mourn my son. 3.15.3: I take refuge in the imperishable chest for such and such and such. I take refuge in Prāna for such and such and such. I take refuge in Bhuh for such and such and such. I take refuge in Bhuvah for such and such and such. I take refuge in Svah for such and such and such. 3.15.4: When I said, 'I take refuge in Prāna', (it was because) all these beings, whatsoever exist, are indeed Prāna. So it was in this alone that I took refuge. 3.15.5: Then when I said, 'I take refuge in Bhuh', I said only this: 'I take refuge in the earth, I take refuge in the sky, I take refuge in heaven'. 3.15.6: Then when I said, 'I take refuge in Bhuvah', I said only this: 'I take refuge in Fire, I take refuge in Air, I take refuge in the Sun.' 3.15.7: Then, when I said, 'I take refuge in Svah', I said only this: 'I take refuge in the Rig-Veda, I take refuge in the Yajur-Veda, I take refuge in the Sama-Veda'—yes, that was what I said.

3.16.1: Man, truly, is the sacrifice. His (first) twenty-four years are the morning libation, for the meter Gayatri is made up of twenty-four syllables, and the morning libation is related to the Gayatri meter. With this the Vasus are connected. The Prānas indeed are the Vasus, for they make all this stable. 3.16.2: During this period of life if anything (e.g. illness) causes him pain, he should repeat: 'O Prānas, Vasus, unite this morning libation of mind with the midday libation. May I who am a sacrifice not be lost in the midst of the Vasus who are the Prānas'. He surely recovers from that and becomes healthy. 3.16.3: Now, (his next) forty-four years are the mid-day libation, (for) the meter Tristubh is made up of forty-four syllables, and the mid-day libation is related to the Tristubh meter. With this, the Rudras are connected. The Prānas indeed are the Rudras, for they cause all this (universe) to weep. 3.16.4: During this period of life if anything (e.g. illness) causes him pain, he should repeat: 'O Prānas, Rudras, unite this mid-day libation of mine with the third libation. May I, who am a sacrifice, not be lost in the midst of the Rudras who are the Prānas'. He surely recovers from that and becomes healthy. 3.16.5: Then (his next) forty-eight years are the third libation. The meter Jagati is made up of forty-eight syllables and the third libation is related to the Jagati meter. With this, the Adityas are connected. The Prānas indeed are the Adityas, for they accept all this. 3.16.6: During this period of life if anything (e.g. illness) causes him pain, he should repeat: 'O Prānas, Adityas, extend this third libation of mine to a full length of life. May I, who am a sacrifice, not be lost in the midst of the Adityas who are the Prānas.' He surely recovers from that and becomes healthy. 3.16.7: Knowing this well-known (doctrine of sacrifice) Aitareya Mahidasa said, 'Why do you afflict me thus, me who cannot be so killed.' He lived for one hundred and sixteen years. He, too, who knows thus, lives in vigor for one hundred and sixteen years.

3.17.1: That he (who performs the Purusha sacrifice) feels hunger, that he feels thirst, that he does not rejoice —all these are the initiatory rites of this sacrifice. 3.17.2: And, that he eats that he drinks, that he rejoices—all these approach Upasadas. 3.17.3: And, that he laughs, that he eats, that he behaves as one of a couple—all these approach Stotra and Sastra. 3.17.4: And his austerity, gifts, uprightness, non-violence, and truthfulness—all these are the largesse of this sacrifice. 3.17.5: Therefore people say 'sosyati' (will procreate), and 'asosta' (has procreated). Again, that is the procreation of this, and death is the Avabhrita bath. 3.17.6: Ghora Angirasa expounded this well-known doctrine to Devaki's son Krishna and said, 'Such a knower should, at the time of death, repeat this triad—"Thou art the imperishable, Thou art unchangeable, Thou art the subtle essence of Prāna". (On hearing the above) he became thirst-less. There are these two Rik stanzas in regard to this.

3.17.7: Those knowers of Brahman (who have purified their mind through the withdrawal of the senses and other means like Brahmacharya) see everywhere the supreme light of the ancient One who is the seed of the universe and the light that shines in the Effulgent Brahman. May we too having perceived the highest light which dispels darkness, reach it. Having perceived the highest light in our own heart we have reached that highest Light which is the dispenser of water, rays of light and the Prānas shining in all gods—we have reached that highest light.

It is the light of the Supreme Being that is in the eternal light and in all the luminaries of the galaxies, such as the sun, the moon, and the stars. It is His light that is in wood, lamps, candles, and is the energy in all living beings. His light is behind all lights and the source of all energy in the universe.

3.18.1: The mind is Brahman, thus one should meditate—this is (the meditation) with regard to the body (including the mind). Next, the meditation with regard to the gods—the Ākāsha is Brahman, thus (one should meditate). Both the meditations, with regard to the body and with regard to the gods are being enjoined. 3.18.2: This same Brahman has four feet. The organ of speech is one foot. Prāna (the organ of smell) is one foot, the eye is one foot and the ear is one foot. This is with reference to the body. Next, with reference to the gods. Agni is one foot, Vayu is one foot, Aditya is one foot and the quarters are one foot. Thus both the meditations, with reference to the body and with reference to the gods, are enjoined. 3.18.3: The organ of speech is one of the four feet of Brahman (called Mind). With the light of fire it shines and warms. He who knows thus, shines and warms with fame and celebrity and with the holy effulgence born of sacred wisdom. 3.18.4: The organ of smell is one of the four feet of Brahman. With the light of air it shines and warms. He who knows thus, shines and warms with fame and celebrity and with the holy effulgence born of sacred wisdom. 3.18.5: The eye is one of the four feet of Brahman. With the light of the sun it shines and warms. He who knows thus, shines and warms with fame and celebrity and with the holy effulgence born of sacred wisdom. 3.18.6: The ear is one of the four feet of Brahman. With the light of the quarters it shines and warms. He who knows thus, shines and warms with fame and celebrity and with the holy effulgence born of sacred wisdom.

3.19.1: The Sun is Brahman—this is the teaching. The further explanation of this (is here given). Before creation, this universe was non-existent. Then it became existent. It grew; it turned into an egg; it lay for a period of one year; (and then) it burst open. Of the two halves of that egg-shell, one was of silver and the other of gold. 3.19.2: Of these, that which was of silver is this earth. That which was of gold is heaven. That which was the outer membrane is the mountains. That which was the inner membrane is the mist together with the clouds. Those which were the veins are the rivers. That which was the water in the lower belly is the ocean. 3.19.3: And that which was born is the yonder sun. After he was born, sounds of the form of loud shouts arose, as also all beings and all desired objects. Therefore at his rise and his every return (or his setting), sounds of the form of loud shouts arise, as also all beings and all desired objects. 3.19.4: He who knows the Sun thus and meditates on it as Brahman, auspicious sounds will hasten to him and continue to delight him—yes, will continue to delight.

2. The cart-man

4.1.1: Om. There lived Janasruti Pautrayana who made gifts with respect, who gave liberally, and who had much food cooked (for others). He built rest-houses all round, thinking, 'Everywhere people will eat of my food'. 4.1.2: Once at night, the swans flew along. Then one swan addressed another swan thus, 'Ho, Ho, O Bhallaksa, Bhallaksa, the effulgence of Janasruti Pautrayana has spread like the heaven. Do not come in touch with it, lest it should scorch you.' 4.1.3: Bhallaksa replied to him, 'lo, how could you so describe him as if he were Raikva with the cart?' 'Of what sort is this Raikva with the cart?' 4.1.4: 'Just as all the lower casts of the dice go over to one who has won the Krita-cast, so does go over to Raikva whatsoever good the creatures do; so also to him who knows what Raikva knows. Such is he who has thus been spoken of by me.' 4.1.5-6: Janasruti Pautrayana overheard those words. As soon as he arose, he said to the attendant, 'Lo, did you praise me like Raikva with the cart?' 'What sort of man is this Raikva with the cart?' (Janasruti repeated the words of the swan): 'Just as all the lower casts of the dice go over to one who has won the Krita-cast, so does go over to Raikva whatsoever good the creatures do; and so also to him who knows what Raikva knows. Such is he who has thus been spoken of by me'. 4.1.7: The attendant, having searched for him, came back thinking, 'I could not find him'. Janasruti said to him, 'Well, where the knower of Brahman should be searched, search there for him'. 4.1.8: (After searching) he came to a man sitting under a cart and scratching eruptions on his skin and, sitting near him, asked him, 'Revered sir, are you Raikva with the cart?' 'Well fellow, yes, I am', he admitted. Thinking 'I have found him', the attendant returned.

4.2.1-2: On hearing this, Janasruti Pautrayana took with him six hundred cows, a gold necklace, and a chariot drawn by mules and went to Raikva and addressed him thus: 'O Raikva, (here are for you) these six hundred cows, this gold necklace, and this chariot drawn by mules. Now, revered sir, instruct me about the deity whom you worship.' 4.2.3: The other man answered him thus: 'Ah, O Shudra, let this gold necklace together with the chariot and the cows remain with you.' Thereupon Janasruti Pautrayana again took with him one thousand cows, a gold necklace, a chariot drawn by mules and his daughter and went over to Raikva. 4.2.4: Janasruti said to him: 'O Raikva, (here are for you) these one thousand cows, this gold necklace, this chariot drawn by mules, this wife, and this village in which you reside. Now, revered sir, please instruct me'. 4.2.5: Taking that princess to be the portal for the conveying of knowledge, Raikva said, 'O Shudra, you have brought all these! Even by this means (i.e. the princess) you will make me talk.' The king gave away to him all those villages in the Mahavrisa country known as Raikvaparna where Raikva lived. Raikva said to him:

4.3.1: Air indeed is the absorber. For when a fire goes out, it is in air that it merges; when the sun sets, it is in air that it merges; when the moon sets, it is in air that it merges.

4.3.2: When water dries up, it is in air that it merges; for air absorbs all these. This is (the doctrine of Samvarga) with reference to the gods. 4.3.3: Next is (the doctrine of Samvarga) with reference to the body: Prāna indeed is the absorber. When one sleeps, speech merges in Prāna, the eye merges in Prāna, the ear merges in Prāna, the mind merges in Prāna: for Prāna, indeed, absorbs all these. 4.3.4: These, indeed, are the two absorbers: Air among the gods and Prāna among the sense-organs. 4.3.5: Once upon a time, while Kapeya Saunaka and Kaksaseni Abhipratarin were being served with food, a celibate student of sacred knowledge begged of them. They did not give him anything. 4.3.6: The Brahmacharin said, 'Prajapati, the one god swallowed up the four great ones; he is the protector of the worlds. O Kapeya, O Abhipratarin, mortals do not see him who dwells variously. Even from him, for whom all this food is meant, you have withheld it.' 4.3.7: Kapeya Saunaka, reflecting on those words, approached him (and said): 'He who is the self of all gods and the creator of all beings, who has undecaying teeth, who is the devourer, who is the wise one, who is himself never eaten (but) who devours even those who are not food; and hence (the knowers) describe his magnificence as immeasurable—such, indeed, is the Brahman, O Brahmacharin, whom we worship'. (Then he told the servants): 'Give him food'. 4.3.8: They gave him food. Now, these five and the other five, together becoming ten, constitute the Krita (dice-cast). Therefore (i.e. because the number ten applies to both), these ten are the food or Virat dwelling in all the ten quarters, and these are (the enjoyer) Krita. This Virat, of the form of ten deities, again, is the eater of food (as Krita); by him all this is perceived. He who sees thus, by him also all this is perceived, and he becomes as eater of food.

3 Satyakama Jabala and Seva

4.4.1: Once upon a time Satyakama Jabala addressed his mother Jabala, 'Mother, I desire to live the life of a celibate student of sacred knowledge in the teacher's house. Of what lineage am I?' 4.4.2: She said to him, 'My child, I do not know of what lineage you are. I, who was engaged in many works and in attending on others, got you in my youth. Having been such I could not know of what lineage you are. However, I am Jabala by name and you are named Satyakama. So you speak of yourself only as Satyakama Jabala.' 4.4.3: He went to Haridrumata Gautama and said, 'I desire to live under you, revered sir, as a Brahmacharin; may I approach your venerable self (for the same)?' 4.4.4: Gautama asked him, 'Dear boy, of what lineage are you?' He replied, 'Sir, I do not know of what lineage I am. I asked my mother; she replied, "I, who was engaged in many works and in attending on others, got you in my youth. Having been such, I could not know of what lineage you are. However, I am Jabala by name and you are named Satyakama". So, sir, I am Satyakama Jabala.' 4.4.5: The teacher said to him, 'No one who is not a Brāhmana can speak thus. Dear boy, bring the sacrificial fuel, I shall initiate you as a Brahmacharin, for you have not deviated from truth'. Having initiated him, he sorted out four hundred lean and weak cows and said, 'Dear boy, follow them.' While he was driving them towards the forest Satyakama said, 'I shall not return till it is one thousand.' He lived away for a long time, till they had increased to one thousand.

4.5.1: Then the bull addressed him thus, 'Satyakama!' 'Yes, revered sir', thus he responded, 'Dear boy, we have reached a thousand, take us to the house of the teacher.' 4.5.2: 'Let me instruct you about one foot of Brahman also'. 'Please instruct me, revered sir.' (The bull) said to him, 'The eastern quarter (or direction) is one part, the western quarter is one part, the southern quarter is one part, the northern quarter is one part. This indeed, dear boy, is one foot of Brahman, consisting of four, named the Radiant. 4.5.3: 'He who knows this one foot of Brahman consisting of four parts thus, and meditates on it as the Radiant, becomes radiant in this world. He who knows this one foot of Brahman consisting of four parts thus, and meditates

Chāndogya Upanishad

on it as the Radiant, wins the radiant regions (in the next world).'

4.6.1: 'Fire will tell you of one foot of Brahman'. At dawn of the next day he drove the cows towards the teacher's house. Towards evening, at the place where those cows came together, he kindled the fire there, penned the cows, laid on fuel and sat down near them behind the fire, facing the east. 4.6.2: The fire addressed him, 'Satyakama!' 'Yes, revered sir', he responded. 4.6.3: 'Dear boy, let me instruct you about one foot of Brahman'. 'Please instruct me, revered sir.' (The fire) said to him, 'The earth is one part, the sky is one part, heaven is one part, and the ocean is one part. This indeed, dear boy, is one foot of Brahman, consisting of four parts, named the Endless. 4.6.4: 'He who knows this one foot of Brahman consisting of four parts thus, and meditates on it as the Endless, becomes endless in this world. He who knows this one foot of Brahman consisting of four parts thus, and meditates on it as the Endless, wins the endless (undecaying) regions.'

4.7.1: 'The swan will tell you of one foot of Brahman'. At dawn of the next day, he drove the cows towards the teacher's house. Towards evening, at the place where the cows came together, he kindled the fire there, penned the cows, laid on fuel and sat down near them behind the fire facing the east. 4.7.2: The swan flew to him and addressed him, 'Satyakama!' 'Yes, revered sir', he responded. 4.7.3: 'Dear boy, let me instruct you about one foot of Brahman'. 'Please instruct me revered sir.' (The swan) said to him, 'Fire is one part, the sun is one part, the moon is one part, and lightning is one part. This indeed, dear boy, is one foot of Brahman, consisting of four parts, named the Effulgent. 4.7.4: 'He who knows this one foot of Brahman consisting of four parts thus, and meditates on it as the Effulgent, becomes effulgent in this world. He who knows this one foot of Brahman consisting of four parts thus, and meditates on it as the Effulgent, wins the effulgent regions (of the sun, the moon, etc., in the next world).'

4.8.1: 'Madgu will tell you of one foot of Brahman'. At dawn of the next day, he drove the cows towards the teacher's house. Towards evening at the place where the cows came together, he kindled the fire there, penned the cows, laid on fuel and sat down near them behind the fire facing the east. 4.8.2: The Madgu bird flew to him and addressed him, 'Satyakama!' 'Yes, revered sir', he responded. 4.8.3: 'Dear boy, let me instruct you about one foot of Brahman'. 'Please instruct me, revered sir'. (The Madgu bird) said to him, 'Prāna is one part, the eye is one part, the ear is one part, and the mind is one part. This indeed, dear boy, is one foot of Brahman, consisting of four parts, named the Repository. 4.8.4: 'He who knows this one foot of Brahman consisting of four parts thus, and meditates on it as the Repository, becomes repository (i.e. with proper abode) in this world. He who knows this one foot of Brahman consisting of four parts thus, and meditates on it as the Repository, wins the repository (i.e. extensive) regions (in the next world).'

4.9.1: Satyakama reached the house of the teacher. The teacher addressed him, 'Satyakama!' 'Yes, revered sir', he responded. 4.9.2: 'Dear boy, you shine like a knower of Brahman; who is it that has instructed you?' Satyakama assured him, 'People other than men. But I wish, revered sir, that you would expound it to me. 4.9.3: 'I have definitely heard from persons like your venerable self that the knowledge directly learnt from one's own teacher becomes most beneficial'. The teacher taught him the same thing, and nothing was omitted from this—yes, nothing was omitted.

4. Fire teaches Upakosala

4.10.1: Once upon a time Upakosala Kamalayana lived with Satyakama Jabala the life of a Brahmacharin. He tended his fires for twelve years. Satyakama performed for other disciples the ceremony of completing studies and returning home, but did not perform the ceremony for Upakosala. 4.10.2: The wife of the teacher said to him, 'This Brahmacharin has undergone severe austerities and has tended the fires properly; you should teach him so that the fires may not blame you.' But the teacher went away on a journey without instructing him.

4.10.3: Through mental sufferings Upakosala began to fast. The wife of the teacher said to him, 'O Brahmacharin, do eat; why are you not eating?' He replied, 'In this (very ordinary and disappointed) man (i.e. myself) there are many desires running in various directions; I am full of mental sufferings; so I shall not eat.' 4.10.4: Thereupon the fires said among themselves, 'This Brahmacharin has undergone severe austerities and has tended us properly; come let us instruct him'. They then said to him, 'Prāna (life) is Brahman, Ka (joy) is Brahman, Kha (ether) is Brahman'. 4.10.5: He said, 'I understand that Prāna is Brahman; but I do not understand Ka and Kha.' They said, 'What is Ka, even that is Kha; and what is Kha, even that is Ka'. Then the fires instructed him about Prāna (Brahman) and the Ākāsha within the heart related to it.

4.11.1: Then the Garhapatya fire instructed him: 'Earth, fire, food and the sun (are my forms). The person who is seen in the sun, I am he, I am he, indeed.' 4.11.2: 'He who knows it thus and meditates on it, destroys sinful acts, wins the region (of fire), reaches the full length of life, lives gloriously, and his descendants never perish. We protect him in this world and in the next, who knows it thus and meditates on it.'

4.12.1: Then the Anvaharyapacana fire instructed him: 'Water, the quarters, the stars and the moon (are my forms). The person who is seen in the moon, I am he, I am he indeed. 4.12.2: 'He who knows it thus and meditates on it, destroys sinful acts, wins the region (of fire), reaches the full length of life, lives gloriously, and his descendants never perish. We protect him in this world and in the next, who knows it thus and meditates on it.'

4.13.1: Then the Ahavaniya fire instructed him, 'Prāna, Ākāsha, heaven and lightning (are my forms). The person who is seen in the lightning, I am he; I am he, indeed. 4.13.2: 'He who knows it thus and meditates on it, destroys sinful acts, wins the region (of fire), reaches the full length of life, lives gloriously, and his descendants never perish. We protect him in this world and in the next, who knows it thus and meditates on it.'

4.14.1: The fires said, 'O Upakosala, dear boy, to you (are revealed) this knowledge of the fires and the knowledge of the Atman; but the teacher will tell you the way.' His teacher came back. The teacher addressed him 'Upakosala!' 4.14.2: 'Yes, revered sir', he responded. 'Dear boy, your face shines like that of a knower of Brahman! Who is it that has instructed you?' 'Who should instruct me sir?', said he. Here he concealed the truth, as it were. 'For this reason it is that though they were (formerly) otherwise they are now this wise'. So saying, he hinted at the (part played by the) fires in this matter. 'What did they tell you, dear boy?' 4.14.3: 'This', thus he acknowledged. 'Dear boy, they have told you about the regions only; but I shall tell you the object of your desire (i.e. Brahman). Just as water does not cling to the lotus-leaf, so also sin does not cling to him who knows Brahman thus'. 'Revered sir, please instruct me further'. (The teacher) said to him:

4.15.1: 'This person who is seen in the eye, he is the Atman', said the teacher; 'this is the immortal, the fearless. This is Brahman. Hence, even if one sprinkles clarified butter or water into the eye, it goes away to the edges.' 4.15.2: 'The knowers of Brahman call him as the center of blessings; for all blessings come together in him. All blessings come together in him who knows thus.' 4.15.3: 'He, again, is the vehicle of blessings; for he carries all blessings. He who knows it thus carries all blessings. He who knows it thus carries all blessings.' 4.15.4: 'He again, is the vehicle of light; for he shines in all the regions. He who knows it thus shines in all the regions.'

4.15.5: 'Now, as for such persons, whether the cremation rites are performed or not, they go to light; from light to the day; from the day to the bright fortnight; from the bright fortnight to those six months during which (the sun) rises towards the north; from the months to the year; from the year to the sun; from the sun to the moon; from the moon to the lightning. (From the region of Brahman) a person, who is other than human, (comes and) causes them existing there, to realize Brahman. This is the path of the gods and the path to Brahman. Those who go by this path do not return to this human whirlpool—yes, they do not return.'

The northern path described above is open to those who know Brahma but are not completely Self-realized. Such persons have some trace of dormant desires (or Vāsanā) left. When all desires born of ego are completely eradicated by Self-knowledge, one instantly merges in Braham in this very life after death (Gita 5.26, 18.55, **BrU 4.4.07, MuU 3.2.09, YVa 39.122).** This is called Jeevan-Mukti or Brahma Nirvana. Time of death does not matter for such souls.

4.16.1: He who blows (i.e. air) is indeed the sacrifice, he, moving along, purifies all this. And because moving along he purifies all this, he is the sacrifice. Mind and speech are the two paths of this sacrifice. 4.16.2-3: One of these two paths, the Brahman priest embellishes with the mind. The Hotir, Adhvaryu and Udgatir priests embellish the other with speech. After the Prataranuvaka (the morning recitation) is commenced, and before the Paridhaniya Rik is begun, if the Brahman priest speaks out (breaking silence), then he embellishes only one path (viz. Speech) and the other is injured. Just as a man walking with one leg, or a chariot moving with one wheel suffers injury, so also that sacrifice of this one suffers injury, and when the sacrifice suffers injury, the sacrificer also suffers injury. For having completed the (defective) sacrifice, he becomes a worse sinner. 4.16.4: But, after the Prataranuvaka is commenced and before the Paridhaniya Rik is begun, if the Brahman priest does not break his silence then both the paths are embellished; and neither one is injured. 4.16.5: And just as a man walking with both the legs, or a chariot moving with both the wheels, remains intact, so also the sacrifice of this one remains intact. If the sacrifice remains intact, the sacrificer also remains intact. He becomes great by performing the sacrifice.

4.17.1: Prajapati brooded on the worlds. From them thus brooded upon, he extracted their essences; fire from the earth, air from the sky and the sun from heaven. 4.17.2: He brooded on these three deities. From them thus brooded upon, he extracted their essences: the Riks from fire, the Yajus-mantras from air, and the Saman from the sun. 4.17.3: He brooded on the three Vedas. From them thus brooded upon, he extracted their existences; Bhuh from the Riks, Bhuvah from the Yajus-mantras and Svah from the Samans. 4.17.4: Therefore if the sacrifice is rendered defective on account of the Riks, then with the Mantra 'Bhuh Svaha', (the Brahman priest) should offer an oblation in the Garhapatya fire. Thus verily, through the essence of the Riks, through the virility of the Riks, he makes good the injury of the sacrifice in respect of the Riks. 4.17.5: And if the sacrifice is rendered defective on account of the Yajus, then with the Mantra 'Bhuvah Svaha', (the Brahman priest) should offer an oblation in the Daksinagni. Thus verily, through the essence of the Yajus-mantras, through the virility of the Yajus-mantras, he makes good the injury of the sacrifice in respect of the Yajus-mantras. 4.17.6: And if the sacrifice is rendered defective on account of the Samans, then with the Mantra 'Svah Svaha' (the Brahman priest) should offer an oblation to the Ahavaniya fire. Thus verily, through the essence of the Samans, through the virility of the Saman, he makes good the injury of the sacrifice in respect of the Samans. 4.17.7-8: Just as one would join gold with salt, silver with gold, tin with silver, lead with tin, iron with lead, wood with iron, and wood with leather, even so does (the Brahman priest) make good the injury of the sacrifice through the virility of these regions, of these deities, and of the three Vedas. That sacrifice indeed is healed where there is a Brahman priest knowing thus. 4.17.9: That sacrifice indeed becomes inclined to the north, where there is a Brahman priest knowing thus. It is in reference to the Brahman priest knowing thus that there is this song: 'Whensoever the sacrifice comes back, thither verily does the Brahman priest go (to remedy)'. 4.17.10: Just as the mare protects (the soldier), even so the silent Brahman priest is the only priest who protects the people engaged in rituals. The Brahman priest who knows thus verily protects the sacrifice, the sacrificer, and all the priests. Hence one should appoint as a Brahman priest only him who knows thus, not one who does not know thus—yes, not one who does not know thus.

5.1.1: Om, Verily, he who knows the eldest and the best, surely becomes the eldest and the best. Prana is indeed the eldest and the best (of the organs). 5.1.2: Verily, he who knows the richest, becomes the richest among his own people. Speech is indeed the richest. 5.1.3: Verily, he who knows the stable basis, becomes stabilized in this world and in the next. The eye is indeed the stable basis. 5.1.4: Verily, he who knows prosperity, attains all desires, both divine and human. The ear is indeed prosperity. 5.1.5: Verily, he who knows the abode, becomes the abode of his people. The mind is indeed the abode. 5.1.6: Now, once the five senses disputed among themselves about their personal superiority, saying 'I am superior'. 5.1.7: Those senses approached the father Prajapati and said to him, 'Revered sir, who is the best amongst us?' He replied, 'He amongst you is the best on whose departure the body would appear its worst, as it were.' 5.1.8: Speech departed. Staying a year out, it came back and asked, 'How have you been able to live without me?' (The others replied,) 'Just like the dumb, though not speaking, yet living with the breath, seeing with the eyes, hearing with the ear and thinking with the mind.' (At this) speech entered (the body). 5.1.9: The eye departed. Staying a year out, it came back and asked, 'How have you been able to live without me?' (The others replied,) 'Just like the blind, though not seeing, yet living with the breath, speaking with the organ of speech, hearing with the ear and thinking with the mind.' (At this) the eye entered (the body). 5.1.10: The ear departed. Staying a year out, it came back and asked, 'How have you been able to live without me?' (The others replied,) 'Just like the deaf, though not hearing, yet living with the breath, speaking with the organ of speech, seeing with the eye and thinking with the mind.' (At this) the ear entered (the body). 5.1.11: The mind departed. Staying a year out, it came back and asked, 'How have you been able to live without me?' (The others replied,) 'Just like infants without developed minds, yet living with the breath, speaking with the organ of speech, seeing with the eye and hearing with the ear.' (At this) the mind entered (the body). 5.1.12: Then, as the Prana was about to depart, it uprooted the other senses just as a horse of mettle would uproot the pegs to which it is tethered. They all then came to it and said, 'O revered sir, be our lord, you are the best amongst us; do not depart from the body.' 5.1.13: Then speech said to that one, 'Just as I am the richest, in the same manner are you also the richest'. Then the eye said to that one, 'Just as I am the stable basis, in the same manner are you also the stable basis'. 5.1.14: Then the ear said to that one, 'Just as I am prosperity, in the same manner are you also prosperity.' Then the mind said to that one, 'Just as I am the abode, in the same manner are you also the abode.' 5.1.15: Verily, people do not call them as organs of speech, nor as eyes, nor as ears, nor as minds. But they call them only as Pranas; for the Prana indeed is all these.

5.2.1: He (the Prana) asked, 'What will be my food?' 'Whatever there is here, even (the food) of dogs and birds', replied the senses. Whatever is eaten, all that is the food of Ana. The name "Ana' indeed is self-evident. For him who knows thus there is nothing that is not food. 5.2.2: He asked, 'What will be my garments?' 'Water', replied the senses. Therefore, indeed, those who are about to eat, cover it, both before and after, with water. (He who knows thus) becomes the obtainer of clothes and of upper garments. 5.2.3: Satyakama Jabala imparted this (doctrine of Prana) to Gosruti, the son of Vyaghrapada, and said, 'If anyone should impart this even to a dry stump, then branches would certainly shoot and leaves would sprout from it'. 5.2.4: Next, if that knower of Prana desires to attain greatness, then having consecrated himself on the new moon day, he should, on the full moon night, stir up in a vessel of curd and honey the mash of all herbs and then offer an oblation into the fire on the spot prescribed for offerings, with the Mantra, 'Svaha to the eldest and the best', and throw what remains attached to the ladle into the mash-pot. 5.2.5: With the Mantra "Svaha to the richest', he should offer an oblation into the fire on the spot prescribed for offerings, and throw what remains attached to the ladle into the mash-pot. With the Mantra 'Svaha to what is stable', he should offer an oblation into the fire on the spot prescribed for offerings, and throw what remains attached to the ladle into the mash-pot. With Mantra 'Svaha to prosperity', he should offer an oblation into the fire on the spot prescribed for offerings, and throw what remains attached to the ladle into the mash-pot. With the Mantra 'Svaha to the abode', he should offer an oblation into the fire on the spot prescribed for offerings, and throw what remains attached to the ladle into the mash-pot. 5.2.6: Then, moving a little away and taking the mash-pot in his hands, he should recite (the Mantra): 'You are Ama by name, for all this (universe) rests with you. He (i.e. you as Prāna) is the eldest, the best, the effulgent, and sovereign. May he (i.e. you as Prāna) lead me to the eldest age, to the best position, to effulgence, and to sovereignty. Verily I wish to become all this.' 5.2.7: Then, reciting this Rik-mantra, foot by foot, he should sip. 'We pray for that food pertaining to the Progenitor', saying this (line) he should sip. 'We pray for the food of the effulgent one', saying this he should sip. '(Which is) the best and all-sustaining', saying this he should sip. We readily meditate upon (the form of the deity) Bhaga', saying this and washing the pot shaped like a Kamsa (goblet) or a Camasa (cup), he should drink all. Then he should lie down behind the fire on a skin or on the ground, controlling speech and mind. If he should see a woman (in a dream), he should know that his rite has succeeded. 5.2.8: There is this verse about it: During the performance of the rites for desired results if the performer sees a woman in a dream, then he should recognize fulfillment in this vision in a dream—yes, in this vision in a dream.

5. Svetaketu: five questions

5.3.1: Once Svetaketu, the grandson of Aruna, came to the assembly of the Panchalas. Pravahana, the son of Jivala, enquired of him, 'My boy, has your father instructed you?' 'He has indeed, revered sir'. 5.3.2: 'Do you know where created beings go above from here?' No, revered sir'. 'Do you know the place of parting of the two paths—the path of the gods and the path of the fathers?' 'No, revered sir'. 5.3.3: 'Do you know why the other world is not filled up?' 'No, revered sir'. 'Do you know how, at the fifth oblation, the liquid oblations (or unseen results of action) come to be designated as man?' 'No, indeed, revered sir'. 5.3.4: 'Then why did you say, "I have been instructed"? For, how can he who does not know these things say, "I have been instructed"?' He was distressed and came to his father's place and said to him, 'Revered Sir, without having instructed me properly you said, "I have instructed you".' 5.3.5: 'That nominal Kshatriya asked me five questions, and I was not able to answer even one of them'. The father said, 'Even as you have spoken to me about them, so do I not know even one of them. If I had known them, why should I not have told you?'

5.3.6: Then Gautama went to the king's place. When he arrived, the king made reverential offerings to him. In the morning he presented himself to the king when he was in the assembly. The king said to him, 'O revered Gautama, please ask for a boon of human wealth'. He replied, 'O king, let the human wealth remain with you, tell me those words which you spoke to my boy'. The king was perturbed. 5.3.7: The king commanded him, 'Stay here for a long time.' At the end of the period he said to him, 'Even as you told me, O Gautama, prior to you, this knowledge never went to the Brāhmanas. This is why the expounding of this knowledge belonged to the Kshatriyas in earlier times in all the worlds'. Then he instructed him.

5.4.1: The world yonder is indeed the fire, O Gautama. Of that, the sun is the fuel, the rays are the smoke, the day is the flame, the moon is the embers, and the stars are the sparks. 5.4.2: Into this fire the deities offer the oblation of faith. Out of that oblation King Soma arises.

5.5.1: Parjanya is indeed the fire, O Gautama. Of that, the air is the fuel, the cloud is the smoke, the lightning is the flame, the thunderbolt is the embers, and the rumblings of thunder are the sparks. 5.5.2: Into this fire the deities offer the oblation of King Soma. Out of that oblation rain arises.

5.6.1: The earth indeed is the fire, O Gautama. Of that, the year, is the fuel, Ākāsha is the smoke, night is the flame, the directions are the embers, and the intermediate directions are the sparks. 5.6.2: Into this fire the deities offer the oblation of rain. Out of that oblation food (in the shape of corn) arises.

5.7.1: Man indeed is the fire, O Gautama. Of that, speech is the fuel, Prāna is the smoke, the tongue is the flame, the eye is the embers, and the ear is the sparks. 5.7.2: Into this fire the deities offer the oblation of food. Out of that oblation the seed arises.

5.8.1-2: Woman indeed is the fire, O Gautama. Into this fire the deities offer the oblation of the seed. Out of that oblation the fetus arises.

5.9.1: Thus at the fifth oblation, (the oblation called) water comes to be designated as man. That fetus, covered with water inside the membrane, lies for nine or ten months, and is then born. 5.9.2: Being born, he lives whatever the length of his life may be. When he is dead (to attain the world) as ordained, they carry him from here (for cremation) to fire itself from which alone he came and from which he arose.

Chāndogya Upanishad

5.10.1-2: Among them, those who know thus (this knowledge of the five fires) and those who are devoted to faith and austerity in the forest—they go to light; from light to the day, from the day to the bright fortnight, from the bright fortnight to those six months during which the sun travels northward; from the months to the year, from the year to the sun, from the sun to the moon and from the moon to the lightning. (From the region of Brahman) a person, who is other than human, (comes and) causes them, existing there, to attain Brahman. This is the path of the gods. 5.10.3: But those who living in villages (as householders) practice sacrifices and works of public utility and gift, go to smoke, from smoke to night, from night to the dark fortnight, from the dark fortnight to those months during which the sun travels southward. From there they do not reach the year (like those going the path of the gods). 5.10.4: From the months, (they go) to the region of the fathers, from the region of the fathers to Ākāsha, from Ākāsha to the moon. This (i.e. this moon) is King Soma (the king of the Brāhmanas). This is the food of the deities. This the deities eat. 5.10.5: Residing in that (region of the moon) till they have exhausted (the results of action) they then return again the same way as they came (by the path that is being mentioned). They come to Ākāsha, and from Ākāsha to air. Having become air, they become smoke. Having become smoke they become the white cloud. 5.10.6: Having become the white cloud, they become the (rain-bearing) cloud. Having become the cloud they fall as rain. Then they are born in this world as rice and barley, herbs and trees, sesamum plants and beans. But the release from these is more difficult, for whoever eats the food and sows the seed, they become like him only. 5.10.7: Among them, those who have good residual results of action here (earned in this world and left as residue after the enjoyment in the region of the moon), quickly reach a good womb, the womb of a Brāhmana, or of a Kshatriya or of a Vaisya. But those who have bad residual results of action quickly reach an evil womb, the womb of a dog or of a hog or of a Chandala. 5.10.8: Then, by neither of these two paths, do they go. They, as small creatures, keep repeatedly revolving, subject to the saying 'Be born and die'. This is the third state. Therefore that region (of the moon) is never filled up. Hence one should be disgusted (with this state). There is this verse about it. 5.10.9: One who steals gold, one who drinks wine, one who dishonors the teacher's bed, and one who injures a Brāhmana—all these four fall, as also the fifth one who associates with them. 5.10.10: Moreover, he who knows (worships) these five fires thus, even though he associates with those sinners, is not tainted by sin. He who knows these thus becomes cleansed and pure and obtains the meritorious world—yes, he who knows thus.

6. Knowledge may not be bought or sold

5.11.1: Pracinasala the son of Upamanyu, Satyayajna the son of Pulusa, Indradyumna the son of Bhallavi, Jana the son of Sarkaraksa, and Budila the son of Asvatarasva—these five great householders and great Vedic scholars, having come together, held a discussion on 'What is our Atman? What is Brahman?' 5.11.2: They reflected among themselves, 'Revered sirs, Uddalaka, the son of Aruna, knows well this Vaisvanara Atman. Well, let us go to him'. And they went to him. 5.11.3: Uddalaka reflected, 'These great householders and great Vedic scholars are going to question me; but possibly I shall not be able to tell them everything. However, I shall direct them to another teacher'. 5.11.4: Uddalaka said: 'Revered sirs, at present, Asvapati, the son of Kekaya, is studying this Vaisvanara Atman. Well, let us go to him'. Then they went to him. 5.11.5: When they arrived, the king arranged for each of them separately a welcome with suitable rites. Next morning, on rising, he said to them, 'In my kingdom there is no thief, no miser, no drunkard, no man who has not installed the fire, no ignorant person, no adulterer, so how can there be any adulteress? Revered sirs, I am going to perform a sacrifice. In that as much wealth, sirs, as I give to each single priest, shall I give to you also. Revered sirs, please remain'. 5.11.6: They said, 'The purpose for which a man goes (to another), on that alone he should speak to him. You are, at present, studying the Vaisvanara Atman, please tell us of that. 5.11.7: The king said to them, 'I shall answer you in the morning'. In the morning, they approached him with sacrificial fuel in their hands. The king, without receiving them as initiated pupils, spoke thus:

5.12.1: 'O Aupamanyava, what is the Atman on which you meditate?' He replied, 'Heaven only, O venerable king'. The king said, 'This that you meditate upon as Atman is the Vaisvanara Atman known as "the highly luminous". Therefore in your family are seen the Suta, Prasuta and Asuta libations of Soma-juice.' 5.12.2: 'So you eat food and see what is dear. One who meditates on this Vaisvanara Atman thus, eats food and sees what is dear, and there is in his family the holy effulgence born of sacred wisdom. But this is only the head of the Atman. If you had not come to me your head (a portion) would have fallen down.'

5.13.1: Then the king said to Satyayajna Paulusi, 'O Pracinayogya, what is that Atman on which you meditate?' He replied, 'The sun only, O venerable king'. The king said, 'This that you meditate upon as Atman is the Vaisvanara Atman known as "the multiform". Therefore in your family are seen all kinds of enjoyable things. 5.13.2: 'So, for you are provided a chariot drawn by mules, maid-servants and a gold necklace; so you eat food and see what is dear. One who thus meditates upon this Vaisvanara Atman, eats food and sees what is dear, and there is in his family the holy effulgence born of sacred wisdom. But this is only the eye of the Atman. If you had not come to me you would have become blind.'

5.14.1: Then the king said to Indradyumna Bhallaveya, 'O descendant of Vyaghrapada, what is that Atman on which you meditate?' He replied, 'Air only, O venerable king.' The king said, 'This that you meditate upon as Atman is the Vaisvanara Atman known as "the diversely coursed". Therefore from diverse directions offerings come to you, and various rows of chariots follow you. 5.14.2: 'So you eat food and see what is dear. One who thus meditates upon this Vaisvanara Atman eats food and sees what is dear, and there is in his family the holy effulgence born of sacred wisdom. But this is only the Prāna of the Atman. If you had not come to me your Prāna would have departed'.

5.15.1: Then the king said to Jana, 'O Sarkaraksya, what is that Atman on which you meditate?' He replied, 'Ākāsha only, O venerable king'. The king said, 'This that you meditate upon as Atman is the Vaisvanara Atman known as "the manifold". Therefore are your offspring and wealth manifold. 5.15.2: 'So you eat food and see what is dear. One who thus meditates upon this Vaisvanara Atman, eats food and sees what is dear, and there is in his family the holy effulgence born of sacred wisdom. But this is only the trunk of the Atman. If you had not come to me your trunk would have been shattered'.

5.16.1: Then the king said to Budila Asvatarasvi, 'O Vaiyaghrapadya, what is that Atman on which you meditate?' He replied, 'Water only, O venerable king'. The king said, 'This that you meditate upon as Atman is the Vaisvanara Atman known as "the wealth". Therefore are you endowed with wealth and bodily strength. 5.16.2: 'So you eat food and see what is dear. One who thus meditates upon this Vaisvanara Atman, eats food and sees what is dear, and there is in his family the holy effulgence born of sacred wisdom. But this is only the lower belly of the Atman. If you had not come to me your lower belly would have burst'.

5.17.1: Then the king said to Uddalaka Aruni, 'O Gautama, what is that Atman on which you meditate?' He replied, 'The earth only, O venerable king'. The king said, 'This that you meditate upon as Atman is the Vaisvanara Atman known as "the foundation". Therefore are you well-founded in offspring and cattle'. 5.17.2: 'So you eat food and see what is dear. One who thus meditates upon this Vaisvanara Atman, eats food and sees what is dear, and there is in his family the holy effulgence born of sacred wisdom. But this is only the feet of the Atman. If you had not come to me your feet would have withered away'.

5.18.1: The king said to them, 'All of you (with partial knowledge) eat food knowing the Vaisvanara Atman differently, as it were. But one who thus meditates upon this Vaisvanara Atman as a whole, consisting of parts and self-conscious, eats food in all the worlds, in all the beings, and in all the selves. 5.18.2: Of the aforesaid Vaisvanara Atman, the head is 'the highly luminous', the eye is 'the multiform', the breath is 'the diversely coursed', the trunk is 'the vast', the lower belly is the 'wealth', the feet are the earth ('the foundation'). (Of the enjoyer as Vaisvanara) the chest is the altar, the hairs on the chest are the Kusa grass, the heart is the Garhapatya fire, the mind is the Anvaharyapacana fire, and the mouth is the Ahavaniya fire.

5.19.1: Therefore, the food that comes first should be an object of oblation. That eater, when he offers the first oblation, should offer it with the Mantra 'Svaha to Prāna'; thereby Prāna is satisfied. 5.19.2: Prāna being satisfied, the eye is satisfied; the eye being satisfied, the sun is satisfied; the sun being satisfied, heaven is satisfied; heaven being satisfied, whatever is under heaven and the sun is satisfied. Through its satisfaction the eater himself is satisfied. (He is satisfied) also with offspring, cattle, food, luster and the holy effulgence born of sacred wisdom.

5.20.1: Then, when he offers the second oblation, he should offer it with the Mantra 'Svaha to Vyana'; thereby Vyana is satisfied. 5.20.2: Vyana being satisfied, the ear is satisfied; the ear being satisfied, the moon is satisfied; the moon being satisfied, the quarters are satisfied; the quarters being satisfied, whatever is under the moon and the quarters is satisfied. Through its satisfaction the eater himself is satisfied. (He is satisfied) also with offspring, cattle, food, luster and the holy effulgence born of sacred wisdom.

5.21.1: Then, when he offers the third oblation, he should offer it with the Mantra 'Svaha to Apana'; thereby Apana is satisfied. 5.21.2: Apana being satisfied, speech is satisfied; speech being satisfied, fire is satisfied; fire being satisfied, the earth is satisfied; the earth being satisfied, whatever is under the earth and fire is satisfied. Through its satisfaction the eater himself is satisfied. (He is satisfied) also with offspring, cattle, food, luster and the holy effulgence born of sacred wisdom.

5.22.1: Then, when he offers the fourth oblation, he should offer it with the Mantra 'Svaha to Samana'; thereby Samana is satisfied. 5.22.2: Samana being satisfied, the mind is satisfied; the mind being satisfied, Parjanya (rain god) is satisfied; Parjanya being satisfied, lightning is satisfied; lightning being satisfied, whatever is under lightning and Parjanya is satisfied. Through its satisfaction the eater himself is satisfied. (He is satisfied) also with offspring, cattle, food, luster and the holy effulgence born of sacred wisdom.

5.23.1: Then, when he offers the fifth oblation, he should offer it with the Mantra 'Svaha to Udana'; thereby Udana is satisfied. 5.23.2: Udana being satisfied, the skin is satisfied; the skin being satisfied, the air is satisfied; the air being satisfied, Ākāsha is satisfied; Ākāsha being satisfied, whatever is under the air and Ākāsha is satisfied. Through its satisfaction the eater himself is satisfied. (He is satisfied) also with offspring, cattle, food, luster and the holy effulgence born of sacred wisdom.

5.24.1: If anyone, without knowing this, offers the Agnihotra, it would be just a man removing the live embers and pouring the oblation on the ashes. 5.24.2: But if one, knowing it thus, offers the Agnihotra to Prāna his oblation is poured into all the worlds, all the beings, and all the selves. 5.24.3: So, even as reed-cotton when laid on the fire is burnt up, so are burnt up all the sins of this one who knowing it thus offers the Agnihotra. 5.24.4: Therefore, even if one, who knows thus, offers the remnant of his food to a Chandala, then also that food becomes his offering to the Vaisvanara Atman only. There is this verse about it. 5.24.5: As, in this world, hungry boys gather round their mother, even so all the creatures wait upon the Agnihotra.

6.1.1: Om. Once upon a time there was one Svetaketu, the grandson of Aruna. His father said to him, 'O Svetaketu, live the life of a Brahmacharin. Dear boy, there never is anyone in our family who does not study and is only nominally a Brāhmana.' 6.1.2-3: Having gone (to the teacher's house) when twelve years old, he came back when he was twenty-four old, having studied all the Vedas, conceited, arrogant and regarding himself as very learned. His father said to him, 'Svetaketu, dear boy, you, I see, are conceited, arrogant, regarding yourself as very learned; did you ask for that teaching (about the Supreme Brahman) through which what is unheard becomes heard, what is unthought becomes thought of, what is unknown becomes known?' 'Of what nature, revered sir, is that teaching?' 6.1.4: 'Dear boy, just as through a single clod of clay all that is made of clay would become known, for all modifications is but name based upon words and the clay alone is real; 6.1.5: Dear boy, just as through a single ingot of gold, all that is made of gold would become known, for all modification is but name based upon words and the gold alone is real; 6.1.6: Dear boy, just as through a single nail-parer all that is made of iron would become known, for all modification is but name based upon words and the iron alone is real—such, dear boy, is that teaching.' 6.1.7: 'Surely, my revered teachers did not know it, for if they had known, why should they not have told it to me? However, revered father, teach it to me'. 'Be it so, dear boy', said (the father).

6.2.1: 'In the beginning, dear boy, this was Being alone, one only, without a second. Some say that, in the beginning, this was Non-being alone, one only, without a second. From that Non-being arose Being.' 6.2.2: Aruni said, 'But now, indeed, dear boy, could it be so? How could Being arise from Non-being? In truth, dear boy, in the beginning (before creation), there was Being alone, one only, without a second. 6.2.3: 'That Being willed, "May I become many, may I grow forth." It created fire. That fire willed, "May I become many, may I grow forth". It created water. Therefore whenever a man grieves or perspires, then it is from fire that water issues. 6.2.4: 'That water willed, "May I become many, may I grow forth." It created food. Therefore wherever it rains, abundant food grows there; it is from water that food for eating is produced.

6.3.1: 'Of the aforesaid beings there are only three origins: those born from eggs, born from living beings, and born from sprouts. 6.3.2: 'That deity willed, 'Well, let me, entering into these three deities through this living self (Jivatman), differentiate name and form. 6.3.3: "Of these, let me make each one triplicated", willing thus, this deity entered into these three deities through this living self and differentiated names and forms. 6.3.4: 'It made each one of them threefold. But, dear boy, how each of these three deities becomes threefold (outside the body), know that from me.

6.4.1: 'In fire, the red color is the color of fire; that which is white belongs to water and that which is black belongs to food (earth). Thus vanishes (the idea of) the quality of fire from fire; for all modification is but name based upon words, only the three forms are real. 6.4.2: 'In the sun, the red color is the color of fire, that which is white belongs to water and that which is black belongs to earth. Thus vanishes (the idea of) the quality of the sun from the sun; for all modification is but name based upon words, only the three forms are real. 6.4.3: 'In the moon, the red color is the color of fire, that which is white belongs to water and that which is black belongs to earth. Thus vanishes (the idea of) the quality of the moon from the moon; for all modification is but name based upon words, only the three forms are real. 6.4.4: 'In lightning, the red color is the color of fire, that which is white belongs to water and that which is black belongs to earth. Thus vanishes (the idea of) the quality of lightning from lightning; for all modification is but name based upon words, only the three forms are real. 6.4.5: 'It was indeed on knowing this (triplication) that the ancient great householders and great Vedic scholars said, 'There is, at present, nothing that anyone would point out to us as unheard, unthought or unknown"; for from these they understood everything.

6.4.6: 'Whatever else appeared red, that also they knew to be the color of fire; whatever appeared white, that also they knew to be the color of water; whatever appeared black, that also they knew to be the color of earth. 6.4.7: 'Whatever appeared to be unknown, that also they knew to be a combination of these very deities. But, dear boy, know from me how, on reaching man, each of these three deities becomes threefold.

6.5.1: 'Food, when eaten, becomes divided into three parts. What is its grossest ingredient, that becomes fasces; what is the middling ingredient, that becomes flesh; and what is the subtlest ingredient, that becomes mind. 6.5.2: 'Water, when drunk, becomes divided into three parts. What is its grossest ingredient, that becomes urine; what is the middling ingredient, that becomes blood; and what is the subtlest ingredient, that becomes Prāna. 6.5.3: 'Fire, when eaten, becomes divided into three parts. What is its grossest ingredient, that becomes bone; what is the middling ingredient, that becomes marrow; and what is the subtlest ingredient, hat becomes speech.

Food is called the root of the body-tree. A healthy body and mind are the prerequisites for success in spiritual life. The mind will be healthy if the body is healthy. Persons in the mode of goodness like vegetarian foods. One can also become a noble person by taking vegetarian food because one becomes what one eats.

6.5.4: 'Hence, dear boy, mind is made up of food, Prāna is made up of water, and speech is made of fire. 'Explain it further to me, revered sir'. 'Be it so, dear boy', said the father.

6.6.1: 'Dear boy, of the curd that is being churned that which is the subtlest part rises upwards and that becomes butter. **6.6.2: 'So also, dear boy, of the food that is eaten that which is the subtlest part rises upwards and that becomes the mind.** 6.6.3: 'Dear boy, of the water that is drunk that which is the subtlest part rises upwards and that becomes Prāna. 6.6.4: 'Dear boy, of the fire that is eaten that which is the subtlest part rises upwards and that becomes speech. 6.6.5: 'Hence, dear boy, mind is made up of food, Prāna is made up of water, and speech is made up of fire'. 'Explain it further to me, revered sir'. 'Be it so, dear boy', said the father.

6.7.1: 'Dear boy, man consists of sixteen parts. Do not eat for fifteen days; drink as much water as you like. Prāna is made up of water, and the Prāna of one who drinks water is not cut off. 6.7.2: Svetaketu did not eat for fifteen days. Then he approached him saying, 'What shall I say?' The father said, 'The Riks, the Yajus, and the Samans, dear boy.' 'They do not at all arise in me, sir'. 6.7.3: The father said to him, 'Dear boy, just as a single ember of the size of a firefly, left over from a large burning fire, cannot burn any more than that, even so, dear boy, of your sixteen parts only one part is left over, now by means of that you cannot perceive the Vedas. Eat, then you will understand me'. 6.7.4: He ate and then approached his father. Whatever he asked him, he answered them all. 6.7.5-6: The father said to him, 'Dear boy, just as when a single ember of the size of a firefly left over from a large burning fire, is made to blaze up by adding straw and it burns much more than before, even so, dear boy, of your sixteen parts, only one part remained, and that being nourished by food, has been made to blaze up; and by that you perceive the Vedas now. Hence, dear boy, the mind is made up of food, the Prāna is made up of water, and speech is made up of fire. From his words, (Svetaketu) understood it—yes, he understood it.

6. Svetaketu: nature of sleep

6.8.1: Once Uddalaka Aruni said to his son Svetaketu, 'Dear boy, know from me the true nature of sleep. When a man is said to be sleeping, then, dear boy, he has become united with Being and has attained his own nature. Hence people speak of him as sleeping, for them he has attained his own nature.

6.8.2: 'Just as a bird tied to a string, after flying in various directions and finding no resting place elsewhere, takes refuge at the very place where to it is tied, even so, dear boy, that mind, after flying in various directions and finding no resting place elsewhere, takes refuge in Prāna alone; for the mind, dear boy, is tied to Prāna. 6.8.3: 'Dear boy, know from me (the true nature of) hunger and thirst. When a man is said to be hungry, then (it is to be understood that), water is leading away what has been eaten; (therefore water may be designated as hunger). Just as people speak of the leader of cows, the leader of horses, and the leader of men, even so they speak of water as the leader of food. Hence, dear boy, know this shoot (the body) to be put forth (by a root), for it cannot be without a root. 6.8.4: 'Where could its root be apart from food? Even so, dear boy, with food as the shoot, look for water as the root; with water as the shoot, dear boy, look for fire as the root; with fire as the shoot, dear boy, look for Being as the root. All these creatures, dear boy, have Being as their root, have Being as their abode, and have Being as their support. 6.8.5: 'Again, when a man is said to be thirsty, then (it is to be understood that), fire is leading away what has been drunk: (therefore fire may be designated as thirst). Just as people speak of the leader of cows, the leader of horses, and the leader of men, even so they speak of that fire as the leader of water. Hence, dear boy, know this shoot (water) to be put forth (by a root), for it cannot be without a root. 6.8.6: 'Where could its root be apart from water? Dear boy, with water as the shoot, look for fire as the root; with fire as the shoot, look for Being as the root. All these creatures, dear boy, have Being as their root, have Being as their abode, and have Being as their support. How dear boy, each of these three deities, on reaching man, becomes threefold has been explained to you earlier. When this man is about to depart, dear boy, his speech merges in the mind, mind in Prāna, Prāna in fire and fire in the supreme deity. 6.8.7: 'That Being which is this subtle essence (cause), even That all this world has for its self. That is the true. That is the Atman. That thou art, O Svetaketu.' 'Revered sir, please explain it further to me'. 'So be it, dear boy', said (the father).

7. That thou art, O Svetaketu

6.9.1-2: 'As, dear boy, the bees make honey by collecting juices from different trees and reduce them into one essence, and there, as these juices have no such discrimination as "I am the juice of this tree, I am the juice of that tree"; even so, dear boy, all these creatures having merged into Being, do not know, "We have merged into Being." 6.9.3: 'Whatever these creatures are here in this world, tiger or lion or wolf or boar or worm or flying insect or gadfly or mosquito, that they become again. 6.9.4: 'That Being which is this subtle essence (cause), even That all this world has for itself. That is the true. That is the Atman. That thou art, O Svetaketu.' 'Revered sir, please explain it further to me'. 'So be it, dear boy', said (the father).

After many births, the enlightened one surrenders to My Will by realizing that everything is, indeed, My manifestation. Such a great soul is very rare. **(BG** 7.19) (Also see **BG** 7.07, **18.**66)

The other seven Sanskrit verses of the Vedas, called great sayings are: (1) All this is, of course, the Spirit because everything is born from, rests in, and merges into the Spirit (in ChU 3.**14.**01 of Sāmaveda). (2) All this is Spirit. The Spirit is everywhere. All this universe is, indeed, Supreme Brahman in MuU 2.02.11 of Atharvaveda. The Bible also says: You are gods (John **10.**34). The Vedas and Upanishads declare: (3) Consciousness is Spirit (in AiU 3.03 of Rigveda). (4) I am the Spirit (in BrU 1.04.10 of Yajurveda). (5) You are the Spirit (तत् त्वम् असि in ChU 6.**08.**07 of Sāmaveda). (6) The individual Self (Jivātmā, Jiva) is one and the same with the Absolute (Brahman, Brahma) (in MaU 02 of Atharvaveda) and (7) That which is One has become all these (in Rigveda 8.58.02).

6.10.1-2: 'These eastern rivers, dear boy, flow along to the east and the western ones to the west. They rise from the ocean and merge in the ocean, and become that ocean itself. And there as these rivers do not know themselves as "I am this river, I am that river", even so, dear boy, all these creatures, having come from Being, do not know, "We have come from Being". And whatever these creatures were here, tiger or lion or wolf or boar or worm or flying insect or gad-fly or mosquito, that they become again. 6.10.3: 'That Being which is this subtle essence (cause), even That all this world has for its self. That is the true. That is the Atman. That thou art, O Svetaketu.' 'Revered sir, please explain it further to me'. 'So be it, dear boy', said (the father).

6.11.1: 'Of this large tree, dear boy, if anyone were to strike at the root, it would exude sap, though still living; if anyone were to strike in the middle, it would exude sap, though still living; if anyone were to strike at the top, it would exude sap, though still living. As that tree is pervaded by the living-self, it stands firm, drinking constantly and rejoicing. 6.11.2: 'If the life leaves one branch of this tree, then that branch dries up; if it leaves the second one, then that dries up; it leaves the whole tree, the whole tree dries up.' 6.11.3: The father said, 'Dear boy, know that even so, being left by the living self this body surely dies, but the living self does not die. That Being which is this subtle essence (cause), even That all this world has for its self. That is the true. That is the Atman. That thou art, O Svetaketu.' 'Revered sir, please explain it further to me'. 'So be it, dear boy', said (the father).

6.12.1: 'Bring a fruit from this Banyan tree'. 'Here it is, revered sir'. 'Break it.' 'It is broken, revered sir'. 'What do you see in this?' 'These seeds, small like particles, revered sir'. 'Break one of these, my child'. 'It is broken, revered sir'. 'What do you see in it?' 'Nothing, revered sir'. 6.12.2: The father said to him, 'Dear boy, this subtle essence which you do not perceive, growing from this subtle essence the large Banyan tree thus stands. Have faith, dear boy.' 6.12.3: 'That Being which is this subtle essence (cause), even That all this world has for its self. That is the true. That is the Atman. That thou art, O Svetaketu.' 'Revered sir, please explain it further to me'. 'So be it, dear boy', said (the father).

6.13.1-2: 'Put this salt into water and then come to me in the morning'. He did so. The father said to him, 'Bring the salt, my child, which you put into water at night'. Having searched for it, he did not find it, as it has completely dissolved. 'My child, take a sip from the top of this water. How is it?' 'It is salt'. 'Take a sip from the middle. How is it?' 'It is salt'. 'Take a sip from the bottom. How is it?' 'It is salt'. 'Throw this water away and then come to me'. He did so (and returned saying), 'It is there always'. The father said to him, 'Dear boy, as you do not see what is present in this water though indeed it exists in it, similarly, (Being exists) indeed in this body. 6.13.3: 'That Being which is this subtle essence (cause), even That all this world has for its self. That is the true. That is the Atman. That thou art, O Svetaketu.' 'Revered sir, please explain it further to me'. 'So be it, dear boy', said (the father).

6.14.1: 'Just as, dear boy, (some robber) having brought a man from the Gandhara region with his eyes bound up, might leave him in a very desolate place, and just as that man would shout towards the east, or towards the north, or towards the south, or towards the west, (saying) "I have been brought here with my eyes bound up, I have been left here with my eyes bound up." 6.14.2: 'And as someone might remove his bandage and tell him, "The Gandhara region is in this direction, proceed in this direction" and as he, enquiring his way from village, to village and being instructed and capable of judging by himself would reach the Gandhara region itself, even so, in this world that person knows who has a preceptor. And for him, only so long is the delay as he is not liberated (from the body) and then immediately he is merged in Being. 6.14.3: 'That Being which is this subtle essence (cause), even That all this world has for its self. That is the true. That is the Atman. That thou art, O Svetaketu.' 'Revered sir, please explain it further to me'. 'So be it, dear boy', said (the father).

6.15.1: 'Dear boy, the relatives of a man who is ill assemble round him and ask, "Do you recognize me? Do you recognize me?" As long as his speech is not merged in the mind, the mind in Prāna, Prāna in fire, and fire in the supreme deity, so long does he know them. 6.15.2: 'Then when his speech is merged in the mind, the mind in Prāna, Prāna in fire, and fire in the supreme deity, then he does not know them. 6.15.3: 'That Being which is this subtle essence (cause), even That all this world has for its self. That is the true. That is the Atman. That thou art, O Svetaketu.' 'Revered sir, please explain it further to me'. 'So be it, dear boy', said (the father).

6.16.1: 'Dear boy, (The officers of the king) bring a man, holding him by the hand (while saying) "He has taken something, he has committed a theft, heat the axe for him". If he is doer of that, then he makes himself false. And being addicted to falsehood, he covers himself with falsehood and grasps the heated axe; he is burnt, and then he is punished. 6.16.2: 'If, however, he is not the doer of that, then he makes himself true. And being attached to truth, he covers himself with truth and grasps the heated axe; he is not burnt and then he is released. 6.16.3: 'And as in this case he (the man attached to truth) is not burnt, (similarly a man of knowledge is not born again). That is the true. That is the Atman. That thou art, O Svetaketu.' From his words Svetaketu understood That.

7.1.1: Om. 'Revered sir, teach me,' thus saying Narada approached Sanatkumara. Sanatkumara said to him, 'What you already know, declaring that to me, be my disciple. What is beyond that I shall tell you?' Narada said: 7.1.2: 'Revered sir, I know the Rig-Veda, the Yajur-Veda, the Sama-Veda and the Atharvanas the fourth, the Itihasa-Purana as the fifth, grammar, the rules for the worship of the ancestors, mathematics, the science of portents, the science of treasures, logic, the science of ethics, etymology, the ancillary knowledge of the Vedas, the physical sciences, the science of war, the science of the stars, the science related to serpents, and the fine arts—all this I know, revered sir.' 7.1.3: 'Revered sir, however, I am only a knower of verbal texts, not a knower of Atman. Indeed I have heard from persons like your revered self that a knower of Atman goes beyond grief. I am in such a state of grief. May your revered self take me across it.' Sanatkumara replied to him,' Whatsoever you have studied here, really it is only a name.' 7.1.4: 'Name indeed is Rig-Veda, (so also) Yajur-Veda, Sama-Veda and the Atharvana as the fourth, the Itihasa-Purana as the fifth, grammar, the rules of the worship of the ancestors, mathematics, the science of portents, the science of treasures, logic, the science of ethics, etymology, the ancillary knowledge of the Vedas, the physical science, the science of war, the science of the stars, the science related to serpents, and the fine arts—name alone is all this. Worship the name. 7.1.5: 'He who worships name as Brahman becomes free to act as he wishes in the sphere within the reach of name, he who worships name as Brahman'. (Narada) 'Revered sir, is there anything greater than name?' (Sanatkumara) 'Surely, there is something greater than name'. (Narada) 'Revered sir, communicate it to me.'

7.2.1: 'Speech surely is greater than name. Speech indeed makes us understand the Rig-Veda, Yajur-Veda, Sama-Veda, Atharvana as the fourth, Itihasa-Purana as the fifth, grammar, the rules of the worship of the ancestors, mathematics, the science of portents, the science of treasures, logic, the science of ethics, etymology, the ancillary knowledge of the Vedas, the physical science, the science of war, the science of the stars, the science related to serpents, and the fine arts—also heaven and earth, air and Ākāsha, water and fire, gods and men, cattle and birds, grasses and trees, beasts down to worms, flying insects and ants, merit and demerit, true and false, good and bad, pleasant and unpleasant. Verily, if speech did not exist, neither merit nor demerit would be understood, neither true nor false, neither good nor bad, neither pleasant nor unpleasant. Speech alone makes us understand all this. (Hence) worship speech. 7.2.2: 'He who worships speech as Brahman becomes free to act as he wishes in the sphere within the reach of speech, he who worships speech as Brahman'. 'Revered sir, is there anything greater than speech?' 'Surely, there is something greater than speech'. 'Revered sir, communicate it to me'.

7.3.1: 'Mind surely is greater than speech. Just as the closed hand encompasses two Amalaka, or two Kola, or two Aksa fruits, so does the mind encompasses speech and name. When by mind one intends "Let me learn the Mantras", then he learns; Let me do sacrificial acts", then he does; "Let me desire offspring and cattle", then he desires; "Let me desire this world and the next", then he desires.

Mind indeed is Atman. Mind indeed is the world. Mind indeed is Brahman. Worship the mind. 7.3.2: 'He who worships the mind as Brahman becomes free to act as he wishes in the sphere within the reach of mind, he who worships the mind as Brahman'. 'Revered sir, is there anything greater than mind?' 'Surely, there is something greater than mind'. 'Revered sir, communicate it to me'.

7.4.1: 'Will surely is greater than mind. Verily, when one wills, then he intends in his mind, then he sends forth speech, and he sends it forth in a name. In the name sacred formulas and in sacred formulas the sacrifices become one.' 7.4.2: 'All these, indeed, merge in the will, are made up of the will, and abide in the will. Heaven and earth willed, air and Ākāsha willed, water and fire willed. Through the willing of these, rain wills. Through the willing of rain, food wills. Through the willing of food, Prānas will. Through the willing of Prānas, sacred formulas will. Through the willing of sacred formulas (sacrificial) acts will. Through the willing of (sacrificial) acts, the world wills. Through the willing of the world, all things will. This is will. Worship will. 7.4.3: 'He who worships will as Brahman, he indeed, attains the worlds willed by him—himself being permanent, the permanent worlds; himself being well-founded, the well-founded worlds; himself being undistressed, the undistressed world. He becomes free to act as he wishes in the sphere within the reach of will, he who worships will as Brahman'. 'Revered sir, is there anything greater than will?' 'Surely, there is something greater than will'. 'Revered sir, communicate it to me'.

7.5.1: 'Intelligence surely is greater than will. Verily, when one understands, then he wills, then he intends in mind, then he sends forth speech, and he sends it forth in a name. In the name sacred formulas and in sacred formulas the sacrificed become one. 7.5.2: 'All these, indeed, merge in intelligence, are made up of intelligence and abide in intelligence. Therefore, even if a man who knows much is without intelligence, people speak of him thus, 'He does not exist, nor what he has known; if he were really learned, he would not thus be without intelligence". On the other hand, if a man knowing little is endowed with intelligence, people desire to listen to him also. Intelligence, indeed, is the one center of mergence of all these, intelligence is their soul, and intelligence is their support. Worship intelligence. 7.5.3: 'He who worships intelligence as Brahman, he indeed, attains the worlds of intelligence—himself being permanent, the permanent worlds; himself being well-established, the well-established worlds; and himself being undistressed, the undistressed world. He becomes free to act as he wishes in the sphere within the reach of intelligence, he who worships intelligence as Brahman'. 'Revered sir, is there anything greater than intelligence?' 'Surely, there is something greater than intelligence'. 'Revered sir, communicate it to me'.

7.6.1: 'Contemplation surely is greater than intelligence. The earth contemplates as it were. The sky contemplates as it were. Heaven contemplates as it were. Water contemplates as it were. The mountains contemplate as it were. Gods and men contemplate as it were. Therefore, verily, those who attain greatness among men here, they seem to have obtained a share of the result of contemplation. And those who are small people, they are quarrelsome, abusive and slanderous; but those who are great men, they appear to have obtained a share of the result of contemplation. Worship contemplation. 7.6.2: 'He who worships contemplation as Brahman becomes free to act as he wishes in the sphere within the reach of contemplation, he who worships contemplation as Brahman'. 'Revered sir, is there anything greater than contemplation?' 'Surely, there is something greater than contemplation'. 'Revered sir, communicate it to me'.

7.7.1: 'Understanding surely is greater than contemplation. By understanding alone one understands the Rig-Veda, Yajur-Veda, Sama-Veda, Atharvana as the fourth, Itihasa-Purana as the fifth, grammar, the rules for the worship of the ancestors; mathematics, the science of portents, the science of treasures, logic, the Vedas, the physical science, the science of war, the science of the stars, the science related to serpents, and the fine arts—also heaven and earth, air and Ākāsha, water and fire, gods and men, cattle and birds, grasses and trees, beasts down to worms, flying insects and ants, merit and demerit, true and false, good and bad, pleasant and unpleasant, food and drink, this world and the next — (all this) one understands by understanding alone. Worship understanding. 7.7.2: 'He who worships understanding as Brahman, attains the worlds containing the knowledge of the Scriptures and other subjects. He becomes free to act as he wishes in the sphere within the reach of understanding, he who worships understanding as Brahman'. 'Revered sir, is there anything greater than understanding?' 'Surely, there is something greater than understanding'. 'Revered sir, communicate it to me'.

7.8.1: 'Strength surely is greater than understanding. A single man with strength causes even a hundred men with understanding to tremble. When a man becomes strong, then he rises; rising, he serves; serving, he approaches nearer; approaching nearer, he sees, hears, reflects, understands, acts and realizes. By strength, indeed, the earth stands; by strength, the sky; by strength, heaven; by strength, the mountains; by strength, gods and men; by strength, cattle and birds, grasses and trees, beasts down to worms, flying insects and ants; by strength the world stands. Worship strength. 7.8.2: 'He who worships strength as Brahman becomes free to act as he wishes in the sphere within the reach of strength, he who worships strength as Brahman'. 'Revered sir, is there anything greater than strength?' 'Surely, there is something greater than strength'. 'Revered sir, communicate it to me'.

7.9.1: 'Food surely is greater than strength. Therefore, if one does not eat for ten days, even though he might live, yet, verily, he does not see, does not hear, does not reflect, does not act, and does not realize. But with the coming of food, he sees, hears, reflects, understands, acts and realizes. Worship food. 7.9.2: 'He who worships food as Brahman, he verily attains the worlds supplied with food and drink. He is free to act as he wishes in the sphere within the reach of food, he who worships food as Brahman'. 'Revered sir, is there anything greater than food?' 'Surely, there is something greater than food'. 'Revered sir, communicate it to me'.

7.10.1: 'Water surely is greater than food. Therefore, when there is not good rain, living creatures are in agony (thinking), "Food will be scarce". But when there is good rain, living creatures become joyous (thinking), "Food will abound". Water, indeed, has assumed all these forms—this earth, this sky, this heaven, these mountains, these gods and men, these cattle and birds, grasses and trees, beasts down to worms, flying insects and ants. Water, indeed, has assumed all these forms. Worship water. 7.10.2: 'He who worships water as Brahman obtains all desires and becomes satisfied. He becomes free to act as he wishes in the sphere within the reach of water, he who worships water as Brahman'. 'Revered sir, is there anything greater than water?' 'Surely, there is something greater than water'. 'Revered sir, communicate it to me'.

7.11.1: 'Fire surely is greater than water. It is this fire that having seized the air warms up the Ākāsha. Then people say, "It is hot, it is burning hot, it will surely rain". There, it is fire that shows itself first, and then creates water. It is (because of) this fire that thunders roll, along with lightnings flashing upwards and across; and so people say, "Lightning is flashing, it is thundering, it will surely rain". There, it is fire that shows itself first and then creates water. Worship fire. 7.11.2: 'He who worships fire as Brahman, he, being resplendent himself, attains resplendent worlds, full of light and free from darkness. He becomes free to act as he wishes in the sphere within the reach of fire, he who worships fire as Brahman'. 'Revered sir, is there anything greater than fire?' 'Surely, there is something greater than fire'. 'Revered sir, communicate it to me'.

7.12.1: Ākāsha surely is greater than fire. In Ākāsha, indeed, exist both the sun and moon, lightning, stars and fire. Through Ākāsha one calls, through Ākāsha one hears, through Ākāsha one hears the response. In Ākāsha one rejoices, in Ākāsha one does not rejoice. In Ākāsha a thing is born, and towards Ākāsha it grows. Worship Ākāsha. 7.12.2: 'He who worships Ākāsha as Brahman, he indeed, attains vast worlds full of light, unconfined and spacious. He is free to act as he wishes in the sphere within the reach of Ākāsha, he who worships Ākāsha as Brahman'. 'Revered sir, is there anything greater than Ākāsha?' 'Surely, there is something greater than Ākāsha'. 'Revered sir, communicate it to me'.

7.13.1: 'Memory surely is greater than Ākāsha. Therefore, even if many persons should assemble and if they should have no memory, they surely would not hear any sound, they would not think, they would not know. But surely, should they have memory, then they would hear, then they would think, then they would know. Through memory, indeed, one discerns one's sons, through memory one's cattle. Worship memory. 7.13.2: 'He who worships memory as Brahman becomes free to act as he wishes in the sphere within the reach of memory, he who worships memory as Brahman'. 'Revered sir, is there anything greater than memory?' 'Surely, there is something greater than memory'. 'Revered sir, communicate it to me'.

7.14.1: 'Aspiration surely is greater than memory. Kindled by aspiration, (one's) memory recites the hymns, performs rites, desires sons and cattle, desires this world and the next. Worship aspiration. 7.14.2: 'He who worships aspiration as Brahman, by aspiration all his wishes prosper, his prayers become infallible. He is free to act as he wishes in the sphere within the reach of aspiration, he who worships aspiration as Brahman'. 'Revered sir, is there anything greater than aspiration?' 'Surely, there is something greater than aspiration'. 'Revered sir, communicate it to me'.

7.15.1: 'Prāna surely is greater than aspiration. Just as the spokes of the wheel are fastened to the nave, so is all this fastened to this Prāna. Prāna moves by Prāna, Prāna gives Prāna and it gives Prāna. Prāna is the father, Prāna is the mother, Prāna is the brother, Prāna is the sister, Prāna is the preceptor, Prāna is the Brāhmana. 7.15.2: 'If one answers something harsh to his father, mother, brother, sister, preceptor or a Brāhmana, people say this to him, "Fie on you! You are indeed a slayer of your father, you are indeed a slayer of your mother, you are indeed a slayer of your brother, you are indeed a slayer of your sister, you are indeed a slayer of your preceptor, you are indeed a slayer of a Brāhmana." 7.15.3: 'On the other hand, when the Prāna has departed from them, even if one piles them together, dismembers them with a fork and burns them up, surely people would not say to him, "You are a slayer of your father", nor "you are a slayer of your mother", nor "You are a slayer of your brother", nor "You are a slayer of your sister", nor "you are a slayer of your preceptor", nor "You are a slayer of a Brāhmana". 7.15.4: 'Prāna indeed becomes all these.

He, indeed, who sees thus, thinks thus and knows thus becomes a surpassing speaker. If someone were to say to him, "You are a surpassing speaker", he should say, "Yes, I am a surpassing speaker", he should not deny it.

7.16.1: 'But he really speaks surpassingly who speaks surpassingly with truth'. 'Revered sir, being such, I would speak surpassingly with truth'. 'But one must desire to understand the truth'. 'Revered sir, I desire to understand the truth'.

7.17.1: 'When one understands, then alone does one declare the truth. Without understanding, one does not declare the truth. Only he who understands declares the truth. But one must desire to understand understanding.' 'Revered sir, I desire to understand understanding'.

7.18.1: 'When one reflects, then alone does one understand. Without reflecting one does not understand. Only he who reflects understands. But one must desire to understand reflection.' 'Revered sir, I desire to understand reflection'.

7.19.1: 'When one has faith, then alone does one reflect. Without faith, one does not reflect. Only he who has faith reflects. But one must desire to understand faith'. 'Revered sir, I desire to understand faith'.

7.20.1: 'When one has steadfastness, then alone does one have faith. Without steadfastness, one does not have faith. Only he who has steadfastness has faith. But one must desire to understand steadfastness.' 'Revered sir, I desire to understand steadfastness.'

7.21.1: 'When one acts, then alone does one become steadfast. Without acting, one does not become steadfast. Only on acting does one become steadfast. But one must desire to understand activity'. 'Revered sir, I desire to understand activity'.

7.22.1: 'When one obtains happiness', then alone does one act. Without obtaining happiness one does not act. Only on obtaining happiness does one act. But one must desire to understand happiness'. 'Revered sir, I desire to understand happiness'.

7.23.1: That which is infinite, is alone happiness. There is no happiness in anything finite. The infinite alone is happiness. But one must desire to understand the infinite'. 'Revered sir, I desire to understand the infinite'.

7.24.1: 'In which one sees nothing else, hears nothing else, understands nothing else, that is infinite. But that in which one sees something else, hears something else, understands something else, is the finite. That which is infinite, is alone immortal, and that which is finite, is mortal'. 'Revered sir, in what is that infinite established?' 'On its own greatness or not even on its own greatness'. 7.24.2: 'Here in this world people call cows and horses, elephants and gold, servants and wives, fields and houses, "greatness". I do not speak thus (of greatness), for in that case one thing would be established in another. What I do say is thus:

7.25.1: 'That infinite alone is below. That is above. That is behind. That is in front. That is to the south. That is to the north. That alone is all this. So next is the teaching in regard to the self-sense. I alone am below. I am above. I am behind. I am in front. I am to the south. I am to the north. I alone am all this. 7.25.2: 'So now is the teaching through Atman. Atman alone is below. Atman is above. Atman is behind. Atman is in front. Atman is to the south. Atman is to the north. Atman alone is all this. Verily, he it is who sees thus, and understands thus, has pleasure in Atman, delight in Atman, union in Atman, joy in Atman. He becomes Self-sovereign; he becomes free to act as he wishes in all the worlds. But those who know otherwise than this are ruled by others and live in perishable worlds; they are not free to act as they wish in all the worlds.

7.26.1: Verily, for him alone, who sees thus, reflects thus and understands thus, Prāna springs from Atman, aspiration from Atman, memory from Atman, Ākāsha from Atman, fire from Atman, water from Atman, appearance and disappearances from Atman, food from Atman, strength from Atman, understanding from Atman, contemplation from Atman, intelligence from Atman, will from Atman, mind from Atman, speech from Atman, name from Atman, hymns from Atman, rites from Atman, all this (springs) from Atman alone. 7.26.2: 'There is this verse about it: "He who sees this does not see death nor illness nor any sorrow. He who sees this sees all things and obtains all things in all ways." 'He is one, becomes threefold, fivefold, sevenfold and also ninefold. Then again he is called the elevenfold, also a hundred- and-ten-fold and also a thousand-and-twenty-fold. **"When nourishment is pure, reflection and higher understanding become pure. When reflection and higher understanding are pure, memory becomes strong. When memory becomes strong, there is release from all the knots of the heart.** The revered Sanatkumara showed to Narada, after his impurities had been washed off, the further shore of darkness. People call Sanatkumara as Skanda—yes, they call him Skanda.

8.1.1: Om. Now, in this city of Brahman, there is a mansion in the shape of a small lotus; in it is a small inner Ākāsha. What is within that, that should be sought; that indeed, one should desire to understand. 8.1.2-3: If the disciples should say to him, 'In this city of Brahman in which is a small mansion in the shape of a lotus and in the small inner Ākāsha within—what is it that lies there which should be sought, which one should desire to understand?'—he should say in reply, 'As large indeed as is this Ākāsha, so large is that

Ākāsha in the heart. Within it, indeed, are contained both heaven and earth, both fire and air, both the sun and the moon, lightning and the stars. Whatever there is of him in this world and whatever is not, all that is contained within it.' 8.1.4: If they should say to him, 'If in this city of Brahman is contained all this, all beings and all desires, then what is left of it when old age overtakes it or when it perishes?' 8.1.5: He should say, 'It (the Brahman called inner Ākāsha) does not age with the ageing of the body, it is not killed by the killing of this. This (Ākāsha) is the real city of Brahman, in it are contained the desires. This is the Atman, free from evil, free from old age, free from death, free from sorrow, free from hunger, free from thirst, whose desire is of the truth, whose resolve is of the truth. Just as in this world, the subjects follow as they are commanded and whatever province they desire, be it a country or a part of the field, on that they live. (So the ignorant depend upon others for enjoying the fruits of their Karma). 8.1.6: 'Just as here on earth the world which is earned by work perishes, even so there in the other world, the world which is earned by righteous deeds perishes. So those who depart from here without having understood the Atman and these true desires, for them there is no freedom to act as they wish in all the worlds. But those who depart from here, having understood the Atman and these true desires, for them there is freedom to act as they wish in all the worlds.'

8.2.1: If he becomes desirous of the world of fathers, by his mere will, fathers arise. Possessed of that world of fathers he feels happy and exalted. 8.2.2: And if he becomes desirous of the world of mothers, by his mere will, mothers arise. Possessed of that world of mothers he feels happy and exalted. 8.2.3: And if he becomes desirous of the world of brothers, by his mere will, brothers arise. Possessed of that world of brothers he feels happy and exalted. 8.2.4: And if he becomes desirous of the world of sisters, by his mere will, sisters arise. Possessed of that world of sisters he feels happy and exalted. 8.2.5: And if he becomes desirous of the world of friends, by his mere will, friends arise. Possessed of that world of friends he feels happy and exalted. 8.2.6: And if he becomes desirous of the world of perfumes and garlands, by his mere will, of perfumes and garlands arise. Possessed of that world of perfumes and garlands he feels happy and exalted. 8.2.7: And if he becomes desirous of the world of food and drink, by his mere will, food and drink arise. Possessed of that world of food and drink he feels happy and exalted. 8.2.8: And if he becomes desirous of the world of song and music, by his mere will, song and music arise. Possessed of that world of song and music he feels happy and exalted. 8.2.9: And if he becomes desirous of the world of women, by his mere will, women arise. Possessed of that world of women he feels happy and exalted. 8.2.10: Whatever provinces he is attached to and whatever desirable objects he desires by his mere will, they get. Possessed of that he feels happy and exalted.

8.3.1: These same are the true desires covered by the untrue. Although the desires are true, they are covered by the untrue. For whosoever of one's people departs from here in this world one does not get him back to see. 8.3.2: But those of his people, whether they are alive or dead and whatever else one desires but does not get, all that one finds by going there (into the Atman, the Ākāsha in the heart); for here, indeed, are those true desires of his covered by the untrue. Just as, though people who do not know the field walk again and again over the treasure of gold hidden underground but do not find it, even so all these creatures here, though they go daily into the Brahman-world, yet do not find it, for they are carried away by the untrue. 8.3.3: This Atman verily is in the heart. Its etymological explanation is this. This (Atman) is in the heart, hence it is the heart. He who knows thus (indeed goes daily into the heavenly world. 8.3.4: Now that serene and happy being, rising out of this body and reaching the highest light, appears in his own true form. This is the Atman, said the teacher. This is the immortal, the fearless. This is Brahman. Verily, the name of this Brahman is the True. 8.3.5: These are indeed the three syllables, 'sa', 'ti', 'yam'. What is 'sa', that is the immortal, and what is 'ti', that is the mortal, and what is 'yam', with it one holds the two together. Because with it one holds the two together, therefore it is 'yam'. Verily, he who knows thus goes to the heavenly world.'

8.4.1: Now, this Atman is the dyke, the embankment for the safety of these worlds. This dyke, neither the day nor the night crosses, nor old age nor death nor sorrow, nor merit nor demerit. All evils turn back from it, for this Brahman-world is free from evil. 8.4.2: Therefore, verily, on reaching this dyke, if one was blind he ceases to be blind; if wounded, he ceases to be wounded, if afflicted- he ceases to be afflicted. Therefore, verily, on reaching this dyke, even night becomes day, for this Brahman-world is ever illumined. 8.4.3: But only those who attain according to the instruction this Brahman-world through Brahmacharya, to them belongs this Brahman-world. For them there is freedom to act as they wish in all the worlds.

8.5.1: Now, what people call sacrifice is really Brahmacharya, for only by means of Brahmacharya does the knower attain that world. And what people call worship (Ista) is really Brahmacharya, for only by worshipping with Brahmacharya does one attain the Atman. 8.5.2: Now, what people call the sacrificial session is really Brahmacharya, for only by means of Brahmacharya does one obtain one's salvation from Being. And what people call the vow of silence is really Brahmacharya for only through Brahmacharya does one understand the Atman and then meditate. 8.5.3:

Chāndogya Upanishad

Now, what people call a course of fasting is really Brahmacharya, for this Atman never perishes which one attains by means of Brahmacharya. And what people call the life of a hermit is really Brahmacharya, for verily Ara and Nya are the two oceans in the Brahman-world in the third heaven from here and therein is the lake Airammadiya, and there is the Aparajita (unconquered) city of Brahma, and there is the gold hall specially built by the Lord. 8.5.4: Therefore only those who attain the two oceans, Ara and Nya, in the Brahman-world by means of Brahmacharya, only to them belongs this Brahman-world and for them there is freedom to act as they wish in all the worlds.

8.6.1: Now, these arteries which belong to the heart exist filled with the juice of a fine substance which is reddish-brown, white, blue, yellow and red. The yonder sun indeed is reddish-brown, he is white, he is blue, he is yellow, he is red. 8.6.2: Just as an extending highway runs between two villages, this as well as that, even so the rays of the sun go to both these worlds, this as well as that. They spread out of the yonder sun and enter into these arteries. Out of these arteries they spread and enter into the yonder sun. 8.6.3: Therefore when one is thus sound sleep, composed, serene so that he knows no dreams, then he enters into (the Ākāsha of the heart through) these arteries. Then no evil touches him for then he is filled with the light of the sun. 8.6.4: Now, when one is thus reduced to a weakened condition, those who sit around him say, 'Do you know me? Do you know me?' As long as he has not departed from this body, so long he knows them. 8.6.5: But when he thus departs from this body, then he proceeds upwards through those very rays, (if a knower) he surely goes up meditating on Om or (does not got up if he is not a knower). As long as it takes for the mind to travel, in that (short) time, he goes to the sun. That indeed is the door to the world (of Brahman), an entrance for the knowers and a shutting out for the ignorant. 8.6.6: There is this verse about it: A hundred and one are the arteries of the heart; one of them leads up to the crown of the head. Passing upwards through that, one attains immortality, while the other arteries serve for departing in various other directions—yes, serve for departing.

8. Indra and virochana

8.7.1: The Atman which is free from evil, free from old age, free from death, free from sorrow, free from hunger and thirst, whose desire is of the truth, whose resolve is of the truth, he should be sought, him one should desire to understand. He who has found out and who understands that Atman attains all the worlds and all the desires. Thus spoke Prajapati. 8.7.2: Both the gods and the demons heard this and said, 'Well, let us seek that Atman by seeking which one attains all the worlds and all the desires.' Then Indra alone from among the gods went out and so did Virochana from among the demons. Then without communicating with each other, they both came into the presence of Prajapati, fuel in hand. 8.7.3: For thirty-two years they lived there the disciplined life of a celibate student of sacred knowledge. Then Prajapati asked them, 'Desiring what have you been living?' They replied, 'The Atman which is free from evil, free from old age, free from death, free from sorrow, free from hunger and thirst, whose desire is of the truth, whose resolve is of the truth, he should be sought, him one should desire to understand. He who has found out and who understands that Atman attain all the worlds and all the desires—these are known to be the words of your revered self. Desiring that Atman we have been living.' 8.7.4: Prajapati said to them, 'The person which is seen in the eye is the Atman'. He added, 'This is the immortal, the fearless. This is Brahman'. 'But, revered sir, he who is perceived in water and he who in a mirror, which of these is the Atman?' It is he himself that is perceived in all these', replied Prajapati.

8.8.1: 'Look at yourself in a pan of water and whatever you do not understand of the Atman, tell me that'. Then they looked in a pan of water. Prajapati asked them, 'What do you see?' They replied, 'Revered sir, we both see the self entirely as we are, the very image, even to the very hairs and nails.' 8.8.2: Then Prajapati said to them, 'Having become well adorned, well dressed and well groomed, look into the pan of water.' They too, having become well adorned, well dressed and well groomed, looked into the pan of water. Then Prajapati asked them, 'What do you see?' 8.8.3: They replied, 'Just as we are ourselves, revered sir, well adorned, well dressed and well groomed, even so are both these, revered sir, well adorned, well dressed and well groomed.' 'This is the Atman', said he, 'this is the immortal, the fearless. This is Brahman'. They both went away satisfied in their hearts. 8.8.4: Then Prajapati looked at them and said, 'They are going away without having perceived, without having understood the Atman. Whosoever will follow such a doctrine be they gods or demons, they will be foiled.' Now, Virochana, satisfied in his heart, went to the demons and declared this doctrine to them. 'Here the (bodily) self alone is to be worshipped, the self is to be attended upon. Here it is only by worshipping the self and attending upon the self that one obtains both the worlds, this as well as the yonder.' 8.8.5: Therefore, even to this day, here people say of one who is not a giver, who has no faith, who does not perform sacrifices, 'Oh, he is a demon'; for this is the doctrine of the demons. They adorn the body of the deceased with enjoyable things, clothes and ornaments for, by this, they think, they will win the other world.

8.9.1: But Indra, even before reaching the gods, saw this difficulty: 'Just as this (reflected self) becomes well adorned when this body is well adorned, well dressed when the body is well dressed, well-groomed when the body is well groomed, even so this (reflected self) also becomes blind when the body is blind, one-eyed when the body is one-eyed, crippled when the body is crippled, and it perishes when this body perishes. I see no good in this.' 8.9.2: He came back again, fuel in hand. Prajapati asked him, 'Desiring what, O Indra, have you come back, since you went away satisfied in your heart, along with Virochana?' Indra replied, 'Revered sir, just as this (reflected self) becomes well adorned when this body is well adorned, well dressed when the body is well dressed, well-groomed when the body is well groomed, even so this (reflected self) also becomes blind when the body is blind, one-eyed when the body is one-eyed, crippled when the body is crippled, and it perishes when this body perishes. I see no good in this. 8.9.3: 'So is it indeed, O Indra', said Prajapati; 'However, I shall explain this further to you. Live here for another thirty-two years.' He lived there for another thirty-two years. Then Prajapati said to him:

8.10.1-2: Prajapati said, 'He who moves about in dreams, he is the Atman. He is the immortal, the fearless. He is Brahman'. Indra went away satisfied in his heart. But even before reaching the gods he saw this difficulty: 'Even though this (dream-self) is not blind when this body is blind, nor one-eyed when the body is slain, nor has running nose and eyes when the body has running nose and eyes, yet it is as if they kill it, as if they chase it, it becomes conscious of pain, as it were, and even weeps, as it were. I see no good in this'. 8.10.3-4: He came back again, fuel in hand. Prajapati asked him, 'Desiring what, O Indra, have you come back, since you went away satisfied in your heart?' He replied, 'Revered sir, even though this self is not blind when this body is blind, nor one-eyed when the body is one-eyed, nor suffers defects from the defects of the body, nor is slain when the body is slain, nor has running nose and eyes, yet it is as if they kill it, as if they chase it, it becomes conscious of pain as it were, and even weeps, as it were. I see no good in this'. 'So is it indeed, O Indra', said Prajapati; 'However, I shall explain this further to you. Live here for another thirty-two years.' He lived there for another thirty-two years. Then Prajapati said to him:

8.11.1: Prajapati said, 'He who is fully asleep, composed, serene and knows no dream, he is the Atman. He is the immortal, the fearless. He is Brahman'. Indra went away satisfied in his heart. But even before reaching the gods he saw this difficulty: 'In truth this one does not know himself now as "I am he", nor indeed these beings. It seems as if he has gone to annihilation. I see no good in this'. 8.11.2: He came back again, fuel in hand. Prajapati asked him, 'Desiring what, O Indra, have you come back, since you went away satisfied in your heart?' He replied, 'Revered sir, in truth this one does not know himself as "I am he", nor indeed these beings. It seems as if he has gone to annihilation. I see no good in this'. 8.11.3: 'So is it indeed, O Indra', said Prajapati; 'However, I shall explain this further to you and none other than this. Live here for another five years.' He lived there for another five years. That makes one hundred and one years and so with regard to that, people say thus, 'Verily, for one hundred and one years Indra lived with Prajapati the disciplined life of a celibate student of sacred knowledge". Then Prajapati said to him:

8.12.1: 'O Indra, mortal indeed is this body, held by death. But it is the support of this deathless, bodiless Atman. Verily, the embodied self is held by pleasure and pain. Surely, there is no cessation of pleasure and pain for one who is embodied. But pleasure and pain do not indeed touch one who is bodiless. 8.12.2-3: Bodiless is air; and white cloud, lightning, thunder, these also are bodiless. Now as these arise out of the yonder Ākāsha, reach the highest light and appear each with its own form, even so this serene one rises out of this body, reaches the highest light and appears in his own form. He is the Highest Person. There he moves about, laughing, playing, rejoicing with women, vehicles or relations, not remembering this body in which he was born. As an animal is attached to a chariot, even so is the Prāna attached to this body. 8.12.4: Now, where the sight merges in Ākāsha (inside the eye, i.e., the black pupil of the eye), (there exists) that which is the person in the eye; and the eye is only for (his) seeing. And he who knows 'I smell this', is the Atman; the nose is for smelling. And he who knows 'I speak this', is the Atman, the organ of speech is for speaking. And he who knows 'I hear this', is the Atman; the ear is for hearing. 8.12.5: And he who knows 'I think this', is the Atman, the mind is his divine eye. Through this divine eye of the mind he verily sees these desired objects which are in the Brahman-world, and rejoices. 8.12.6: 'Verily, this is the Atman whom the gods worship. Therefore all the worlds and all the desired objects are held by them. He obtains all the worlds all the desired objects, who having known that Atman (from the teacher and the scriptures) understands it.' Thus spoke Prajapati—yes, thus spoke Prajapati.

8.13.1: From the dark I attain to the variegated from the variegated I attain to the dark. Shaking off evil as a horse his hairs, shaking off the body as the moon frees itself from the mouth of Rahu, I, having fulfilled all ends, obtain the eternal Brahman-world—yes, I obtain it.

8.14.1: Verily, what is called Ākāsha is the revealer of name and form. That within which they are, is Brahman, that is the immortal, that is the Atman. 'I attain to the assembly-hall and abode of Prajapati. I am the glory of the Brāhmanas, the glory of the Kshatriyas, the glory of the Vaisyas. I wish to attain that glory. I am the glory of the glories. May I never go to that which is reddish-white and toothless yet devouring and slippery—yes, may I never go to it.'

8.15.1: Brahma expounded this to Prajapati. Prajapati to Manu and Manu to his descendants. He who has read the Veda according to the prescribed rule, in the time left over after performing his duties to the teacher, he who after having come back from the teacher's house, settles down in his household, continues the study of the Veda in a clean place, and has virtuous sons and disciples, he who withdraws all his senses into the Atman, who practices non-injury to all beings except in places specially ordained, he who behaves thus throughout his life reaches the world of Brahman and does not return again—yes, he does not return again.

Om! Let my limbs and speech, Prāna, eyes, ears, vitality and all the senses grow in strength. All existence is the Brahman of the Upanishads. May I never deny Brahman, nor Brahman deny me. Let there be no denial at all: Let there be no denial at least from me.

May the virtues that are proclaimed in the Upanishads be in me, who am devoted to the Atman; may they reside in me.

Om! Shantih! Shantih! Shantih!!

Here ends the Chandogyopanishad, as contained in the Sama-Veda.

Chandogya Upanishad

Commentary

by Swami Nirmalananda Giri

The Glory of Om

In this commentary I will be mostly using the translation of Swami Prabhavananda. In his translations of some Upanishads Swami Prabhavananda omitted some parts, many that were in such obscure language that any attempt at translation would really only be speculation. He also omitted very repetitious passages and those that dwelt with matters irrelevant to the knowledge of Brahman and the Self. That is why in the references to the verses of this Upanishad there will be some jumping around. However, Prabhavananda omitted some passages that I think are extremely important. So I will be supplementing his translation.

Meditation on Om

"One should meditate on the syllable Om, the Udgītha. Of this, the explanation follows." (Chandogya Upanishad 1.1.1)

This leaves us little doubt as to what the author (or authors) of the Chandogya Upanishad consider the subject of prime importance: meditation on Om. **"Udgītha" is the technical, ritual term for Om when It is sung aloud in Vedic recitation.** So in the subsequent verses I am just going to put Om wherever Udgītha occurs.

The supreme essence

"The essence of man is speech. The essence of speech is the hymns of the Rig Veda. Their essence is the hymns of the Sama Veda. The essence of the Sama Veda is Om." (Chandogya Upanishad 1.1.2)

That which marks human beings out from the lesser forms of evolution is the power of vak—of symbolic, creative speech. Most animals make some kinds of sounds that indicate their feelings, but only humans have symbolic words that recount and stimulate both thought and behavior: This is the power of logos spoken of in Greek philosophy and Eastern Christian writings. It is not just a simple trait, but a virtual intellectual ocean that separates us from other sentient beings on earth. It is, as said, a product of evolution, and skill in speech is the mark of an evolved human being, though the most important ability is that of creative thought/ conceptualization. Vak is what makes us human.

The highest form of Speech is that of the hymns of the Rig Veda that were revealed in meditation untold thousands of years ago to the Vedic Rishis (Seers). The highest of those hymns were collected into the Sama Veda, whose text is marked (pointed) for devotional singing. And the supreme essence of the Sama Veda hymns is the single syllable: OM. In many texts it is stated that to intone Om is to recite all the Vedic hymns. Therefore:

"The syllable Om which is called Udgītha, is the quintessence of the essences, the supreme, deserving of the highest place." (Chandogya Upanishad 1.1.3) This can be said, because Om is the Primal Word, the Original Sound, the First Word "spoken" by God, and by which all that "is" was created, and is being sustained and evolved at this very moment. **The Vedic Seers long ago stated: "In the beginning was Prajapati [God the Creator], with Him was the Word, and the Word was truly the Supreme Brahman."** (*Prajapati vai idam agra asit. Tasya vak dvitiya asit. Vag vai paramam Brahman.* Krishna Yajurveda, Kathaka Samhita, 12.5, 27.1; Krishna Yajurveda, Kathakapisthala Samhita, 42.1; Jaiminiya Brāhmana II, Samaveda, 2244) **This was much later paraphrased in the opening verses of the Gospel of Saint John: "In the beginning was the Word, and the Word was with God, and the Word was God.**

The same was in the beginning with God." (John 1:1,2)

Chandogya Upanishad 2.23.3 says that Brahma the creator concentrated his awareness on the worlds he had projected and: "From them, thus brooded upon, issued forth [as their essence] the syllable Om. Just as all the parts of the leaf, are permeated by the ribs of the leaf, so are all the words permeated by the syllable Om. Verily, the syllable Om is all this—yes, the syllable Om is verily all this."

Everything is contained in Om, as other Upanishadic texts enumerate, including all the possible states of consciousness, the expanse of time (past, present, future), the three worlds (physical, astral, causal)—ALL. The Upanishadic teaching is that Om is identical with Brahman Itself. How then can we regard It as anything other than "the quintessence of the essences, the supreme, deserving of the highest place"?

The divine union

"Speech [Vak] and Breath [Prāna] taken together form a couple. This couple is joined together in the syllable Om. Whenever a couple come together, they, indeed, fulfill each other's desire." (Chandogya 1.1.5.6)

Fulfiller of desires

"He who meditates upon Om knowing it thus (as the fulfiller), verily becomes a fulfiller of all the desirable ends. That verily is the syllable of assent, for whenever one assents to a thing, one says only 'Om'. Assent alone is prosperity. He who meditates upon Om, knowing it thus (as endowed with the quality of prosperity), verily becomes one who increases all the desirable ends." (Chandogya Upanishad 1.1.7,8)

This is important for two reasons. First, that **Om contains within Itself creative power, and IS Creative Power.** Naturally, we must both know how to employ It and to be of such a level of consciousness that we can do with It what God does with It. This is certainly possible. I have known yogis who could heal with Om and do many other "magical" things that were really quite normal for the person who knew how. That is why this section is concluded with these words:

"**Whatever is performed with knowledge, faith and meditation (on Om) becomes more effective**. Up to this truly is the explanation of (the greatness of) this syllable Om." (Chandogya Upanishad 1.1.10)

The second important point is that the yogi need not be a person who lives in a bare subsistence manner, unworldly, impractical and indifferent to all material things including his body. The opposite is true. In the eighth chapter of this Upanishad we find these verses: "If the sage desires to see his fathers of the spirit-world, lo, his fathers come to meet him. In their company he is happy. And if he desires to see his mothers of the spirit-world, lo, his mothers come to meet him. In their company he is happy. And if he desires to see his brothers of the spirit-world, lo, his brothers come to meet him. In their company he is happy. And if he desires to see his sisters of the spirit-world, lo, his sisters come to meet him. In their company he is happy. And if he desires to see his friends of the spirit-world, lo, his friends come to meet him. In their company he is happy. And if he desires heavenly perfumes and garlands, lo, heavenly perfumes and garlands come to him. In their possession he is happy. And if he desires heavenly food and drink, lo, heavenly food and drink come to him. In their possession he is happy. And if he desires heavenly song and music, lo, heavenly song and music come to him. In their possession he is happy. Indeed, whatsoever such a knower of Brahman may desire, straightway it is his; and having obtained it, he is exalted of men." (Chandogya Upanishad 8.2.1-10)

Such is the real yogi, the true adept. I remember a recording of Paramhansa Yogananda in which he spoke about how many mortgages he had paid off, how much property he had bought, and how large a "family" he had supported for decades. "I could have kept away a million dollars and no one would have known," he said, speaking of the abundance that had come to him after enduring great hardship and remaining faithful to the ideals he had been sent to America to teach and practice. (A Bengali song in his honor says: "Going far away you taught dharma. And that dharma which you taught, you showed perfectly in your life.") Then he told his hearers that despite all the financial outlay, he only had a little box that was never empty by God's grace, and he never bothered to count how much was in it. One of India's greatest yogis was Janaka, whose name is invoked as the symbol of tremendous wealth as well as wisdom. They speak of Janaka in India as we do of Midas in the West.

Such is Om; such are those that meditate upon It.

The Gods and Om

Throughout the Upanishads, Gita, and other spiritual texts we find references to gods—in Sanskrit: devas. A Brief Sanskrit Glossary defines deva in this way: "A shining one,' a god—greater or lesser in the evolutionary hierarchy; a semi-divine or celestial being with great powers, and therefore a 'god.' Sometimes called a demi-god. Devas are the demigods presiding over various powers of material and psychic nature. In many instances 'devas' refer to the powers of the senses or the sense organs themselves."

The sun

"Now the meditation on Om with reference to the gods is described. One should meditate on the sun as Om.

Verily, when he rises, he sings aloud for the sake of all creatures." (Chandogya Upanishad 1.3.1)

We should skip ahead a little bit to continue this subject.

"Now, that which is Om **is verily Pranava and that which is Pranava is Om.** The yonder sun is Om and also Pranava, for he moves along pronouncing 'Om.'" (Chandogya Upanishad 1.5.1) That is, the energy of the sun is a manifestation of Om. Scientists have only recently discovered this phenomenon. On page 16 of the July 2004 issue of *National Geographic* we find this: "Bubbles the size of Texas cover the sun's face…. Called granules, the short-lived cells of plasma carry heat to the surface through convection, the same way water boils in a pot. The rise and fall of granules creates sound waves, which cause the sun to throb like a drum every five minutes."

In The Word That is God we find the following comment: "All plant, animal, and human life on this planet depends upon the sun. It is the subtle powers of sunlight which stimulate growth and evolution. Sunlight particularly stimulates the activity of the higher centers in the brain, especially that of the pineal gland. Even in the depths of the earth a sensitive man can tell when the sun rises and sets above him. The sun truly awakens us in the deepest sense. As the germinating seed struggles upward toward the sun and out into its life-giving rays, so all higher forms of life reach out for the sun, which acts as a metaphysical magnet, drawing them upward and outward toward ever-expanding consciousness. Sunlight is the radiant form of Om. The sun initiates the entire solar system into Om. Human beings are solar creatures, therefore to intone Om is the most natural things they can do." Later the Upanishad says: **"Reflect upon Om as the rays of the sun." (Chandogya Upanishad 1.5.2)**

Further on we find a section that speaks of the divine Person (Purusha) who ensouls and enlivens the sun: Ishvara. "Now, that Person, effulgent as gold, who is seen within the sun, who is with golden beard and golden hair, is exceedingly effulgent even to the very tips of his nails. His eyes are bright like a red lotus. He is above all evils. (Verily, he who knows thus rises above all evils.) He is Om. Moreover, he controls the worlds which are above that sun, as also the desires of the gods." (Chandogya Upanishad 1.6.6-8)

Even further on we are told that Om is like the flower of the sun. When the yogi-bees "pressed this Pranava, from It, thus pressed, issued forth as juice: fame, splendor of limbs, alertness of the senses, virility, and nourishment." (Chandogya Upanishad 3.5.2)

The most important aspect of the solar connection with Om is found in the eighth section of the Upanishad. There it speaks of the nadis, the subtle energy channels that function in the subtle bodies of human beings. Then it says that "Just as an extending highway runs between two villages, this as well as that, even so the rays of the sun go to both these worlds, this as well as that. They spread out of the yonder sun and enter into these nadis. Out of these nadis they spread and enter into the yonder sun." (Chandogya Upanishad 8.6.2) Regarding one who meditates on Om, the Upanishad continues: "When he thus departs from this body, then he proceeds upwards through those very rays. He surely goes up meditating on Om. As long as it takes for the mind to travel, in that time he goes to the sun. That indeed is the door to the world of Brahman, an entrance for the knowers and a shutting out for the ignorant." (Chandogya Upanishad 8.6.5) Those who pass through the sun are free from the compulsion to rebirth on the earth. Om!

The breath and Om

The connection between the sun and our breath is next described. "This breath and that sun are the same. Therefore one should meditate on this breath and that sun as Om." (Chandogya Upanishad 1.3.2) This is why in Om Yoga we join our intonations of Om with the breath.

The Upanishad continues: "Now with reference to the body: One should meditate on the breath as Om, for he moves along pronouncing 'Om.' Thinking thus, sing praise to Om as the manifold prānas. Now, that which is Om, is verily Pranava; and that which is Pranava, is Om—so one should think." (Chandogya Upanishad 1.5.3-5)

Escaping death

Now we have a parable about rising above the realm of death: samsara.

"One should meditate on the syllable Om. Of this the explanation follows. Verily, the gods, being afraid of death, took refuge in the three Vedas. Just as a fisherman would see a fish in water, so did Death observe the gods in the Vedic hymns. They, too, knowing this, arose and entered Om. **This syllable Om is indeed immortality and fearlessness. Having entered into Om the gods became immortal and fearless. He who worships this syllable knowing it thus, enters this syllable which is immortality and fearlessness.** And having entered it, he becomes immortal by that amrita [Om], by which the gods became immortal." (Chandogya Upanishad 1.4.1-5)

The devas (gods) are all the aspects of the human being. Those who seek life and immortality in external rites—indeed, in anything other than Brahman—will be caught in the net of death just like fish in the fisherman's net. But when they take refuge in meditation of Om they rise above the realm of even the possibility of death. Of course this may also be a story of highly evolved beings who found that they were still subject to death in the higher worlds, being forced to drop the subtle bodies proper to those realms and enter bodies on lesser levels or worlds. At the Mahapralaya, the Great Universal Dissolution, all the worlds are shaken and dissolve away. The wise, knowing that, do not content themselves with living in carefree and beautiful wish-fulfilling worlds, but busy themselves with tapasya to ascend beyond relativity. And they do this through meditation on Om. And so should we.

The Sages and Om

The Upanishad gives some very interesting views on Om in the form of a discussion between three sages. We will look at a condensed version.

"In ancient times there were three proficient in Om: Silaka the son of Salavat, Caikitayana of the Dalbhya family and Pravahana the son of Jivala. They said, 'We are proficient in Om. If you agree, let us enter on a discussion of Om.' 'Let it be so', saying this they sat down." (Chandogya Upanishad 1.8.1-2)

Ether (Akāsha)

Om is a sound rising from the heart of all things; and the element of ether, which is its highest form, is consciousness, is the basis of all sound. (Ultimately, **Om and consciousness are the same** thing.) A Brief Sanskrit Glossary defines akāsha in this way: "Ether; space; sky; literally: 'not visible.' **The subtlest of the five elements (pancha-bhuta), from which the other four arise.** It is all-pervading, and is sometimes identified with consciousness—chidakasha. It is the basis of sound (shabda), which is its particular property." This being so, the dialogue proceeds as follows: "What is the essence of this world?' Akāsha. All these beings arise from akāsha alone and are finally dissolved into akāsha; because akāsha alone is greater than all these and akāsha is the support at all times." (Chandogya Upanishad 1.9.1)

Remember, Om is the subject of this discussion, and since akāsha is the foundation of sound, it moves on, with this: "It is this Om which is progressively higher and better. This again is endless. He who, knowing thus, meditates upon the progressively higher and better Om, obtains progressively higher and better lives and wins progressively higher and better worlds." (Chandogya Upanishad 1.9.2)

Om is the thread that runs through all levels of existence; It is the core of all worlds, emanating from the Absolute that is beyond them all. By meditating on Om we ascend higher and higher, passing through the states of consciousness that correspond to higher and higher worlds. Whatever the state of mind we are established in at the time of death, it will take us into the corresponding world. "Whatever state of being [bhavam] he remembers when he gives up the body at the end, he invariably goes to that state of being, transformed into that state of being." (Bhagavad Gita 8:6)

There is another aspect to this. In meditation, **our perceptions of Om become subtler and subtler.** From being a mental repetition sounding just like it would if we were speaking aloud, it becomes softer and softer, even whisper like, eventually become a silent ideation or conceptualization while mysteriously remaining a complete word. **This mutation takes place as our consciousness is moving into higher and higher states of being or bhavas.** Our experiencing of this is experiencing Om and the states of awareness inherent in It.

The conclusion

The Upanishad sums it up like this:

"Atidhanvan, the son of Sunaka, having taught this to Udarasandilya, said, 'As long as among your descendants, this knowledge of Om continues, so long their life in this world will be progressively higher and better than ordinary lives. And in that other world also their state will be similar'. He who knows and meditates thus—his life in this world surely becomes progressively higher and better, and so also his state in that other world—yes, in that other world." (Chandogya Upanishad 1.9.3-4)

Four Things God REALLY Wants You to Know

Have you ever seen, or been given, a little leaflet entitled "Four Things God Wants You To Know"? When I was young, long ago, it was quite a popular tool of Fundamentalist Protestants. It had four statements—mostly about sin, death, and hell—backed up with Bible quotations. Usually there was a place to sign on the back saying you were willing to let God save you. And that was it! Salvation for the masses. Here in the Chandogya Upanishad we find the real four things we all need to know.

Duty and realization

"The requirements of duty [dharma] are three. The first is sacrifice, study, almsgiving; the second is austerity; the third is life as a student in the home of a teacher and the practice of continence. Together, these three lead one to the realm of the blest. But he who is firmly established in the knowledge of Brahman achieves immortality." (Chandogya Upanishad 2:23:1)

The basis of dharma, of life that leads to spiritual unfoldment has three elements which need scrutiny, each in turn.

Sacrifice, study, and almsgiving. Sacrifice (yajna) means formal religious observance, especially the offering of the daily activities to God, hopefully leading to the perfect offering of oneself to God—Ishwarapranidhāna. Study means just that, but study of spiritual texts, of the wisdom of the enlightened, and pondering the ways to incorporate that teaching into one's own life. This is serious application to holy knowledge and its personal assimilation. Almsgiving (dāna) means giving of time and money to the welfare of others. It is also the cultivation of generosity as a trait of mind and heart. These three are discussed in the Bhagavad Gita, especially in chapter seventeen, as absolute necessities on the spiritual path, never to be abandoned—not even by the renunciate. For these are not part of worldly life, but essentials of spiritual life.

Austerity—tapasya—is spiritual discipline, including control of mind, body, the factors of external life, and especially meditation. It is an entire reshaping and purification of the inner and outer life, not a mere dabbling or dalliance. It is total in its scope, and therefore total in its effect.

Life as a student in the home of a teacher and the practice of continence. It is a fact that the earlier we begin spiritual cultivation the more likely we are to persevere and therefore succeed. In the ancient culture of India from an early age everyone lived as a religious student in the house of a recognized spiritual teacher. Although the teacher imparted a great deal of practical, world-oriented knowledge, the primary subject was always spiritual life and development through spiritual practice and religious activities. Since the student remained in the teacher's house until the attainment of adulthood, brahmacharya, sexual continence, was considered a fundament requisite—so much so that the student was called a brahmachari: one who observes continence.

In the West this system was totally unknown in the Indian form, but through the centuries it was not uncommon for monasteries and convents to permit children to live there and study, some becoming monastics and others leaving and leading a secular life. The Franciscan Order had "minor seminaries" in which young boys began preparation for religious life, especially the priesthood, from a very young age. If one decided that he did not wish to eventually be a monk or priest he usually returned home and continued an ordinary course of study.

But here in the West the majority of those following Sanatana Dharma come to it as adults. They can engage in sacrifice, study, charity, and spiritual practice, but what about this factor, which the Upanishad says is a requirement of dharma? Besides the general study of the basic scriptures of India, such persons will need to devote themselves to a particular form of spiritual cultivation. For example, someone can take up the study of teachings relating to a specific approach, such as the familiar paths of karma, bhakti, and jnana. They may center their attention on a particular teacher, such as Shankara, Ramanuja, Sri Ramakrishna, Vivekananda, Ramana Maharshi, Paramhansa Yogananda, Swami Bhaktivedanta, or a contemporary teacher, of which there are many. Even if a teacher is no longer in the body, through study and application of his teaching they can be his student. The "home" of a teacher is not a building or ashram, but that teacher's level of spiritual awareness. It is not easy to live in that real home, but it can and must be done. Only those who attune themselves to the teacher's consciousness are true disciples. Physical proximity of itself means nothing. In India I have seen people that lived for decades in an ashram, often personally attending on or traveling with the teacher—and many of them never really met the teacher once on the level that counts.

For all students of whatever form or situation, brahmacharya is needed. A teacher that does not tell them that right from the start is no real teacher at all.

The blessed and the Blesser

"Together, these three lead one to the realm of the blest. But he who is firmly established in the knowledge of Brahman achieves immortality."

Honesty in spiritual life is a necessity, on the side of the teacher and the student. True spiritual teaching is not a matter of marketing, of appealing to the consumer. Therefore facts that may not be palatable or comforting are always to be found wherever truth is being taught. Degenerate religion revels in adjusting and dubbing down it teachings in order to gain more adherents, and therefore more power and money. True religion always follows the fundamental principle that the seeker conforms to the teaching, not the other way around. All of us really need to get this through our heads and into our hearts—and thereby into our lives.

I say this because we see that the Upanishadic sage tells us the truth about what has been commended to us: they will take us into the "realm of the blest." Now, he does not mean the earthlike "heaven" of most religions, but the realm of the wise and holy who have evolved to the point where earthly rebirth is no longer needed. They—and those who ascend there—are liberated from that bondage, but they are still subject to rebirth in the higher worlds, of which there is a seemingly infinite number. So, painless as it is, and happy as are the worlds involved in our subtle births and deaths, we are still bound and subject to departing and returning. It is a higher and happy portion of the evolutionary ladder, but still not our transcendental Home beyond the ladder for which attainment we originally came forth into relative existence. So we must assiduously engage in the sacred three in order that we may at least become freed from earthly bonds, but always keeping in mind that there is something more needed: the knowledge of (not just about) Brahman. And we should be striving for that as well. So there really should be four elements in our endeavor.

Only the knower of Brahman has immortality, for only he is freed from birth and death in all forms.

The Light Within The Light of the Self

"The light that shines above the heavens and above this world, the light that shines in the highest world, beyond which there are no others—that is the light that shines in the hearts of men." (Chandogya Upanishad 3:13:7) Gambhirananda: "Now, that Light which shines beyond this heaven, beyond the whole creation, beyond everything, in the highest worlds which are unsurpassingly good, it is certainly this which is the light within a person."

It is the Atma-Jyoti, the Light of the Self, which is also Divinity Itself. As a student of the Upanishadic wisdom through his Master, Jesus, Saint John wrote: "This then is the message which we have heard of him [Jesus], and declare unto you, that God is light." (I John 1:5) That Light is purely spiritual (Spirit, actually) beyond the light we see in this world, but which nevertheless is also a manifestation or extension of that Light, as is the entire creation. In all the worlds—and beyond all the worlds—it is the One Light that shines in, and as, all. What a glorious concept! A truth as profound as it is simple. "The Lord shall be unto thee an everlasting light, and thy God thy glory." (Isaiah 60:19) This was the Essence of teaching which Jesus received even in infancy.

Original Christianity—which was identical with Sanatana Dharma—taught that the Divine Light "was the light of men....the true Light, which lighten every man" (John 1:4, 9) without exception. That Light cannot be alienated from us, but is ever the essence of our existence, making us "the children of light." (John 12:36) This is the real Gospel, the Good News, of real religion.

The Light that IS Brahman

This Light is transcendent because God is transcendent—and so are we! Because: "Truly has this universe come forth from Brahman. In Brahman it lives and has its being. Assuredly, all is Brahman. Let a man, freed from the taint of passion, worship Brahman alone." (Chandogya Upanishad 3:14:1a) Again Gambhirananda: "All this is Brahman. This is born from, dissolves in, and exists in That. Therefore, one should meditate by becoming calm." Really, what can—or need be—said about this incredible assertion: ALL is Brahman?

What we can consider is the final part, the practical advice, which in the Sanskrit text is only two words: *shanta upasita*. Literally, they mean: "Draw near peacefully" or: "Go near peace-fully." *Upasana* means to sit or draw near, and is usually understood to mean either worship or meditation. In the Greek original of the New Testament the word translated "prayer" is *prosevki*, which also means to draw near. The Greek word translated "worship" is *proskuneo*, which has the same meaning.

The important thing to realize is that true worship and meditation are both an inner process, for God is the light that shines within each one of us, as the first verse quoted points out. So to draw near to that light we must turn within. As Jesus said: "Neither shall they say, Lo here! or, lo there! for, behold, the kingdom of God is within you." (Luke 17:21)

The inner search must be done *shanta*—peacefully. This is a major key in yoga. All meditation must be done calmly and carefully, otherwise it will be impossible to perceive and assimilate the subtle states of awareness which meditation should produce. The mind must be as still as a mirror to really meditate, and meditation alone produces that stillness. Meditation is being described by Saint Paul when he says: "We all, with open face beholding as in a mirror the glory of the Lord, are changed into the same image from glory to glory." (II Corinthians 3:18) That is why in the book of Revelation, which Paramhansa Yogananda said was a book about yoga, it says that a "sea of glass" like a great mirror is before the throne of God, and that the saints "stand" upon it. This symbolizes the perfectly still mind of the yogi by which he experiences higher realities. (Revelation 4:6, 15:2)

The yogi's will

Now the second half of the verse we just examined: "A man is, above all, his will. As is his will in this life, so does he become when he departs from it. Therefore should his will be fixed on attaining Brahman." (Chandogya Upanishad 3:14:1b)

This is surely one of the most important statements in the Upanishads. The will is the highest faculty we possess. It is higher even than the intellect, for we often say: "I won't think about that right now..." and we do not, because the will controls it. The only thing higher than the will is the Self. The will approaches closer to the Self than any other aspect of our being. This is so important, because the quality of our religion and our yoga is determined by which aspect is the basis of our belief and practice.

We have five levels or "bodies." They are: 1) the physical, material body (annamaya kosha), 2) the magnetic or bio-energetic body (prānamaya kosha), 3) the sensory mind (manomaya kosha), 4) the intelligent mind, the intellect (jnanamaya kosha), and 5) the will (anandamaya kosha). These also correspond to the five elements: earth (prithvi), water (apa), fire (agni), air (vayu), and ether (akasha) which are also the seats of the five senses—smell, taste, sight, touch, and hearing.

The will is the anandamaya kosha, which corresponds to the ether element, whose special faculty is sound (shabda), both the passive faculty of hearing and the active faculty of speech. Which is why the highest yoga is based on Sound—specifically, the highest sound: Om. Om Yoga is the way to correct and develop the will. Since we *are* our will according to the Upanishad, it must be made alive through the continual japa and meditation of the Pranava, the Word of Life: Om. **Only through Om can we gain mastery of the will,** and thereby of ourselves. We must become Om, "the Word that is God" according to the Bhagavad Gita (7:8. "I am the sacred syllable Om." 10:25). By becoming Om, we become God—not in the absolute sense, but in the relative sense of **knowing ourselves as an eternal part of God, identical in essence, even though not the Whole.**

If in this life we become united to Brahman, when we leave this world we will go to Brahman. "Then Satyakama, son of Shibi, asked him [the Rishi Pippalada]: 'Venerable Sir, what world does he who meditates on Om until the end of his life, win by That?' To him, he said: 'That which is the sound Om, O Satyakama, is verily the higher and the lower Brahman. Therefore, with this support alone does the wise man reach the one or the other.'…If he meditates on the Supreme Being [Parampurusha] with the Syllable Om, he becomes one with the Light, the Sun. He is led to the world of Brahman. He sees the Person that dwells in the body, who is higher than the highest life. …That the wise one attains, even by the mere sound Om as support, That which is tranquil, unaging, immortal, fearless, and supreme." (Prashna Upanishad 5.1,2,5,7) "When a man leaves his body and departs,…let him take refuge in steady concentration, uttering the sacred syllable Om and meditating upon me. Such a man reaches the highest goal." (Bhagavad Gita 8:12, 13) You can't get more detailed—or more authoritative—than that.

"Therefore should his will be fixed on attaining Brahman," concludes this verse. For as Krishna said: "When a yogi has meditated upon me unceasingly for many years, with an undistracted mind, I am easy access to him, because he is always absorbed in me." (Bhagavad Gita 8.14)

The Self Within

"The Self, who is to be realized by the purified mind and the illumined consciousness, whose form is light, whose thoughts are true; who, like the ether, remains pure and unattached; from whom proceed all works, all desires, all odors, all tastes; who pervades all, who is beyond the senses, and in whom there is fullness of joy forever—he is my very Self, dwelling within the lotus of my heart." (Chandogya Upanishad 3:14:2)

Rejoicing in the Self

It can reasonably be felt that the Bhagavad Gita is more important than the Upanishads because it not only embodies their teachings, it provides practical advice for their personal realization. This is also my opinion, but the Upanishads are certainly indispensable for us who seek the Goal. One of their most wonderful aspects—and one that I have never heard mentioned in my nearly half a century of Sanatana Dharma study—is their marvelous ecstatic exulting in the wonder and glory of the Self. Just reading such joyful declarations produces a powerful stirring of the will towards perseverance in the divine search. This verse is one such rapturous affirmation and well worth our savoring carefully.

The Self, who. The Self is a Who, NOT a What. That is, the Self is a conscious Person—or more accurately a person who IS consciousness itself. Of course, the Self—individual or Universal—is not the ego, a conditioned personality, but a changeless consciousness. It is certainly true that the Self is not "personal" or even a "person" in the way we know those terms. It is a transcendent reality, of one essence with the Absolute Reality. But it is Conscious and It is Real. This is bedrock truth. Countless ages of realization are behind this principle. We may not understand it fully or flawlessly, but that is only our human limitation. IT is Eternal Truth. That is the truth being presented in this verse, a truth that brings profound joy to those who realize it. It is said that Shiva sits immersed in the Self, but that sometimes he arises and dances, singing: "O! Who I am! Who I am!"

Is to be realized. We REALIZE the Self, we do not "find" It because it is ever present—It is us. That is, we enter into and experience our eternal nature. We have always had it, but have lost touch with it. There is nothing to reach out for; rather we need to regain perception of it. It is more "here and now" than anything else, because It IS the Here and Now. It is only a matter of seeing, of experiencing It—and not as an object but as the Subject. Ultimately, it is beyond description, but what can be said is glorious.

By the purified mind. "Mind" does not mean the sensory mind (manas), or even the intellect (buddhi), but the principle of consciousness itself (prajna). The simile of a mirror is very apt here. Covered with thick dust and dirt, the mirror is no more than a lump of earth or a slab of wood. But the more the debris is removed, the more things are seen on its surface, until it shines forth in its reflective nature. In the same way our consciousness—or rather the "glass" that covers it—must be cleansed so there is no obstruction to our perception of the Self. That is why Jesus said: "Blessed are those that are pure (*katharos*: clean, clear, pure) at the center of their being (*kardia*: heart, core, center), for they shall see God." (Matthew 5:8) And Saint John said: "Every man that has this hope in him purifies himself, even as he is pure." (I John 3:3) The path of this necessary purification is fully outlined in the Yoga Sutras (Yoga Darshan) of Patanjali.

And the illumined consciousness. The Self is consciousness that is swayam prakash—self illumined. That is, Its very nature is Light (Jyoti). By Its presence it illuminates all its upadhis—Its various bodies. Being Life as well as Light, it also makes them "live" through Its nearness to them, just as the presence of Brahman makes the worlds "alive." But it, too, is illumined and enlivened by its essential unity with the Supreme Light, the Supreme Life: Brahman. So it both illumines and is illumined.

Whose form is light. The word Form should really be in quotes, for neither Brahman nor the Atman have a form in the way that is understood in relative existence. Their nature is Light, and although they are inaccessible to the senses, in a mysterious way they can be perceived or intuited as Light. I once heard a great yogi of India speaking of how it was possible to "see" the Self as a blinding light that soothed rather than burned the eyes. "Suppose a thousand suns should rise together into the sky: such is the glory of the Shape of Infinite God." (Bhagavad Gita 11:12)

Whose thoughts are true. Actually, the word is *satyasankalpa*, which means a lot more than "true thoughts." For after all, God does not have thoughts, because He has no mind—and the same is true of the Self. A being that *knows* does not need to *think*—actually cannot think. Sankalpa means an act of will, resolution, or intention. This is the nearest we can get to some idea of the movement of consciousness that takes place when God wills or determines something. So we will have to leave it there. Whatever it may be in the consciousness of Brahman, the Upanishad assures us that it is always Sat—absolutely true or real. True, in the sense that it is in total keeping with the nature of Brahman; real, in the sense that is always results in something. "So shall my word be that goes forth out of my mouth: it shall not return unto me void, but it shall accomplish that which I please, and it shall prosper in the thing whereto I sent it." (Isaiah 55:11)

Who, like the ether, remains pure and unattached. This divine Self is said to be ākāshātmā, which Shankara defines as: "one whose nature is like that of space...all pervasive, subtle, and free from form." Just as the sky contains suns, planets, atmosphere, clouds, smoke, and suchlike, yet is utterly untouched and unaffected by them, so the Self is free from any effects from its continuous rebirths and their experiences. The Self has no karma or conditionings, and so is like the ether at all times.

From whom proceed all works. It is a fundamental tenet of the Upanishads and the Gita that the Self never acts. So when the Upanishad uses the term sarvakarma—"all karma"—it is to be taken in the context of Sankhya, the philosophy behind them. Sankhya declares that all action takes place only through the proximity of the Self. That the energy bodies (prakriti) in which the Self is encased are like the iron that is heated and expands through the nearness of fire, or like the globes so popular at state fairs in which the little flags rotate because of light shining on them. So all actions occur through the presence of the Self, but are not done by the Self.

All desires. All movements of will or intention (the higher nature of "desire") are made possible by the Self, by Its transforming influence. But, as with action, the Self does not produce them.

All odors, all tastes. The same is true of the senses and the impressions they convey to the mind. The Self causes them to function and be perceived—again, not through actually "making" them happen, but through simply being there. The prime idea in these three phrases is that all "life" takes place through the Self being present. The Self does not "live" in a relative sense, but is the "life-giver" in the ultimate sense. This is but part of Its wonder.

Who pervades all. This underscores what has just been said. It is the all-pervasive Presence of the Self that causes all phenomena to occur.

Who is beyond the senses. This is said over and over in the scriptures, but it is put here within the context of the realization of the Self. We must turn inward to find the Self, and in that turning we must get beyond the senses. Those who are finding God do not abound in visions, chills, levitations, revelations, surging of energies, cataclysmic experiences, sweepings of emotions, and all such that are nothing but distractions that can NEVER lead to Reality. All phenomena must be left far behind, and we must "walk in the sky" that is free of all clouds—we must expand into consciousness that is free from all types of "experience" and even "existence" in the relative sense. For centuries people have amused themselves with "mystical" experiences and phenomena, remaining ignorant and earthbound despite their psychic powers and aura of "holiness." We must seek for the One. And to do that we must abandon the Many.

In whom there is fullness of joy forever. If we could only get this truth through our heads and into our hearts! In God alone is the perfection of happiness, love, peace, and all goodness—and in nothing or nowhere else. It is, however, not enough to momentarily touch or enter the joy of the Self. We must be established in It. By that I mean we must totally enter into It, encompass that Consciousness and be encompassed by It. When this is done, our realization is permanent. It will never be lost or diminished in any way. In the Bible this is spoken of as entering or possessing our "inheritance." It is forever.

He is my very Self. Although we identify with so much from life to life, this which the Upanishads have so carefully described is our true Self, and that alone should be our identity. This is made possible through the realization of the Self—not intellectually, but as a state of eternal Being.

Dwelling within the lotus of my heart. Since the Self is there, in the depths of our being: "Only that yogi whose joy is inward, inward his peace, and his vision inward shall come to Brahman and know Nirvana." (Bhagavad Gita 5:24)

The all-encompassing Self

"Smaller than a grain of rice is the Self; smaller than a grain of barley, smaller than a mustard seed, smaller than a canary seed, yes, smaller even than the kernel of a canary seed. Yet again is that Self, within the lotus of my heart, greater than the earth, greater than the heavens, yes, greater than all the worlds." (Chandogya Upanishad 3:14:3)

The Atman transcends time and space, is always beyond them. Consequently the Self cannot really be described as large or small. It is beyond such dualities, and beyond any attempt at measurement. Why, then does the Upanishad say what has just been cited? It is indicating to us that there is nothing which is not pervaded by the Self—there is nothing so small or so large that it is "outside" of the Self. Rather, the Self encompasses all relative being as well as the absolute. However large or small something may be, the Self is present within it to the fullest degree.

("The kernel of a canary seed" is not a reference to bird seed, but to the Shyamaka seed that is extremely small and its kernel is infinitesimal.)

The Self encompasses all worlds—all levels of creation. In modern times we know that the physical universe is beyond all conception, it is so vast. Even so, the Self is much greater. But this is true only because It is part of the Supreme Self Who spoke through Krishna to Arjuna, saying: "But what need have you, Arjuna, to know this huge variety? Know only that I exist, and that one atom of myself sustains the universe." (Bhagavad Gita 10:42)

The Self is within our heart, and within that Self is contained all the worlds. So we carry Infinity within ourselves. No wonder the pinnacle of the spiritual quest is called self-realization.

The great summing-up

Now the Upanishad wraps and sums it all up, saying: "He from whom proceed all works, all desires, all odors, all tastes; who pervades all, who is beyond the senses, and in whom there is fullness of joy forever—he, the heart-enshrined Self, is verily Brahman. I, who worship the Self within the lotus of my heart, will attain him at death. He who worships him, and puts his trust in him, shall surely attain him." (Chandogya Upanishad 3:14:4a) It is those who "worship" the Self by constantly being intent on the Self through the inward focusing of their japa and meditation of Om, that will shed all false identities and enter into the truth of the Self—if not in this life, then at the time of leaving the body and ascending into higher consciousness.

Even the Upanishads recognize the value of citing spiritual authorities, for the second half of this verse says: "Said the seer Sandilya: At the moment of death a knower of Brahman should meditate on the following truths: *Thou art imperishable. Thou art the changeless Reality. Thou art the source of life.*" (Chandogya Upanishad 3:14:4b) This is possible for those who have made Self-knowledge the central and paramount factor of their life's work. Those who have come to know the Self through profound meditation and constant remembrance of Om, will then know that they are imperishable, changeless, and Life itself.

Krishna

Then a most interesting statement is made: "This highest knowledge, the knowledge of Brahman, having drunk of which one never thirsts, did **Ghora Angirasa teach to Krishna**, the son of Devaki." (Chandogya Upanishad 3:17:6) By this we know that Krishna himself is the embodiment of the Upanishadic wisdom, and was therefore qualified to give the teachings of the Bhagavad Gita, which has been called the cream and the essence of the Upanishads.

Satyakama

Now we come to a very interesting part of the Chandogya Upanishad which consists of stories of seekers who came to know Brahman.

A feature that will seem odd to Western readers is the instruction of some of the seekers by animals and even by the forces of nature. Any explanation I might give is purely speculative and not worth much, but here they are:

1. The accounts are simply symbolic parables, the animals and nature forces symbolizing powers within the yogis.

2. These are not actual events, but dreams which the yogis had—this, too, is a matter of symbolism.

3. They are intuitions occurring to the yogis as they pondered the animals and the natural forces, wanting to understand the ideas behind them—for the universe is entirely ideational in nature. I do not think that any of these are very satisfactory, so I prefer to just focus on the spiritual teaching and let the rest go by, the way we crack the shell and throw it away, keeping the nut inside which is nourishing. One thing is, evident, though, the pure-hearted will be instructed by other means if human teachers fail to do so (or even be available).

Truthfulness (satya), a foundation of yoga, is taught here in the story of Satyakama.

A case of identity

"One day the boy Satyakama came to his mother and said: 'Mother, I want to be a religious student [brahmachari]. What is my family name [gotra]?' 'My son,' replied his mother, 'I do not know. In my youth I was a servant and worked in many places. I do not know who was your father. I am Jabala, and you are Satyakama. Call yourself Satyakama Jabala." (Chandogya Upanishad 4:4:1, 2)

This is no small thing. At the time of Satyakama it was essential for the teacher (acharya) to know the caste of the student, for the instruction given was according to the student's caste so as to prepare him for his distinctive life within the society of that era. In this way children were prepared to live the life of Brahmin priests and teachers, Kshatriya administrators and warriors, and Vaishya artisans and merchants. (Shudras—servants—were not accepted in the schools, since education was deemed pointless for their mode of life.) It is true that in very ancient times a student's caste was finally determined during his education, according to his aptitudes and inclinations, but he started out being considered of the caste of his parents. Later caste was solely a matter of heredity. Whichever era this story took place in, the father's caste had to be known.

Complicating the whole thing was the matter of gotra. Gotra means clan, family, or lineage, and all the castes were divided in gotras. This, too, could determine what the student would be taught, because different gotras had their own dharma shastras—scriptures which set forth the social and religious rules for members of that gotra. Sometimes these texts governed such minutiae as the student's style of hair, mode and color of clothing, and even the type of wood their staff should be made of and how long it should be. Those born completely outside such a system may consider this all meaningless complications, but it was not so at the time the Upanishad was written, and we should realize the seriousness of all this, even if we do not feel the same way.

Anyhow, Satyakama needed to know his caste and his gotra. Since his mother was a servant, a Shudra, he "should" not be accepted anyway, and on top of it he was illegitimate—a total bar to assimilation by society on any level, including education. But Satyakama thirsted for knowledge, and with the single-minded intent of a child dared to approach the great sage Gautama, something even those of highest caste might hesitate to do.

Truth

"Thereupon the boy went to Gautama and asked to be accepted as a student. 'Of what family are you, my lad?' inquired the sage. Satyakama replied: 'I asked my mother what my family name was, and she answered: "I do not know. In my youth I was a servant and worked in many places. I do not know who was your father. I am Jabala, and you are Satyakama. Call yourself Satyakama Jabala!" I am therefore Satyakama Jabala, sir.' Then said the sage: 'None but a true Brahmin would have spoken thus. Go and fetch fuel, for I will teach you. You have not swerved from the truth.'" (Chandogya Upanishad 4.4.3-4)

Here we see that character, composed of karma and samskara, was the basis for caste in the Upanishadic age. Truthfulness is a prime trait of a Brahmin, as is indicated here. Though Prabhavananda translates: "None but a true Brahmin would have spoken thus," the literal meaning is: "A non-Brahmin will not be able to say this." This is extremely powerful, for it not only indicates that a true Brahmin is in such a purified state that it is impossible for him to not speak the truth—and speak it fully—it also indicates that a Brahmin will not have the ego that would prevent him speaking truthfully and plainly regarding himself in all aspects of his life. For him there is no ego-based shyness or embarrassment of any sort. A Brahmin will never seek to hide anything about himself by speech or silence. As yogis we must seek to be perfect Brahmins.

The realization

Now I will summarize what is a rather wordy and sometimes obscure text. (You can read it yourself in

4:4:3 to 4:8:1-4, and you will see what I mean.)

Satyakama, at the instruction of his guru, Gautama, lived some years in the forest. During that time, from various sources he learned in stages that the entire cosmos is a manifestation of Brahman, though only a "particle" of Brahman. Even though I say he "learned" this, it was not learning in the ordinary, intellectual sense. Rather it was direct experience gained in the depths of meditation. Thus Satyakama KNEW Brahman, and KNEW Brahman was manifesting as all the worlds, and at the same time transcending them all.

The return

"At last the youth arrived at the home of his master and reverently presented himself before him. As soon as Gautama saw him, he exclaimed: 'My son, your face shines like a knower of Brahman. By whom were you taught?' 'By beings other than men,' replied Satyakama; 'but I desire that you too should teach me. For I have heard from the wise that the knowledge that the teacher imparts will alone lead to the supreme good.' Then the sage taught him that knowledge, and left nothing out." (Chandogya Upanishad 4:9:1-3)

This reminds us of the radiant Buddha walking down the road after his enlightenment. Like Gautama, a Brahmin met him and also saw the divine radiance and asked him: "Who are you?" Continuing to walk on, Buddha simply said: "I am awake."

Although he possessed the perfect knowledge of Brahman (Brahma-jnaana), Satyakama wisely asked that Gautama should teach him. For he knew that his perceptions might be either incorrect or incomplete, and he wanted to check them by hearing from the lips of an enlightened Master. This is the way of the wise; they are always aware that they may not have perfect knowledge or experience. It is only the ignorant that insist they know the truth and have no need of testing. As Dion Fortune remarked in one of her books, those who are deluded will hysterically insist on the veracity of their "revelations," even being violent verbally and physically in defense of those delusions. On the other hand, a person who has had valid experiences and garnered true wisdom from them will speak of such things very apologetically—even hesitantly—frequently commenting that they realize their experiences may be delusions or they may be mistaken in their understanding of them even if they are real. Because of his sobriety and humility Satyakama was worthy (and capable) of being instructed fully in the wisdom of the sages (rishis). And so he was.

Such is an ideal spiritual aspirant.

Upakosala

Now we come to the story of another student: "Upakosala dwelt as a student in the house of Satyakama for twelve years. Though the teacher let other disciples return to their homes after they had been duly taught the way of truth, Upakosala was not allowed to depart. The wife of Satyakama entreated her husband to finish teaching him in order that he might go home like the rest, but Satyakama not only refused to do so but went off on a journey. At this Upakosala was so sad and sick at heart that he could not eat. The teacher's wife plied him with food, and in everything treated him with tender affection, but to no avail. At last the boy cried out to her: 'O mother, my heart is still so impure; I am too unhappy to eat!" (Chandogya Upanishad 4:10:1-3)

The mind of Upakosala

Satyakama did not let Upakosala return home because he had not learned all that was necessary for leading a fully dharmic life according to the scriptural precepts. It is interesting that Upakosala does not consider that his failing is an academic one, but rather one of interior disposition. This shows his fundamental worthiness. "My heart is still so impure" is a misleading translation. The text actually says: "In this person there are these many desires which tend towards many things—I am filled with them." (He spoke in the third person because he was objective in analyzing himself. This indicates his lack of egotism.)

This reminds us of the following from the life of Jesus: "He entered into a certain village: and a certain woman named Martha received him into her house. And she had a sister called Mary, which also sat at Jesus' feet, and heard his word. But Martha was cumbered about much serving, and came to him, and said, Lord, dost thou not care that my sister hath left me to serve alone? Bid her therefore that she help me. And Jesus answered and said unto her, Martha, Martha, thou art careful and troubled about many things: But one thing is needful: and Mary hath chosen that good part, which shall not be taken away from her." (Luke 10:38-42)

Upakosala understood this (and Jesus must have studied this Upanishad in India), realizing that although desires may not be negative or foolish, yet they pull us in many directions, whirling us around and confusing our minds and depleting our life energies. *Only when the mind is fixed on the One can the many be safely attended to.*

Why did the sage leave this boy to his sorrow? Those who see with earthly eyes and think only earthly thoughts often accuse the saints of being heartless or even cruel. But they know what they are doing, and are aware that their actions are needed. When Jesus told his disciples that he would be leaving them, they were unhappy. So he said: "Because I have said these things unto you, sorrow hath filled your heart. Nevertheless I tell you the truth; It is expedient for you that I go away: for if I go not away, the Comforter will not come unto you; but if I depart, I will send him unto you." (John 16.6-7) Vivekananda once commented: "A man harms his disciples by staying too long with them," for they do not develop the independence needed to pursue spiritual life. Swami Sivananda often sent his disciples away to engage in spiritual practice or spiritual work. Even at the time of his leaving this world, few "old" disciples were present.

There was a man who very much wanted spiritual instruction from one of Sri Ramakrishna's disciples, but that man sent him to another disciple, who sent him to still another—and that one refused him, too. Becoming very upset, even angry and bitter, the man left Calcutta and returned home. That very night he awoke, feeling that someone was in his room. Indeed there was: Sri Ramakrishna himself in living, physical form! He touched the man, blessing him, and gave him spiritual instruction. The next time that man saw one of his "refusers," he was told: "We knew you were destined to receive personal instruction from Thakur himself; that is why we did not teach you ourselves."

The teaching

And so it was with Upakosala. Through a voice from the sacred fire Brahman became his teacher. Here is how:

"Then a voice from out the fire which he was tending said: 'This life is Brahman. The sky is Brahman. Bliss is Brahman. Know thou Brahman!' 'I know that life is Brahman,' replied Upakosala. 'But that the sky is Brahman, or that bliss is Brahman, I do not know.' Again came the voice from out the fire, this time explaining that by sky was meant the lotus of the heart, wherein dwells Brahman, and that by bliss was meant the bliss of Brahman. 'Both,' said the voice, 'refer to Brahman'; and, continuing, it taught Upakosala thus: 'Earth, food, fire, sun—all these that you worship—are forms of Brahman. He who is seen in the sun—that one am I. He who dwells in the east, in the north, in the west, and in the south, he who dwells in the moon, in the stars, and in water—that one am I. He who dwells in the sky and makes the lightning his home— that one also am I. Know well the true nature of the world that it may never do you harm.' Thereupon the fire, which had been only an earthly fire with which to prepare sacrifices, assumed a new aspect, and became the Lord himself. The earth was transformed; life was transformed; the sun, the moon, the stars, the lightning—everything was transformed, and deified. And thus it was that to Upakosala the true nature of all things was revealed." (Chandogya Upanishad 4:10:4,5; 4:11:1,2; 4:12:1, 2; 13:1, 2; 14:1)

This is thoroughly clear, and needs no comment, except to say that here we see the nature of enlightenment as a total transformation of perception. And that is one of the greatest teachings of this Upanishad.

The final words

"In due time Satyakama returned home. When he saw Upakosala, he said: 'My son, your face shines like one who knows Brahman. Who has taught you?' 'Beings other than men,' replied Upakosala. Then said Satyakama: 'My son, what you have learned is true. True also is this that I teach you now. Lo, to him who knows it shall no evil cling, even as drops of water cling not to the leaf of the lotus: He who glows in the depths of your eyes—that is Brahman; that is the Self of yourself. He is the Beautiful One, he is the Luminous One. In all the worlds, forever and ever, he shines!'" (Chandogya Upanishad 4.14.2-3; 4.15.1 and 4)

Nothing more can or need be said.

The story of Svetaketu

Now we come to the best known and most valued section of the Upanishads: the story of Svetaketu and his learning about Brahman—and also his own Self. Prabhavananda has wisely condensed the narrative as it contains a great deal of repetition which at one time in India was considered high literary style (as the Pali Sutras of Buddhism show).

Learning that was ignorance

"When Svetaketu was twelve years old, his father Uddalaka said to him, 'Svetaketu, you must now go to school and study. None of our family, my child, is ignorant of Brahman.'" (Chandogya Upanishad 6:1:1) What a blessed time it must have been when education was aimed at the attainment of Brahma-jnana!

"Thereupon Svetaketu went to a teacher and studied for twelve years. After committing to memory all the Vedas, he returned home full of pride in his learning." (Chandogya Upanishad 6:1:2)

Yes, yes, yes, we all have read over and over that the Vedas are the basis of Sanatana Dharma, and that "belief in the Vedas" makes one a Hindu. But this is not the perspective of the Upanishads or the Bhagavad Gita. Vedic study is constantly being decried by them as worthless—so what does that say about the Vedas? (Which, by the way, are said to be three, not four.) Just calling them Shabda Brahman—the Sound Brahman—does not make them so. (Anyhow, anyone who reads the Upanishads and Gita knows that Om is the Shabda Brahman!) In the same way in the Bible we find the prophets, including David in the Psalms, denouncing the ways of the Law and deriding those who follow it. (The Essenes declared that the Law, the Torah, had been corrupted and brought into line with the ways of the ignorant religions of the nations which surrounded and intimidated Israel.)

However we may look at the question, there is no doubt that twelve years of Vedic study had left Svetaketu both ignorant and arrogant.

"His father, noticing the young man's conceit, said to him: 'Svetaketu, have you asked for that knowledge by which we hear the unhearable, by which we perceive the unperceivable, by which we know the unknowable?' 'What is that knowledge, sir?' asked Svetaketu." (Chandogya Upanishad 6:1:3)

Here we have three words: *Ashrutam, amatam, and avijnatam* that are most important. Ashrutam means "the unheard," amatam means "the unthought" or "the unconceived," and avijnatam means "the unknown." They also mean "the unhearable," "the unthinkable," and "the unknowable." These are epithets of Brahman, the Absolute Being. Not only do we not at this moment hear, think of, or know Brahman, we *cannot* do so—not through the mind, that is. But we can know Brahman directly at the core of our Self. When we go beyond the usual perceptors into the Knower...then we will hear without hearing, think without thought, and know without knowing. For it will be a matter of BEING alone. In other words, we must be yogis.

The Knowledge

Uddalaka now tells Svetaketu: "My child, as by knowing one lump of clay, all things made of clay are known, the difference being only in name and arising from speech, and the truth being that all are clay; as by knowing a nugget of gold, all things made of gold are known, the difference being only in name and arising from speech, and the truth being that all are gold—exactly so is that knowledge, knowing which we know all." (Chandogya Upanishad 6:1:4-6)

This is pretty straightforward, but it has an interesting implication. Uddalaka says that if we know one lump of clay or one nugget of gold we will know all clay and gold. The Self (Atman) and Brahman are absolutely one, yet the Self is limited in Its scope, whereas Brahman is limitless—and willing to share that limitlessness with us. Therefore the way to know the Paramatman, Brahman, is to know the Jivatman, the individual Self. Once we know the part we know the Whole. There is more to it than this, because in that knowing we participate in the infinite Being of Brahman. This is a matter of yoga and beyond the scope of language to express or explain. That is why the Kena Upanishad says: "He truly knows Brahman who knows him as beyond knowledge; he who thinks that he knows, knows not. The ignorant think that Brahman is known, but the wise know him to be beyond knowledge." (Kena Upanishad 2:3) In response Svetaketu says:

"But surely those venerable teachers of mine are ignorant of this knowledge; for if they had possessed it, they would have taught it to me. Do you therefore, sir, give me that knowledge.' 'Be it so,' said Uddalaka." (Chandogya Upanishad 6:1:7)

The ONE

"In the beginning there was Existence, One only, without a second. Some say that in the beginning there was nonexistence only, and that out of that the universe was born. But how could such a thing be? How could existence be born of non-existence? No, my son, in the beginning there was Existence alone—One only, without a second." (Chandogya Upanishad 6.2.1-2)

In the beginning—and evermore—there was SAT: Existence; Reality; Being: Brahman, the Absolute, Pure Being. And this Sat was *ekam, evam, adwityam*: one only, without a second. This Absolute Unity is all that ever has been or that can ever be. This is a major principle of Sanatana Dharma, one that is not easy to always keep in mind since we find ourselves immersed in the experience of duality. But when through self-purification and the practice of yoga we sweep aside this delusive curtain we will see the One and know It within our own Self (atman) as its inmost essence. The Sat is always One, not one among many, and is absolutely indivisible. Duality cannot arise in It to any degree.

This being so, Uddalaka warns Svetaketu away from the mistaken idea that there was an original Nothing from which came Something. Certainly, Brahman is No Thing, but that is a far cry from Nothing. Rather, it is Everything. This is important to us for two reasons. First, if originally there was nothing, then when we return to our primal state we will be annihilated, "become" nothing. And, indeed, there are those who believe and even yearn for this. But it is not so. Second, for us raised in Western religion, it points out the absurdity of the theological principle that God created the world *ex nihil*—from nothing.

Since this second proposition is merely an intellectual perception, it is not particularly negative, but the first one is, for it deludes us as to what our ultimate state is meant to be. And it is perfectly possible to enter into an empty, jada state of unconscious inertia that can be mistaken for Nirvana, that is often wrongly translated "annihilation" or "extinguishment."

The "Many"

"He, the One, thought to himself: Let me be many, let me grow forth. Thus out of himself he projected the universe; and having projected out of himself the universe, he entered into every being. All that is has its self in him alone. Of all things he is the subtle essence. He is the truth. He is the Self. And that, Svetaketu, THAT ART THOU. 'Please, sir, tell me more about this Self.' 'Be it so, my child.'" (Chandogya Upanishad 6:2:3a; 6:3:2; 6:8:7)

This is extremely important. Brahman did not "create" anything: It projected everything out of Its own being—and not as a separate entity, for It is within everything as its sole Reality, as its Self, as its subtle Essence.

You might be interested to know that this was the original teaching of Christianity. In the New Testament the word translated "made" in speaking of the origin of the universe is *ginomai*, which means to be generated—not made from nothing. It also means to arise or be assembled from something already existing. The expression "only-begotten" is *monogenis*, coming from the same root word. In *The Apostolic Constitutions*, one of the earliest liturgical texts of Christianity, God is said to have "brought forth all things as from a treasure house"—not from nothing.

After saying all these amazing things, Uddalaka enunciates the highest wonder: *Tat Twam Asi*: THOU ART THAT. This is the pinnacle of the Upanishads—of all the wisdom scriptures of India. This awesome truth that behind and beneath it all, including our own Self, is THAT, is Brahman. "Of all things he is the subtle essence. He is the truth. He is the Self."

Svetaketu asked to hear more. In a sense there was no more, but there could be more affirmations of the single truth. So:

The unknowing

"As the bees make honey by gathering juices from many flowering plants and trees, and as these juices reduced to one honey do not know from what flowers they severally come, similarly, my son, all creatures, when they are merged in that one Existence, whether in dreamless sleep or in death, know nothing of their past or present state, because of the ignorance enveloping them—know not that they are merged in him and that from him they came. Whatever these creatures are, whether a lion, or a tiger, or a boar, or a worm, or a gnat, or a mosquito, that they remain after they come back from dreamless sleep. All these have their self in him alone. He is the truth. He is the subtle essence of all. He is the Self. And that, Svetaketu, THAT ART THOU. 'Please, sir, tell me more about this Self.' 'Be it so, my son.'" (Chandogya Upanishad 6:9:1-4)

All of us in relative existence are enveloped in ignorance. That should not be hard to accept! But whatever the background or past of any sentient being, of whatever level, in dreamless sleep and death they all return to Brahman. But their enveloping ignorance prevents them from knowing where they are, the way a submarine keeps those inside from being wet. So they are not enlightened in any way, though so close to the Light from whence they came. Although in that state they have no self-concept, no identity with their present level of evolution, when they awake from sleep or return from death to rebirth, they find themselves in the form that corresponds to their inner development. And of course they immediately get lost in the dream and start wandering around, never really coming to rest anywhere. Yet at all times they are within Brahman and ARE Brahman.

Svetaketu wants more, so his father repeats what he has said from another angle.

"The rivers in the east flow eastward, the rivers in the west flow westward, and all enter into the sea. From sea to sea they pass, the clouds lifting them to the sky as vapor and sending them down as rain. And as these rivers, when they are united with the sea, do not know whether they are this or that river, likewise all those creatures that I have named, when they have come back from Brahman, know not whence they came. All those beings have their self in him alone. He is the truth. He is the subtle essence of all. He is the Self. And that, Svetaketu, THAT ART THOU. 'Please, sir, tell me more about this Self.' 'Be it so, my child.'" (Chandogya Upanishad 6:10:13)

Svetaketu asks for more.

The all-pervading Source

"If someone were to strike once at the root of this large tree, it would bleed, but live. If he were to strike at its stem, it would bleed, but live. If he were to strike at the top, it would bleed, but live. Pervaded by the living Self, this tree stands firm, and takes its food; but if the Self were to depart from one of its branches, that branch would wither; if it were to depart from a second, that would wither; if it were to depart from a third, that would wither. If it were to depart from the whole tree, the whole tree would wither. Likewise, my son, know this: The body dies when the Self leaves it—but the Self dies not. All that is has its self in him alone. He is the truth. He is the subtle essence of all. He is the Self. And that, Svetaketu, THAT ART THOU. 'Please, sir, tell me more about this Self.' 'Be it so.'" (Chandogya Upanishad 6:11:1-3)

Everything is alive, but only because the Living Self, Brahman, inhabits it. If that Presence is withdrawn, then death results. Therefore when the Self leaves the body, the body dies, but not the Self. Yet see how backwards we are in the West. We think that it is being in the body that makes a person alive, that when they leave the body they die. Absolutely backwards! Not only that, we continue to treat the body as the person, dressing it up, putting makeup on it, fixing its hair and putting in a satin-lined box and mourning over it. Even crazier, we will first have drained out its blood and pumped formaldehyde into it. Then we put the box in a concrete box in a grave and pile dirt on top of it, heap flowers on it, and leave. But we keep coming back to "visit" the "dead" with more flowers and even talk to the body as though it were the still-living person who has long ago departed from the body. Now, if that is not insane, tell me what is? And it is not only sanctioned by our stupid religions, it is encouraged by them, especially those that disdain prayers for the departed.

More, says Svetaketu.

The subtle Essence

"Bring a fruit of that Banyan tree."

"Here it is, sir."

"Break it."

"It is broken, sir."

"What do you see?"

"Some seeds, extremely small, sir."

"Break one of them."

"It is broken, sir."

"What do you see?"

"Nothing, sir."

"The subtle essence you do not see, and in that is the whole of the tree. Believe, my son, that that which is the subtle essence—in that have all things their existence. That is the truth. That is the Self. And that, Svetaketu, THAT ART THOU. 'Please, sir, tell me more about this Self.' 'Be it so.'" (Chandogya Upanishad 6:12:1-3)

This is easily understood. What I would like to point out is the fact that Uddalaka says "the whole of the tree" is in the Divine Essence. It is not part in and part out, as we think in the West, believing that part of us is material and part is spirit, or that part of us lives in this world and part of us in the spiritual world. These distinctions are products of ignorance. There is only The ONE. At all times.

In response to Svetaketu's request, Uddalaka produces another object lesson.

"Put this salt in water, and come to me tomorrow morning."

Svetaketu did as he was bidden. The next morning his father asked him to bring the salt which he had put in the water. But he could not, for it had dissolved. Then said Uddalaka:

"Sip the water, and tell me how it tastes."

"It is salty, sir."

"In the same way," continued Uddalaka, "though you do not see Brahman in this body, he is indeed here. That which is the subtle essence—in that have all things their existence. That is the truth. That is the Self. And that, Svetaketu, THAT ART THOU. 'Please, sir, tell me more about this Self,' said the youth again. 'Be it so, my child.'" (Chandogya Upanishad 6:13:1-3)

For some reason Prabhavananda did not translate this fully. In the original text Uddalaka asks Svetaketu to taste the water from the top, the middle, and the bottom of the bowl. Each time he finds it salty. The idea is that Brahman pervades the entire field of relative existence, AS that field. And we are That.

Svetaketu wants to hear more.

Teaching needed

"As a man may be blindfolded, and led away, and left in a strange place; and as, having been so dealt with, he turns in every direction and cries out for someone to remove his bandages and show him the way home; and as one thus entreated may loosen his bandages and give him comfort; and as thereupon he walks from village to village, asking his way as he goes; and as he arrives home at last—just so does a man who meets with an illumined teacher obtain true knowledge. That which is the subtle essence—in that have all beings their existence. That is the truth. That is the Self. And that, O Svetaketu, THAT ART THOU. 'Please, sir, tell me more about this Self.' 'Be it so, my child.'" (Chandogya Upanishad 6:14:1-3)

The teaching here is of major import. We can know we are blind and lost and need to see and go back home, but it stops there. We have to be made to see and shown the way. This can only happen when we find the teachings of enlightened Masters. If we can meet such a Master face-to-face, our good fortune is incalculable. Over forty years have passed since I received the blessing and wisdom of the first Masters of my acquaintance, and some decades since the last one spoke with me. Yet those memories are my heart's rosary which I can go over and vividly return in memory to those days. I do not have to believe books: I have seen living embodiments of Sanatana Dharma and listened to their words, many of them addressed personally to me. However, I have spent many, many more hours reading the printed teachings of some of those great Masters, and many more Masters that I have only "met" in books.

However the teachings come to us, it is the application that matters. I saw a lot of do-nothings circulating around the Masters who just played groupie until the Master died and then they wasted their time grieving over the loss of something they never really had, and waiting for the Master to "give the green light" (a quote from one of them) so they could die and go to the Master's "loka" and be with him forever. Small chance! They were not really with the Master in life, so why in death?

What I want to assure you is that truth is always truth. If you learn mathematics from a teacher or a book it is the same. Further, this Upanishadic simile does not inculcate the guru-disciple enslavement that is considered so essential for enlightenment. Yes, one person did take away the bandage and point out the way, but notice that "thereupon he walks from village to village, asking his way as he goes." So he has many teachers, not just one. And it should be the same with us. "Loyalty" to a single teacher should not be a blindfold on the eyes of our soul. All Masters are living, and as Yogananda said, we should realize that all Masters are one and not make differences between them. (He is speaking of Masters, though, not just teachers.)

Ultimately, even the teachers are just the mouth-pieces of Brahman, of our own ultimate Self.

At his request, Svetaketu now receives one last instruction.

Forgetting and remembering

"When a man is fatally ill, his relations gather round him and ask, 'Do you know me? Do you know me? Now until his speech is merged in his mind, his mind in his breath, his breath in his vital heat, his vital heat in the Supreme Being, he knows them. But when his speech is merged in his mind, his mind in his breath, his breath in his vital heat, his vital heat in the Supreme Being, then he does not know them. That which is the subtle essence—in that have all beings their existence. That is the truth. That is the Self. And that, O Svetaketu, THAT ART THOU."

(Chandogya Upanishad 6:15:1-3)

When we merge with Brahman in Mahasamadhi—the great exit of death—then all that we "knew" and believed in is nothing to us: only Brahman remains for us to know and identify with. The long journey is over, Reality gained at last. All that was enslaving and misery-producing, all the trivia and folly of relativity, is over forever. No return engagement! No return trip ticket! Home at last; home forever. Home in Infinity; Life to a degree undreamed of by us for ages beyond calculation. For the final time we close our external eyes to open the eye of spirit. My grandmother asked me to have a song entitled "We'll Say Goodnight Here, But Good Morning Up There" sung at her funeral. It certainly is "night" here and eternal "morning" in God. But attaining it is not so simple as the song implies. Nevertheless, one day—beyond all time—it will happen to us all. Then we will really know: That which is the subtle essence—in that have all beings their existence. That is the truth. That is the Self. And THAT ART THOU."

The Essence of the Mind and Prāna

Sometimes the longer Upanishads branch off from the central subject and explore a byway or two. This happened in the preceding dialogue between Uddalaka and Svetaketu. Uddalaka began expounding the origin of various components of the human being, including the mind, the manas, which is the sensory mind, the field of energy which conveys the impressions of the sensory impulses of the brain. It is part of our astral bodies, but since it consists of the grossest of astral substance, it is integrated, even interlaced, with the material body and brain. According to Uddalaka the energy of the mind is derived from the physical body. Here are his words:

"Food, when eaten, becomes divided into three parts. What is its grossest ingredient, that becomes feces; what is the middling ingredient, that becomes flesh; and what is the subtlest ingredient, that becomes mind." (Chandogya Upanishad 6.5.1-2)

From this we see how important diet is, for the very substance of the mind is the essential energy of the food we eat. For that reason we must be very careful both as to what we eat and what its vibration might be.

For example, we should avoid meat, fish, eggs, alcohol, nicotine, and mind-influencing drugs—that should be obvious to the yogi. But we must also be careful about the vibration of acceptable food, for if it is a vehicle of negative vibrations it will be poisonous to the mind. When food is cooked or handled, the vibrations of the cook and the handler enter into it, for cooked food is very receptive to vibrations. Usually a prayer or blessing will neutralize any negative energies attached to food, but not always, especially if the cook or handler were mentally disturbed. Restaurant food can be a problem for that reason, and also because the food may be cooked in the same oil in which meat has been cooked, or may have been touched by meat in some way in the restaurant kitchen.

Prāna, the subtle life force in the yogi's body, must also be kept pure, as it affects everything in the physical and astral bodies, and has a major influence on meditation, during which the prānas must be as pure and subtle as possible, since the mental energies and the prāna interact with one another intimately. About the prāna, Uddalaka says: "Water, when drunk, becomes divided into three parts. What is its grossest ingredient, that becomes urine; what is the middling ingredient, that becomes blood; and what is the subtlest ingredient, that becomes Prāna." (Chandogya Upanishad 6.5.1-2) What is said about water stands for any liquid, and we must be as careful about that as about our food.

"Hence, mind is made up of food, Prāna is made up of water." (Chandogya Upanishad 6.5.4)

Then he repeats this, giving examples.

"Of the curd [yogurt] that is being churned that which is the subtlest part rises upwards and that becomes butter. So also, of the food that is eaten that which is the subtlest part rises upwards and that becomes the mind. Of the water that is drunk that which is the subtlest part rises upwards and that becomes Prāna....Hence, mind is made up of food, Prāna is made up of water." (Chandogya Upanishad 6.6.1-3-4)

This is extremely valuable knowledge for everyone, but especially for the yogi, as we see that food and drink have a direct effect on the mind and vital force within.

Narada

Now we come to the account of the great sage Narada and his inquiries made to the great Master, Sanatkumara. This contains a lot of rhetoric and repetition, so I will omit some of the first fifteen sections of the seventh chapter of the Chandogya Upanishad as translated by Swami Prabhavananda.

The ladder to reality

"Narada once came to Sanatkumara and asked to be taught. To Sanatkumara's question, 'What have you already studied?' Narada replied that he had studied all the branches of learning—art, science, music, and philosophy, as well as the sacred scriptures. 'But,' said he, 'I have gained no peace. I have studied all this, but the Self I do not know. I have heard from great teachers like you that he who knows the Self overcomes grief. Grief is ever my lot. Help me, I pray you, to overcome it." (Chandogya Upanishad 7:1:1-4)

This contains a cardinal truth: there is no peace or real happiness outside the knowledge of the Self (atma jnana). Those who wish to end all sorrow must seek that knowledge. Such is the assertion of the great teachers of humanity.

First Sanatkumara taught Narada the ascending steps of reality which we must perfect before we can know the ultimate Reality: that which we hear from others, the faculty of speech, the mind, will, intelligence, meditation, and the wisdom gained from direct spiritual experience.

The Eternal Truth

"Then said Sanatkumara: 'But, verily, he is the true knower—who knows eternal Truth.'

'Revered sir, I wish to be a true knower.' 'Then ask to know of that infinite Reality.' 'Sir, I ask to know of it.'" (Chandogya Upanishad 7:16:1)

There are two simple points here. The first is that only the knower of Brahman really knows anything. Only those that know Eternal Being are jnanis—knowers. This is a necessary perspective for those that set out to seek the Absolute, for unless they hold to this outlook they may become distracted along the way and settle for less, or even begin actively seeking the less.

The second point is that the seeker must ask a qualified teacher for teaching, that it will not just be dropped in his hands. Asking is the heart of seeking. An equally important point is implied here: a qualified teacher will not teach unless asked. Somewhere I have mentioned that this was one of my first lessons learned during my first trip to India. I found that fools and fakes went into teaching mode the moment they saw me and being grinding out the philosophical cliches—along with the hints that I should arrange a world tour for them to end in America the Land of Opportunity. Since nineteenth-century translations of the Upanishads had the teacher addressing the disciple as "my dear," these ignoramuses and charlatans always called me "my dear" upon meeting me. In contrast, the real teachers and Masters were kind and most polite, asking me about my purpose in coming to India and where I had been, and suchlike. But they never said a word about either philosophy or yoga. If I asked them for wisdom upon our first meeting, they spoke sparingly in an almost diffident way, in no way pushing their words at me or trying to impose their views on me. (Some would not even answer the first time they were questioned. One teacher only told me anything after I had inquired three times in a row.) After more contact, they would become very free with me and answer my questions gladly. But still they never volunteered anything. I always had to ask. This is the mark of a genuine teacher. So Narada had to declare his desire to know Infinite Reality.

Steps on the path

Next Swami Prabhavananda gives a kind of digest of several verses.

"It is only when a man has realized eternal Truth that he declares it. **He who reflects upon it realizes it. Without reflection it is not realized. And only he who has faith and reverence reflects on eternal Truth.** And only he who attends on a teacher gains faith and reverence. And only he attends on a teacher who struggles to achieve self-control. And only he struggles to achieve self-control who finds joy in it. Ask to know of this joy.' 'Sir, I ask to know of it.'" (Chandogya Upanishad 7:16:1-22:1)

This list starts at the top and goes to the bottom, and are the steps to realization according to Sri Sanatkumara.

It is only when a man has realized eternal Truth that he declares it. Only one who has realized the Eternal Truth of the Brahman-Self can truly declare It. All others just speak rumor and speculation. So if we want spiritual authority we will have to seek out those that have found Truth and embody it. For their very words will convey awakening and empowerment to the worthy hearer. That is why Jesus made the remarkable statement: "The words that I speak unto you, they are spirit, and they are life." (John 6:63) This is not true of the words of ordinary teachers.

He who reflects upon it realizes it. Without reflection it is not realized. This does not mean mere intellectual thought, just pondering on ideas about Brahman. The word *matih* means thinking of something, reflecting upon it because of love, of great affinity, for it. (Shankara says this in his commentary.) The meaning is that the worthy seeker is purified enough in intellect to intuit both Brahman and his eternal relation with Brahman. As a result a spontaneous inner "recognition" of Brahman arises, along with a reaching out for the experience of Brahman as Reality. Just as a magnet draws metal to itself, so the yogi begins to experience the pull of the Infinite, and loves the drawing and the possibility of the final union. Brahman becomes the most cherished object of his heart, and Its reality is never absent from his consciousness. This is a sign of his nearness to realizing Brahman.

And only he who has faith and reverence reflects on eternal Truth. The worthy yogi is not a casual weekender, paddling his feet in the ocean of Infinity. Rather, he is one in whom intuitive conviction of the reality of God and the necessity of finding God has arisen. This insight motivates him from the depths of his own being.

And only he who attends on a teacher gains faith and reverence. Actually, the text says nothing about a teacher, just the word-*nishtha*, which means steadiness. But Shankara in his commentary says that it indicates the steadfast seeking of a teacher's wisdom "for acquiring knowledge of Brahman." So Prabhavananda has translated accordingly. We have already considered that we may have recourse either to a living teacher or the teachings of a realized Master. It is contact with the "vibrations" of a teacher that enable faith to arise in us. Sometimes only the sight of a Master is needed for awakening to begin—even seeing a picture or photograph. Something is stirred deep within, often impressions from a previous life. Wonderful as that may be, it is steadfastness in inwardly and outwardly approaching the teacher that is needed for success in our search.

And only he attends on a teacher who struggles to achieve self-control. For disciple means one who is engaging in discipline. Things do not come automatically or easily to the seeker. That must be faced. And paths that pretend to automatically and easily produce realization are fake. Discipline—*willing discipline*—is an absolute requisite for spiritual attainment. Otherwise any effort expended is most likely to be useless. A lot of cultish seekers labor and slave and deprive and torment themselves and end up getting nowhere. But they are not truly disciplined in the sense of intelligent understanding and effort put forth in the context of a viable tradition.

And only he struggles to achieve self-control who finds joy in it. This is a signal trait of the worthy seeker: he find joy in the seeking, and rejoices in having at last found the way to real finding. The way is one of discipline and purification, and he loves every bit of it, however it may pain the ego, for he knows it leads to the end of uncertainty and suffering. Such a seeker does not sigh and grudgingly do what is necessary. That kind will not persevere—and good riddance. No, he is like the men Jesus told about: "The kingdom of heaven is like unto treasure hid in a field; the which when a man hath found, he hideth, and for joy thereof goeth and selleth all that he hath, and buyeth that field. Again, the kingdom of heaven is like unto a merchant man, seeking goodly pearls: who, when he had found one pearl of great price, went and sold all that he had, and bought it." (Matthew 13:44-46) They gladly gave all they had. Such are those who find joy in the struggle for self-mastery and Self-realization. Saint Paul says that Jesus himself: "for the joy that was set before him endured the cross, despising the shame, and is set down at the right hand of the throne of God." (Hebrews 12:2)

"Ask to know of this joy." "Sir, I ask to know of it." Certainly many people seek higher reality as a result of disillusionment and suffering. Some merely seek the cessation of suffering, but the wiser actively seek the joy that is the nature of Brahman.

The source of joy

"The Infinite is the source of joy. There is no joy in the finite. Only in the Infinite is there joy. Ask to know of the Infinite.' 'Sir, I ask to know of it." (Chandogya Upanishad 7:23:1)

This is not an easy lesson to learn: that there is no joy outside of the Infinite Brahman; there is no joy outside of our own Self. The meditator knows how difficult this his, for the mind keeps running after utter trivia in meditation, turning from the way to ananda and thinking of those things that only bring suffering even though the mind delights in the idea of them. Fool's gold is preferred by the mind to real gold. This is an addiction incredibly hard to be cured. The first step is asking about the Infinite, as this verse shows.

Experiencing the Infinite

What now follows is not a definition of the Infinite, because that is impossible since It is beyond conceptualization, and therefore beyond words. But it is possible to give a hint about the experience of the Infinite, even though it will be more of a neti-neti (not this-not that) approach.

"Where one sees nothing but the One, hears nothing but the One, knows nothing but the One— there is the Infinite. Where one sees another, hears another, knows another—there is the finite. The Infinite is immortal, the finite is mortal.' 'In what does the Infinite rest?' 'In its own glory— nay, not even in that. In the world it is said that cows and horses, elephants and gold, slaves, wives, fields, and houses are man's glory—but these are poor and finite things. How shall the Infinite rest anywhere but in itself?' (Chandogya Upanishad 7.24.1-2)

I know I have said it elsewhere, but I must say it here: **nowhere in the entire world can there be found teachings equal to those of the Upanishads.** And these two verses are proof of that.

"Where one sees another, hears another, knows another—there is the finite," can be understood in two ways, both of which are correct. First, if someone sees anything besides the Infinite, then he is not perceiving the Infinite, for when the Infinite is perceived, all else either disappears or is seen as the Infinite Itself. Second, if anyone sees anything other than his Self—which is one with the Infinite—he is not seeing the Infinite.

"How shall the Infinite rest anywhere but in itself?" This is also true of those who have realized the Infinite.

Where is the Infinite?

"The Infinite is below, above, behind, before, to the right, to the left. I am all this. This Infinite is the Self. The Self is below, above, behind, before, to the right, to the left. I am all this. One who knows, meditates upon, and realizes the truth of the Self—such one delights in the Self, revels in the Self, rejoices in the Self. He becomes master of himself, and master of all the worlds. Slaves are they who know not this truth." (Chandogya Upanishad 7:25:1-2)

The knower of the Infinite

"He who knows, meditates upon, and realizes this truth of the Self, finds that everything—primal energy, ether, fire, water, and all other elements—mind, will, speech, sacred hymns and scriptures—indeed the whole universe—issues forth from it. It is written: 'He who has realized eternal Truth does not see death, nor illness, nor pain; he sees everything as the Self, and obtains all.' The Self is one, and it has become all things.

"When the senses are purified, the heart is purified; when the heart is purified, there is constant and unceasing remembrance of the Self; when there is constant and unceasing remembrance of the Self, all bonds are loosed and freedom is attained. Thus the venerable Sanatkumara taught Narada, who was pure in heart, how to pass from darkness into light." (Chandogya Upanishad 7:26:1-2)

Nothing really needs to be said in commentary. What is needed is the resolve to follow the example of Narada and attain the same realization.

Within the Lotus of the Heart

The Chidakasha within

"Within the city of Brahman, which is the body, there is the heart, and within the heart there is a little house. This house has the shape of a lotus, and within it dwells that which is to be sought after, inquired about, and realized. What then is that which, dwelling within this little house, this lotus of the heart, is to be sought after, inquired about, and realized?" (Chandogya Upanishad 8:1:1-2)

The body is the abode of Brahman and the Self. The core-center of each relative, sentient being is its heart. And within the heart is a *dahara*, a dwelling; and within that dwelling is pure akasha, ether or space. But it is not the akasha that is one of the five primal elements (panchabhuta), but rather the Chidakasha: **the space of Consciousness.** In other words, the inmost dweller of the heart is Brahman Itself. Such is the import of these verses according to Shankara. So it is Brahman "which is to be sought after, inquired about, and realized."

The inner cosmos

"As large as the universe outside, even so large is the universe within the lotus of the heart. Within it are heaven and earth, the sun, the moon, the lightning, and all the stars. What is in the macrocosm is in this microcosm." (Chandogya Upanishad 8:1:3)

How is this possible? Because space, like time, is only an idea, only an experience, not a reality. Infinity is within each one of us. I have had various experiences of this fact, but here is an account I wrote down some years ago.

"While meditating one day all ordinary physical sensation vanished. Spatial relation ceased to exist and I found myself keenly aware of being beyond dimension, neither large nor small, but infinite (for infinity is beyond size). Although the terminology is inappropriate to such a state, to make it somewhat understandable I have to say that I perceived an infinity of worlds 'within' me. Suns—some solo and others surrounded by planets—glimmered inside my spaceless space. Not that I saw the light, but I felt or intuited it. Actually, I did not 'see' anything—and yet I did. It is not expressible in terms of ordinary sense experience, yet I must use those terms. I experienced myself as everything that existed within the relative material universe."

I was experiencing the mirror-image of the cosmos that exists within the Chidakasha in the heart. No one had ever told me about this, so at first I was at a loss to figure it out. But then in a moment the truth flashed into my mind. When much later I read these words of the Chandogya Upanishad I realized how amazing and invaluable is yoga. The yogi can realize for himself the things written in the wisdom texts of India. He can both experience and understand the meaning of the experience—and all from within.

And yet...

"All things that exist, all beings and all desires, are in the city of Brahman; what then becomes of them when old age approaches and the body dissolves in death? Though old age comes to the body, the lotus of the heart does not grow old. At death of the body, it does not die. The lotus of the heart, where Brahman exists in all his glory—that, and not the body, is the true city of Brahman. Brahman, dwelling therein, is untouched by any deed, ageless, deathless, free from grief, free from hunger and from thirst. His desires are right desires, and his desires are fulfilled." (Chandogya Upanishad 8:1:4-5)

The mystic Angelus Silesius wrote that if he could die, then God would die; that if he could cease to exist, God would cease to exist. Such was his absolute understanding of the identity of the Self and God. Since this is so, the Upanishad tells us that the Immortal is within us, whatever the condition of the body. Moreover, the desires of that Self are *satyakama*, true desires, and Its will is *satyasankalpa*, true will. So if we will center our consciousness in the Self, we will not have worry about desire or will— they will be Sat: revealers of the Real.

True desire and will

Having spoken of true desire and true will as properties of the Self, the Upanishad now outlines the practical aspect of such.

"As here on earth all the wealth that one earns is but transitory, so likewise transitory are the heavenly enjoyments acquired by the performance of sacrifices. Therefore those who die without having realized the Self and its right desires find no permanent happiness in any world to which they go; while those who have realized the Self and its right desires find permanent happiness everywhere." (Chandogya Upanishad 8:1:6)

The desires and intentions of those who have not realized the Self, even if seemingly fulfilled, eventually evaporate and come to nothing. But it is vastly different for those who know the Self and act and will accordingly.

"If the sage desires to see his fathers of the spirit-world, lo, his fathers come to meet him. In their company he is happy.

"And if he desires to see his mothers of the spirit-world, lo, his mothers come to meet him. In their company he is happy.

"And if he desires to see his brothers of the spirit-world, lo, his brothers come to meet him. In their company he is happy.

"And if he desires to see his sisters of the spirit-world, lo, his sisters come to meet him. In their company he is happy.

"And if he desires to see his friends of the spirit-world, lo, his friends come to meet him. In their company he is happy.

"And if he desires heavenly perfumes and garlands, lo, heavenly perfumes and garlands come to him. In their possession he is happy.

"And if he desires heavenly food and drink, lo, heavenly food and drink come to him. In their possession he is happy.

"And if he desires heavenly song and music, lo, heavenly song and music come to him. In their possession he is happy.

"Indeed, whatsoever such a knower of Brahman may desire, straightway it is his; and having obtained it, he is exalted of men." (Chandogya Upanishad 8:2:1-10)

This is lengthy and perhaps not too obvious of meaning. The idea is that the realized person has access to and embodies all that is positive from his past lives, both persons and karmic conditions. This being so, he can obtain anything he desires and wills in the present and the future. Yet "he is exalted of men" in a different manner than the dead and departed "greats" of human history. He is exalted in the Self, in Brahman, in Absolute Being.

The hallmark of Sanatana Dharma is its thorough practicality, its good sense, and its demonstrable truth. So the Upanishad next says:

The obstacle and its removal

"The fulfillment of right desires is within reach of everyone, but a veil of illusion obstructs the ignorant. That is why, though they desire to see their dead, their beloved, they cannot see them.

"Do we wish for our beloved, among the living or among the dead, or is there aught else for which we long, yet, for all our longing, do not obtain? lo, all shall be ours if we but dive deep within, even to the lotus of the heart, where the Lord dwells. Yes, the object of every right desire is within our reach, though unseen, concealed by a veil of illusion.

"As one not knowing that a golden treasure lies buried beneath his feet, may walk over it again and again, yet never find it, so all beings live every moment in the city of Brahman, yet never find him, because of the veil of illusion by which he is concealed." (Chandogya Upanishad 8:3:1-2)

Meditation is the key to the treasure house! So the Upanishad next says:

"The Self resides within the lotus of the heart. Knowing this, devoted to the Self, the sage enters daily that holy sanctuary.

"Absorbed in the Self, the sage is freed from identity with the body and lives in blissful consciousness. The Self is the immortal, the fearless; the Self is Brahman. This Brahman is eternal Truth." (Chandogya Upanishad 8:3:3-4)

Om!

Crossing the Boundary

The Boundary-Self

"The Self within the heart is like a boundary which divides the world from THAT. Day and night cross not that boundary, nor old age, nor death; neither grief nor pleasure, neither good nor evil deeds. All evil shuns THAT. For THAT is free from impurity: by impurity can it never be touched." (Chandogya Upanishad 8:4:1)

Setuh literally means a dam. In the experience of conditioned beings within the realm of relativity, the individual Self or jivatman acts as a boundary between Its Supreme Self, Brahman, the Paramatman, and the world of samsara. This is a very interesting fact, made even more interesting by the fact that I have never encountered it except here in this section of the Chandogya Upanishad.

We may think of the Self as a sea wall. On one side is the vast ocean of Brahman, and on the other side is the "earth" of material form and change. On one side the wall is experiencing the wetness of the sea, and on the other the dryness of earth. That in which the individual finds himself immersed only applies to that "side" of his being. However much we may experience birth, death, change, and all that attends them, they never touch the realm of Brahman. Conversely, although we are living in—and as—Brahman, samsara never touches that. Samsara and Brahman are mutually exclusive of one another. But we participate in the "worlds" of both, in a sense linking them with one another. Presently we are centered in samsara, experiencing our own Self as a barrier to Reality. But that barrier can be crossed, so the Upanishad continues:

"Wherefore he who has crossed that boundary, and has realized the Self, if he is blind, ceases to be blind; if he is wounded, ceases to be wounded; if he is afflicted, ceases to be afflicted. When that boundary is crossed, night becomes day; for the world of Brahman is light itself." (Chandogya Upanishad 8:4:2)

That is so powerful and obvious that there is no place for comment, other than to point out that the conditions listed from which the knowers of the Self are freed are really only illusions, just mirages. The Self being Real, such illusions vanish when It is known.

The way across the boundary

"And that world of Brahman is reached by those who practice continence [brahmacharya]. For the knower of eternal truth knows it through continence. And what is known as worship [yajna], that also is continence. For a man worships the Lord by continence, and thus attains him." (Chandogya Upanishad 8:4:3; 8:5:1)

You cannot get more clear than this! Brahmacharya is THE way to the realm of Brahman (Brahmaloka). Certainly, sexual continence is the core of brahmacharya, but it is really self-restraint on all levels—discipline. This is it: there is no other way to qualify for union with Brahman than through brahmacharya. Yoga is an essential for that union, but frankly the practice of yoga is worthless without brahmacharya. The proof of that is the American and European yoga "scenes." Nothing is coming of it spiritually, only profiteering and self-delusion.

Brahmacharya is the necessary worship-sacrifice to know God. As the Beloved Disciple wrote: "Every man that hath this hope in him purifieth himself, even as he is pure." (John 3:3) Why claim to follow Sanatana Dharma if the teachings of the Upanishads and the Gita are not followed, but ignored and despised and degraded? But there is more.

Liberation

"What is called salvation is really continence. For through continence man is freed from ignorance. And what is known as the vow of silence, that too is continence. For a man through continence realizes the Self and lives in quiet contemplation." (Chandogya Upanishad 8:5:2)

Perhaps I should explain a bit about this fulsome assurance that brahmacharya will accomplish everything.

We, like God, are incarnate in a field of energy which we are intended to evolve just as God evolves the cosmos. When the evolution is completed, that is enlightenment and liberation. This process requires the total application of the inner and outer powers (energies) of the individual, powers that are devastatingly dissipated through sensory experience, emotion, and desire—especially lust. It is like a machine that requires a certain amount of voltage, or an engine that cannot run without the right amount of fuel. This is a purely pragmatic proposition, having nothing to do with concepts of right, wrong, good, bad, or any kind of moral valuation. For example, sex is not dirty, it is destructive. Anything that diverts or dissipates the powers needed for evolution-enlightenment is to be avoided. It is not a "sin" but a hindrance, a distraction. For this reason the intelligent yogi is at all times vigilantly disciplined—in other words, a brahmachari or brahmacharini. Those who do not wish to pay the price of enlightenment are free to pass it by. No one is under coercion. To seek freedom the yogi must be free in that decision (sankalpa) and in the requisite disciplines for success in seeking.

The necessity for brahmacharya is an absolute.

Forest-dwellers

"What people call dwelling in the forest [aranyayanam], that is continence." This is the first sentence of Chandogya Upanishad 8:5:3.

Most yogis have an inward pull to the forest life, to live in the midst of real nature away from the noise and poisons of city life as well as the noise and pollutions of human society. The Gita describes the yogi as "remaining in solitude, alone" (6:10), and having "distaste for crowds of men" (13:10). Whether this is a samskara or an intuition, it will be found in nearly all serious yogis.

One of my best friends was constantly going out into the wilds and risking life and limb so he would meditate far from any other human being. I am not exaggerating about the risks he took. One time he was literally starving, and even wrote a note to anyone that might find his body, saying that it was his unwise ways that caused his death, and yoga should not be blamed. He had been taken into the wilderness by another man, but he had left his original camp and gone farther into the forest. So when the man came back after some weeks to check on him, he could not be found. As my friend was lying on the ground, preparing to die, suddenly that man came walking up and asked: "Where is that woman?" Hardly able to speak, my friend asked his own question: "What woman?" "That woman with the long black hair in the orange dress! If I hadn't followed her, I couldn't have found you." At first my friend was flummoxed, but then he reached in his pack for his photograph of Paramhansa Yogananda. "Is that the 'woman'?" he asked, holding it out to the man. "Yes, that's her!" the man replied. The Master certainly honored my friend's forest-yearning, however impractical.

Solitude is a matter of interior condition. The incredible Russian Orthodox saint, Saint John of Kronstadt, not only never slept, he was never alone more than two hours in twenty-four. Yet a man who knew him very well said: "Father John was always alone." In contrast are those that go miles away from any human being and take the whole world and its population right with them. The teaching of the Upanishad is that Brahmacharya is the way to accomplish true inner solitude and quiet.

Immortality

"In the world of Brahman there is a lake whose waters are like nectar, and whosoever tastes thereof is straightway drunk with joy; and beside that lake is a tree which yields the juice of immortality. Into this world they cannot enter who do not practice continence. For the world of Brahman belongs to those who practice continence. They alone enter that world and drink from that lake of nectar. For them there is freedom in all the worlds." (Chandogya Upanishad 8:5:3-4) Since Brahman is beyond materiality and even any kind of subtle name and form, these verses are speaking symbolically of the immortality-bestowing effects of union with Brahman—which can only be effected by those that practice brahmacharya. (Shankara agrees with me in his commentary.) The meaning is pretty obvious: those who enter the ocean of Brahman and "drink" will be filled with bliss, made immortal with the Immortality of Brahman, and will have access to all the worlds of relative existence and mastery in those worlds. Those who find the Absolute do not lose the relative, for the relative is a manifestation of the Absolute.

The core idea, like the preceding verses, is the necessity of brahmacharya.

Devas and Demons Seeking the Self

"It was said of old: 'The Self, which is free from impurities, from old age and death, from grief, from hunger and thirst, which desires nothing but what it ought to desire, and resolves nothing but what it ought to resolve, is to be sought after, is to be inquired about, is to be realized. He who learns about the Self and realizes it obtains all the worlds and all desires.'" (Chandogya Upanishad 8.7.1)

This is the very heart of Sanatana Dharma: the Self must be known, otherwise all is lost. Sri Ramakrishna said it quite directly: the purpose of human life is knowing God, so those who do not strive to know God are wasting their life. This is the Truth of truth.

Gods and demons

"The gods [devas] and demons [asuras] both heard of this truth, and they thought to themselves,

'Let us seek after and realize this Self, so that we may obtain all the worlds and all desires.'

Thereupon Indra from the gods, and Virochana from the demons, went to Prajapati, the renowned teacher." (Chandogya Upanishad 8.7.2)

The sixteenth chapter of the Bhagavad is devoted to the idea that human beings are divided into two types: divine (daivic) and demonic (asuras). It should be carefully studied by those who see higher consciousness, for it is bedrock truth. Here in the

Upanishad we are given an exposition of the two natures by means of a story.

It may seem that the gods and demons had a common goal: to "obtain all the worlds and all desires," but that is not so. It was certainly the aim of the demons, but the gods desired the realization of the Self, although they certainly knew that "all the worlds and all desires" come to a knower of the Self as a kind of side effect. As Jesus later said in Israel: "Seek ye first the kingdom of God, and his righteousness; and all these things shall be added unto you." (Matthew 6:33)

The difference in the reactions of gods and demons can be seen today quite glaringly. Multitudes of demons throughout the world are spouting that "we are all God" and "everything is God," but with a complete misunderstanding of such statements. For, being entrenched in the ego and material consciousness, they have no idea of the real nature of "we" and "everything." In the same way they have no comprehension of what the divine unity expounded in Advaita (Non-duality) really means, interpreting it according to their own ignorance and limitations, reducing it to a string of childish cliches. Demons have a marked facility for trivializing anything, and degradation is their particular skill.

Approaching Prajapati

Anyhow, Indra the king of the gods, and Virochana, king of the demons, both went to Brahma, to Prajapati the Creator. "For thirty-two years they lived with him as pupils. Then Prajapati asked them why they had both lived with him so long. 'We have heard,' they replied, 'that one who realizes the Self obtains all the worlds and all desires. We have lived here because we want to learn of this Self." (Chandogya Upanishad 8.7.3)

This verse has a lesson, not very obvious, yet nonetheless important for us. The two seekers lived with— or near—the teacher for many years, without asking for what they desired. This is because the teacher should know the disciple and the disciple the guru. When one of my friends, Dr. Mukherji, met his guru, Sri Swami Purnananda of Assam, he was astonished at his evident greatness and asked to become his disciple. "Not at all," the master answered. "You must come to know me well, and I must know you well. Visit me as often as you can and live with me for as much time as you can manage. Then after three years of observing each other we can talk about you learning yoga from me." What a contrast with the drum-beating, self-promoting gurus of today, including those that pretend to have high standards for accepting disciples, but really try to ensnare everyone their eyes rest upon. And here we see that Indra and Virochana after thirty-two years had not even brought up the subject of instruction.

(We need not take so long, but we should be very careful and not rush into accepting the teachings of anyone. That is one of the value of books. We can read them and discard them if we find them worthless without any conflict with the teacher. And we can apply them without becoming the teacher's slave or dependent on him.)

Now we observe the first step in the discovery of the nature of the Self. It is not uncommon in the ancient texts for the truth to be presented as a kind of ladder, starting with either a dim perception of the truth or even a complete misunderstanding and leading upward bit by bit until the complete truth is comprehended. Just why this was done has not been said. Perhaps it was to show that even mistaken or partial ideas were to be seen as steps on the way to perfect understanding. Or it may have been as a kind of yardstick by which the level of development of a person might be known. On the other hand it may have been a showing of the logical progression of thought on a subject. However it may be, this account is part of that tradition.

The body—the Self

"Then said Prajapati: 'That which is seen in the eye—that is the Self. That is immortal, that is fearless, and that is Brahman.'

"Sir,' inquired the disciples, 'is that the Self which is seen reflected in the water, or in a mirror?'

"The Self is indeed seen reflected in these," was the reply.

"Then Prajapati added, 'Look at yourselves in the water, and whatever you do not understand, come and tell me about it.'

"Indra and Virochana gazed on their reflections in the water, and returning to the sage, they said: 'Sir, we have seen the Self; we have seen even the hair and the nails.'

"Then Prajapati bade them don their finest clothes and look again in the water. This they did, and returning to the sage, they said: 'We have seen the Self, exactly like ourselves, well adorned and in our finest clothes.'

"To which Prajapati rejoined: 'The Self is indeed seen in these. The Self is immortal and fearless, and it is Brahman.' And the pupils went away well pleased." (Chandogya Upanishad 8.7.4; 8.8.1-3)

Brahma asked the two inquirers to have experience for themselves, which they did. Notice, that they were the first to put forth the idea that the body "which is seen reflected in the water, or in a mirror" was the Self. The teacher agreed. Puzzling as it seems there is a great lesson here. It is better to be mistaken on our own than to have the truth imposed on us. I have known of teachers in India agreeing to very silly ideas or proposals put forth by disciples because they wanted them to learn for themselves the error of their thoughts. This is absolutely unique to India, and surely one of the reasons why so many disciples have become masters in their own right. It is better for an idea to be ours, even if wrong, than to bow to the belief of another, even if it is more correct. The Gita (3:35) says: "Better one's own dharma though deficient than the dharma of another well performed….the dharma of another invites danger," and this applies to personal philosophy, as well. Only when we have the freedom to make wrong conclusions will we develop the capacity for right conclusions. Intellectual integrity is of the utmost necessity, however most religionists are opposed to it.

Indra and Virochana "went away well pleased." And this is normal. The whole world is happy in delusions and illusions. So a religion or philosophy that "satisfies" us, "answers all our questions," and in which we are "happy" may be completely worthless. But we need to discover that for ourselves. Though their conclusions were wrong, twice in this passage Brahma has told them that Brahman is immortal and fearless. In this way he planted the seed of truth in their minds.

"But Prajapati, looking after them, lamented thus: 'Both of them departed without analyzing or discriminating, and without truly comprehending the Self. Whosoever follows a false doctrine of the Self will perish.'

"Now Virochana, satisfied for his part that he had found out the Self, returned to the demons and began to teach them that the body alone is to be worshipped, that the body alone is to be served, and that he who worships the body and serves the body gains both worlds, this and the next. Such doctrine is, in very truth, the doctrine of the demons!" (Chandogya Upanishad 8.8.4-5)

The assertion that "whosoever follows a false doctrine of the Self will perish" is crucial. It tells us that thoughts really are things and they lead us to a revelation of their nature: if false, to confusion and delusion, and if true, to the True. Jesus said: "According to your faith be it unto you." (Matthew 9:29) Literally we are creating the world of our personal life sphere. As we think it to be, so it will tend to be, though much depends on the strength of our mind and the intensity put forth in exercising its creative power. Brahma let them hold a wrong concept of the Self because they had to discover the right concept for themselves. This is hard for those brought up in coercive religion to accept, but it is true. The nursery rhyme is right: "Leave them alone and they will come home." But only in the East will this faith in the individual be found. Wherever we find it in the West it is but a ray of the Eastern Light—but none the less valuable for that.

Body-worship, which is really only body-enslavement, is the "faith" of those possessing demonic nature, and they literally do die for it. When demons think about yoga it is always Hatha Yoga—"Virochana Yoga." The myriads of "yoga studios" in the West are the haunts of the children of Virochana.

"But Indra, on his way back to the gods, realized the uselessness of this knowledge. 'As this Self,' he reasoned, 'seems to be well adorned when the body is well adorned, well dressed when the body is well dressed, so will it be blind when the body is blind, lame when the body is lame, deformed when the body is deformed. When the body dies, this same Self will also die! In such knowledge I can see no good.' So he returned to Prajapati and asked for further instruction. Prajapati required him to live with him for another thirty-two years, after which time he taught him thus. (Chandogya Upanishad 8.9.1-3)

In Eastern Christianity they say that it is the nature of demons to fall and never rise, and of human beings to fall and rise and fall and rise over and over again. In the same way it is the nature of human demons to adopt an error and hold to it throughout their life. But it is the nature of devic human beings to keep sifting through their ideas, discarding the ones they discover to be mistaken, and using the ones that are true as steps to even more—and higher—truth. Since Indra was not a demon, even before he got back to Indraloka he understood the fallacy of identifying the body with the Self. His reasoning is quite clear. So he returned to Brahman for another period of time, after which he was again instructed.

The astral body—the Self

Brahma told him: "That which moves about in dreams, enjoying sensuous delights and clothed in glory, that is the Self. That is immortal, that is fearless, and that is Brahman.' Pleased with what he had heard, Indra again departed. But before he had reached the other gods he realized the uselessness of this knowledge also. 'True it is,' he thought to himself, 'that this Self is not blind when the body is blind, nor lame or hurt when the body is lame or hurt. But even in dreams it is conscious of many sufferings. So in this doctrine also I can see no good." (Chandogya Upanishad 8.10.1-2)

In the conscious, waking state it is the physical body, including the physical brain, that dominates our consciousness, but in the dream state it is the astral body and brain that come into function and dominate our awareness. This astral body leaves the physical body at death, so it is usually mistaken for the Spirit-Self by the various religions. But, as Indra realized, this cannot be if the definition of the Self formulated by the ancient rishis of India is believed to be accurate. We must go a step higher.

OM TAT SAT

The causal body—the Self

"So he went back to Prajapati for further instruction. Prajapati now bade him live with him for another thirty-two years, and when the time had passed taught him, saying, 'When a man is sound asleep, free from dreams, and at perfect rest—that is the Self. The Self is immortal and fearless, and it is Brahman.'

"Indra went away. But before he had reached his home, he felt the uselessness even of this knowledge. 'In reality,' thought he, "one does not know oneself as this or as that while asleep. One is not conscious, in fact, of any existence at all. The state of one in deep sleep is next to annihilation. I can see no good in this knowledge either.'

"So once more Indra went back to Prajapati, who bade him stay with him yet five years." (Chandogya Upanishad 8:10:3-4; 8:11:1-3)

In dreamless sleep the causal body is dominant, and even in India there are people who try to identify it with the Self, and equate the dreamless sleep state with the eternal state of the Self. This is because of the extreme subtlety of that condition. Here, too, Indra's reasoning is as clear as it is inevitable.

It is significant that Brahma only required a residence of five years this last time. Obviously Indra is so near the truth that a longer time of purification is not required.

The Self as It is

And when the time had passed, he made known to him the highest truth of the Self, saying: "This body is mortal, always gripped by death, but within it dwells the immortal Self. This Self, when associated in our consciousness with the body, is subject to pleasure and pain; and so long as this association continues, freedom from pleasure and pain can no man find. But as this association ceases, there cease also the pleasure and the pain. Rising above physical consciousness, knowing the Self to be distinct from the senses and the mind—knowing it in its true light—one rejoices and is free." (Chandogya Upanishad 8:12:1-2)

This is as inspiring as it is simple: freedom and bliss (not mere pleasure) are the attributes of the Self— and of those who know the Self. Therefore Brahma concluded his teaching of Indra with these words:

"The gods, the luminous ones, meditate on the Self, and by so doing obtain all the worlds and all desires. In like manner, whosoever among mortals knows the Self, meditates upon it, and realizes it—he too obtains all the worlds and all desires." (Chandogya Upanishad 8.12.6)

End of Commentary

2. Brihadaranyaka Upanishad

This forms the last six chapters of Shatapatha Brahman of the Shukla-YajurVeda. This is the biggest of the major Upanishads by its size as well as substance.

Translated by Swami Madhavananda Published by Advaita Ashram, Kolkatta.

Om! That (Brahman) is infinite, and this (universe) is infinite. The infinite proceeds from the infinite. (Then) taking the infinitude out of the infinite (universe), It still remains as the infinite (Brahman) alone.

Om! Shantih! Shantih! Shantih!

1.1.1: Om! The head of the sacrificial horse is the dawn, its eye the sun, its vital force the air, its open mouth the fire called Vaisvanara, and the body of the sacrificial horse is the year. Its back is heaven, its belly the sky, its hoof the earth, its sides the four quarters, its ribs the intermediate quarters, its members the seasons, its joints the months and fortnights, its feet the days and nights, its bones the stars and its flesh the clouds. Its half-digested food is the sand, its blood-vessels the rivers, its liver and spleen the mountains, its hairs the herbs and trees. Its forepart is the ascending sun, its hind part the descending sun, its yawning is lightning, its shaking the body is thundering, its making water is raining, and its neighing is voice. 1.1.2: The (gold) vessel called Mahiman in front of the horse, which appeared about it (i.e. pointing it out), is the day. Its source is the eastern sea. The (silver) vessel Mahiman behind the horse, which appeared about it, is the night. Its source is the western sea. These two vessels called Mahiman appeared on either side of the horse. As a Haya it carried the gods, as a Vajin the celestial minstrels, as an Arvan the Asuras, and as an Asva men. The Supreme Self is its stable and the Supreme Self (or the sea) its source. 1.2.1: There was nothing whatsoever here in the beginning. It was covered only by Death (Hiranyagarbha), or Hunger, for hunger is death. He created the mind, thinking, 'Let me have a mind'. He moved about worshipping (himself). As he was worshipping, water was produced. (Since he thought), 'As I was worshipping, water sprang up', therefore Arka (fire) is so called. Water (or happiness) surely comes to one who knows how Arka (fire) came to have this name of Arka. 1.2.2: Water is Arka. What was there (like) forth on the water was solidified and became this earth. When that was produced, he was tired. While he was (thus) tired and distressed, his essence, or luster, came forth. This was Fire.

1.2.3: He (Viraj) differentiated himself in three ways, making the sun the third form, and air the third form. So, this Prāna (Viraj) is divided in three ways. His head is the east, and his arms that (north-east) and that (south-east). And his hind part is the west, his hip-bones that (north-west) and that (southwest), his sides the south and north, his back heaven, his belly the sky, and his breast this earth. He rests on water. He who knows (it) thus gets a resting place wherever he goes. 1.2.4: He desired, 'Let me have a second form (body).' He, Death or Hunger, brought about the union of speech (the Vedas) with the mind. What was the seed there became the Year (Viraj). Before him there had been no year. He (Death) reared him for as long as a year, and after this period projected him. When he was born, (Death) opened his mouth (to swallow him). He (the babe) cried 'Bhan!' That became speech. 1.2.5: He thought, 'If I kill him, I shall be making very little food.' Through that speech and the mind he projected all this, whatever there is—the Vedas Rig, Yajus and Saman, the meters, the sacrifices, men and animals. Whatever he projected, he resolved to eat. Because he eats everything, therefore Aditi (Death) is so called. He who knows how Aditi came to have this name of Aditi, becomes the eater of all this, and everything becomes his food. 1.2.6: He desired, 'Let me sacrifice again with the great sacrifice'. He was tired, and he was distressed. While he was (thus) tired and distressed, his reputation and strength departed. The organs are reputation and strength. When the organs departed, the body began to swell, (but) his mind was set on the body. 1.2.7: He desired, 'Let this body of mine be fit for a sacrifice, and let me be embodied through this', (and entered it). Because the body swelled (Asvat), therefore it came to be called Asva (horse). And because it became fit for a sacrifice, therefore the horse sacrifice came to be known as Asvamedha. He who knows it thus indeed knows the horse sacrifice. (Imagining himself as the horse and) letting it remain free, he reflected (on it). After a year he sacrificed it to himself, and dispatched the (other) animals to the gods. Therefore (priests to this day) sacrifice to Prajapati the sanctified (horse) that is dedicated to all the gods. He who shines yonder is the horse sacrifice; his body is the year. This fire is Arka; its limbs are these worlds. So these two (fire and the sun) are Arka and the horse sacrifice. These two again become the same god, Death. He (who knows thus) conquers further death, death cannot overtake him, it becomes his self, and he becomes one with these deities.

1.3.1: There were two classes of Prajapati's sons, the gods and the Asuras. Naturally, the gods were fewer, and the Asuras more in number. They vied with each other for (the mastery of these worlds. The gods said, 'Now let us surpass the Asuras in (this) sacrifice through the Udgītha'. 1.3.2: They said to the organ of speech, 'Chant (the Udgītha) for us'. 'All right', said the organ of speech and chanted for them. The common good that comes of the organ of speech, it secured for the gods by chanting, while the fine speaking it utilized for itself. The Asuras knew that through this chanter the gods would surpass them. They charged it and struck it with evil. That evil is what we come across when one speaks improper things. 1.3.3: Then they said to the nose 'Chant (the Udgītha) for us'. 'All right', said the nose and chanted for them. The common good that comes of the nose, it secured for the gods by chanting, while the fine smelling it utilized for itself. The Asuras knew that through this chanter the gods would surpass them. They charged it and struck it with evil. That evil is what we come across when one smells improper things. 1.3.4: Then they said to the eye 'Chant (the Udgītha) for us'. 'All right', said the eye and chanted for them. The common good that comes of the eye, it secured for the gods by chanting, while the fine seeing it utilized for itself. The Asuras knew that through this chanter the gods would surpass them. They charged it and struck it with evil. That evil is what we come across when one sees improper things. 1.3.5: Then they said to the ear 'Chant (the Udgītha) for us'. 'All right', said the ear and chanted for them. The common good that comes of the ear, it secured for the gods by chanting, while the fine hearing it utilized for itself. The Asuras knew that through this chanter the gods would surpass them. They charged it and struck it with evil. That evil is what we come across when one hears improper things. 1.3.6: Then they said to the mind 'Chant (the Udgītha) for us'. 'All right', said the mind and chanted for them. The common good that comes of the mind, it secured for the gods by chanting, while the fine thinking it utilized for itself. The Asuras knew that through this chanter the gods would surpass them. They charged it and struck it with evil. That evil is what we come across when one thinks improper things. Likewise they also touched these (other) deities with evil—struck them with evil. 1.3.7: Then they said to this vital force in the mouth, 'Chant (the Udgītha) for us'. 'All right', said the vital force and chanted for them. The Asuras knew that through this chanter the gods would surpass them. They charged it and wanted to strike it with evil. But as a clod of earth, striking against a rock, is shattered, so were they shattered, flung in all directions, and perished. Therefore the gods became (fire etc.), and the Asuras were crushed. He who knows thus becomes his true self, and his envious kinsman is crushed. 1.3.8: They said, 'Where was he who has thus restored us (to our divinity)?' (and discovered): 'Here he is within the mouth'. The vital force is called Ayāsya Angirasa, for it is the essence of the members (of the body). 1.3.9: This deity is called Dur, because death is far from it. Death is far from one who knows thus. 1.3.10: This deity took away death, the evil of these gods, and carried it to where these quarters end. There it left their evils. Therefore one should not approach a person (of that region), nor go to that region beyond the border, lest one imbibe that evil, death. 1.3.11: This deity after taking away death, the evil of these gods, next carried them beyond death. 1.3.12: It carried the organ of speech, the foremost one, first. When the organ of speech got rid of death, it became fire. That fire, having transcended death, shines beyond its reach. 1.3.13: Then it carried the nose. When it got rid of death, it became air. That air, having transcended death, blows beyond its reach. 1.3.14: Then it carried the eye. When the eye got rid of death, it became sun. That sun, having transcended death, shines beyond its reach. 1.3.15: Then it carried the ear When the ear got rid of death, it became the quarters. Those quarters, having transcended death, remain beyond its reach. 1.3.16: Then it carried the mind. When the mind got rid of death, it became the moon. That moon, having transcended death, shines beyond its reach. So does this deity carry one who knows thus beyond death. 1.3.17: Next it secured eatable food for itself by chanting, for whatever food is eaten, is eaten by the vital force alone, and it rests on that. 1.3.18: The gods said, 'Whatever food there is, is just this much, and you have secured it for yourself by chanting. Now let us have a share in this food.' 'Then sit around facing me', (said the vital force). 'All right', (said the gods and) sat down around it. Hence whatever food one eats through the vital force satisfies these. So do his relatives sit around facing him who knows thus, and he becomes their support, the greatest among them and their leader, a good eater of food and the ruler of them. That one among his relatives who desires to rival a man of such knowledge is powerless to support his dependents. But one who follows him, or desires to maintain one's dependents being under him, is alone capable of supporting them. 1.3.19: It is called Ayāsya Angirasa, for it is the essence of the members (of the body). The vital force is indeed the essence of the members. Of course it is their essence. (For instance), from whichever member the vital force departs, right there it withers. Therefore this is of course the essence of the members. 1.3.20: This alone is also Brihaspati (lord of the Rik). Speech is indeed Brihati (Rik) and this is its lord. Therefore this is also Brihaspati.

1.3.21: This alone is also Brāhmanaspati (lord of the Yajus). Speech is indeed Brahman (yajus), and this is its lord. Therefore this is also Brāhmanaspati. 1.3.22: This alone is also Saman. Speech is indeed Sa, and this is Ama. Because it is Sa (speech) and Ama (vital force), therefore Saman is so called. Or because it is equal to a white ant, equal to a mosquito, equal to an elephant, equal to these three worlds, equal to this universe, therefore this is also Saman. He who knows this saman (vital force) to be such attains union with it, or lives in the same world as it. 1.3.23: This indeed is also Udgītha. The vital force is indeed Ut, for all this is held aloft by the vital force, and speech alone is Gita. This is Udgita, because it is Ut and Gita. 1.3.24: Regarding this (there is) also (a story): Brahmadatta, the great-grandson of Cikitana, while drinking Soma, said, 'Let this Soma strike off my head if I say that

Ayasya Angirasa chanted the Udgītha through any other than this (vital force and speech).' Indeed he chanted through speech and the vital force. 1.3.25: He who knows the wealth of this Saman (vital force) attains wealth. Tone is indeed its wealth. Therefore one who is going to officiate as a priest should desire to have a rich tone in his voice, and he should do his priestly duties through that voice with a fine tone. Therefore in a sacrifice people long to see a priest with a good voice, like one who has wealth. He who knows the wealth of saman to be such attains wealth. 1.3.26: He who knows the gold of this Saman (vital force) obtains gold. Tone is indeed its gold. He who knows the gold of Saman to be such obtains gold. 1.3.27: He who knows the support of this Saman (vital force) gets a resting place. Speech (certain parts of the body) is indeed its support. For resting on speech is the vital force. Some say, resting on food (body). 1.3.28: Now therefore the edifying repetition (Adhyaroha) only of the hymns called Pavamanas. The priest called Prastotir indeed recites the Saman. While he recites it, these Mantras are to be repeated: From evil lead me to good. From darkness lead me to light. From death lead me to immortality. When the Mantra says, 'From evil lead me to good', 'evil' means death, and 'good' immortality; so it says, 'From death lead me to immortality, i.e. make me immortal'. When it says, 'From darkness lead me to light', 'darkness' means death, and 'light', immortality; so it says, 'From death lead me to immortality, or make me immortal'. In the dictum, 'From death lead me to immortality', the meaning does not seem to be hidden. Then through the remaining hymns (the chanter) should secure eatable food for himself by chanting. Therefore, while they are being chanted, the sacrificer should ask for a boon—anything that he desires. Whatever objects this chanter possessed of such knowledge desires, either for himself or for the sacrificer, he secures them by chanting. This (meditation) certainly wins the world (Hiranyagarbha). He who knows the Saman (vital force) as such has not to pray lest he be unfit for this world.

1.4.1: In the beginning, this (universe) was but the self (Viraj) of a human form. He reflected and found nothing else but himself. He first uttered, "I am he" Therefore he was called Aham (I). Hence, to this day, when a person is addressed, he first says, 'It is I,' and then says the other name that he may have. Because he was first and before this whole (band of aspirants) burnt all evils, therefore he is called Purusha. He who knows thus indeed burns one who wants to be (Viraj) before him. 1.4.2: He was afraid. Therefore people (still) are afraid to be alone. He thought, 'If there is nothing else but me, what am I afraid of?' From that alone his fear was gone, for what was there to fear? It is from a second entity that fear comes. 1.4.3: He was not at all happy. Therefore people (still) are not happy when alone. He desired a mate. He became as big as man and wife embracing each other. He parted this very body into two. From that came husband and wife. Therefore, said Yajnavalkya, this (body) is one-half of oneself, like one of the two halves of a split pea. Therefore this space is indeed filled by the wife. He was united with her. From that men were born.

1.4.4: She thought, 'How can he be united with me after producing me from himself? Well let me hide myself'. She became a cow, the other became a bull and was united with her; from that cows were born. The one became a mare, the other a stallion; the one became a she-ass, the other became a he-ass and was united with her; from that one-hoofed animals were born. The one became a she-goat, the other a he-goat; the one became a ewe, the other became a ram and was united with her; from that goat and sheep were born. Thus did he project everything that exists in pairs, down to the ants. 1.4.5: He knew, 'I indeed am the creation, for I projected all this'. Therefore he was called Creation. He who knows this as such becomes (a creator) in this creation of Viraj. 1.4.6: Then he rubbed back and forth thus, and produced fire from its source, the mouth and the hands. Therefore both these are without hair at the inside. When they talk of particular gods, saying, 'Sacrifice to him', 'sacrifice to the other one', (they are wrong, since) these are all his projection, for he is all the gods. Now all this that is liquid, he produced from the seed. That is Soma. This universe is indeed this much—food and the eater of food. Soma is food, and fire the eater of food. This is super-creation of Viraj that he projected the gods, who are even superior to him. Because he, although mortal himself, projected the immortals, therefore this is a super-creation. He who knows this as such becomes (a creator) in this super-creation of Viraj. 1.4.7: This (universe) was then undifferentiated. It differentiated only into name and form—it was called such and such, and was of such and such form. So to this day it is differentiated only into name and form—it is called such and such, and is of such and such form. This Self has entered into these bodies up to the tip of the nails—as a razor may be put in its case, or as fire, which sustains the world, may be in its source. People do not see It, for (viewed in Its aspects) It is incomplete. When It does the function of living. It is called the vital force; when It speaks, the organ of speech; when It sees, the eye; when It hears, the ear; and when It thinks, the mind. These are merely Its names according to functions. He who meditates upon each of this totality of aspects does not know, for It is incomplete, (being divided) from this totality by possessing a single characteristic. The Self alone is to be meditated upon, for all these are unified in It. Of all these, this Self should be realized, for one knows all these through It, just as one may get (an animal) through its foot-prints. He who knows It as such obtains fame and association (with his relatives). 1.4.8: This

Self is dearer than a son, dearer than wealth, dearer than everything else, and is innermost. Should a person (holding the Self as dear) say to one calling anything else dearer than the Self, '(what you hold) dear will die'—he is certainly competent (to say so)—it will indeed come true. One should meditate upon the Self alone as dear. Of him who meditates upon the Self alone as dear, the dear ones are not mortal. 1.4.9: They say: Men think, 'Through the knowledge of Brahman we shall become all'. Well, what did that Brahman know by which It became all? **1.4.10: This (self) was indeed Brahman in the beginning. It knew only Itself as, 'I am Brahman'. Therefore It became all.** And whoever among the gods knew It also became That; and the same with sages and men. The sage Vamadeva, while realizing this (self) as That, knew, 'I was Manu, and the sun'. And to this day whoever in like manner knows It as, 'I am Brahman', becomes all this entire universe. Even the gods cannot prevail against him, for he becomes their self. While he who worships another god thinking, 'He is one, and I am another', does not know. He is like an animal to the gods. As many animals serve a man, so does each man serve the gods. Even if one animal is taken away, it causes anguish, what should one say of many animals? Therefore it is not liked by them that men should know this. 1.4.11: In the beginning this (the Kshatriya and other castes) was indeed Brahman, one only. Being one, he did not flourish. He specially projected an excellent form, the Kshatriya—those who are Kshatriyas among the gods: Indra, Varuna, the moon, Rudra, Parjanya, Yama, Death, and Isana. Therefore there is none higher than the Kshatriya. Hence the Brāhmana worships the Kshatriya from a lower position in the Rajasuya sacrifice. He imparts that glory to the Kshatriya. The Brāhmana is the source of the Kshatriya. Therefore, although the king attains supremacy (in the sacrifice), at the end of it he resorts to the Brāhmana, his source. He who slights the Brāhmana, strikes at his own source. He becomes more wicked, as one is by slighting one's superior. 1.4.12: Yet he did not flourish. He projected the Vaisya—those species of gods who are designated in groups: the Vasus, Rudras, Adityas, Visvadevas and Maruts. 1.4.13: He did not still flourish. He projected the Sudra caste—Pusan. This (earth) is Pusan. For it nourishes all this that exists. 1.4.14: Yet he did not flourish. He specially projected that excellent form, righteousness (Dharma). This righteousness is the controller of the Kshatriya. Therefore there is nothing higher than that. (So) even a weak man hopes (to defeat) a stronger man through righteousness, as (one contending) with the king. That righteousness, as (one contending) with the king. That righteousness is verily truth. Therefore they say about a person speaking of truth, 'He speaks of righteousness', or about a person speaking of righteousness, 'He speaks of truth', for both these are but righteousness. 1.4.15: (So) these (four castes were projected)—the Brāhmana, Kshatriya, Vaisya and Sudra. He became a Brāhmana among the gods as Fore, and among men as the Brāhmana. (He became) a Kshatriya through the (divine) Kshatriyas, a Vaisya through the (divine) Vaisyas and a Sudra through the (divine) Sudra. Therefore people desire to attain the results of their rites among the gods through fire, and among men as the Brāhmana. For Brahman was in these two forms. If, however, anybody departs from this world without realizing his own world (the Self), It, being unknown, does not protect him—as the Vedas not studied, or any other work not undertaken (do not). Even if a man who does not know It as such performs a great many meritorious acts in the world, those acts of his are surely exhausted in the end. One should meditate only upon the world of the Self. He who meditates only upon the world called the Self never has his work exhausted. From this very Self he projects whatever he wants. 1.4.16: Now this self (the ignorant man) is an object of enjoyment to all beings. That he makes oblations in the fire and performs sacrifices is how he becomes such an object to the gods. That he studies the Vedas is how he becomes an object of enjoyment to the Rishis (sages). That he makes offerings to the Manes and desires children is how he becomes such an object to the Manes. That he gives shelter to men as well as food is how he becomes an object of enjoyment to men. That he gives fodder and water to the animals is how he becomes such an object to hem. And that beasts and birds, and even the ants, feed in his home is how he becomes an object of enjoyment to these. Just as one wishes safety to one's body, so do all beings wish safety to him who knows it as such. This indeed has been known, and discussed. 1.4.17: This (aggregate of desirable objects) was but the self in the beginning—the only entity. He desired, 'Let me have a wife, so that I may be born (as the child). And let me have wealth, so that I may perform rites'. This much indeed is (the range of) desire. Even if one wishes, one cannot get more than this. Therefore to this day a man being single desires, 'Let me have a wife, so that I may be born. And let me have wealth, so that I may perform rites.' Until he obtains each one of these, he considers himself incomplete. His completeness also (comes thus): The mind is his self, speech his wife, the vital force his child, the eye his human wealth, for he obtains it through the eye, the ear his divine wealth, for he hears of it through the ear, and the body is its (instrument of) rite, for he performs rites through the body. (So) this sacrifice has five factors—the animals have five factors, the men have five factors, and all this that exists has five factors. He who knows it as such attains all this.

1.5.1: That the father produced seven kinds of food through meditation and rites (I shall disclose). One is common to all eaters. Two he apportioned to the gods.

Three he designed for himself. And one he gave to the animals. On it rests everything—what lives and what does not. Why are they not exhausted, although they are always being eaten? He who knows this cause of their permanence eats food with Pratika (pre-eminence). He attains (identity with) the gods and lives on nectar. These are the verses. 1.5.2: 'That the father produced seven kinds of food through meditation and rites' means that the father indeed produced them through meditation and rites. 'One is common to all eaters' means, this food that is eaten is the common food of all eaters. He who adores (monopolizes) this food is never free from evil, for this is general food. 'Two he apportioned to the gods' means making oblations in the fire, and offering presents otherwise to the gods. Therefore people perform both these. Some, however, say, those two are the new and full moon sacrifices. Therefore one should not be engrossed with sacrifices for material ends. 'One he gave to the animals'—it is milk. For men and animals first live on milk alone. Therefore they first make a new-born babe lick clarified butter or suckle it. And they speak of a new-born calf as not yet eating grass. 'On it rests everything—what lives and what does not' means that on milk indeed rests all this that lives and that does not. It is said that by making offerings of milk in the fire for a year one conquers further death. One should not think like that. He who knows as above conquers further death the very day he makes that offering, for he offers all eatable food to the gods, 'Why are they not exhausted, although they are always being eaten?'—means that the being (eater) is indeed the cause of their permanence, for the produces this food again and again. 'He who knows this cause of their permanence' means that the being (eater) is indeed the cause of their permanence, for he produces this food through his meditation for the time being and rites. If he does not do this, it will be exhausted. 'He eats food with Pratika'; 'Pratika' means pre-eminence; hence the meaning is, preeminently. 'He attains the gods and lives on nectar' is a eulogy. 1.5.3: 'Three he designed for himself' means: the mind, the organ of speech and the vital force; these he designed for himself. (They say), 'I was absent-minded, I did not see it', 'I was absent-minded, I did not hear it'. It is through the mind that one sees and hears. Desires, resolve, doubt, faith, want of faith, steadiness, unsteadiness, shame, intelligence and fear—all these are but the mind. Even if one is touched from behind, one knows it through the mind; therefore (the mind exists). And any kind of sound is but the organ of speech, for it serves to determine a thing, but it cannot itself be revealed. Prāna, Apana, Vyana, Udana, Samana and Ana --- all these are but the vital forces. This body is identified with these—with the organ of speech, the mind and the vital force. 1.5.4: These are the three worlds. The organ of speech is this world (the earth), the mind is the sky, and the vital force is that world (heaven). 1.5.5: These are the three Vedas. The organ of speech is the Rig-Veda, the mind is the Yajur-Veda and the vital force the Sama-Veda. 1.5.6: These are the gods, the Manes and men. The organ of speech is the gods, the mind the Manes, and the vital force men. 1.5.7: These are the father, mother and child. The mind is the father, the organ of speech the mother, and the vital force the child. 1.5.8: These are what is known, what it is desirable to know, and what is unknown. Whatever is known is a form of the organ of speech, for it is the knower. The organ of speech protects him (who knows this) by becoming that (which is known). 1.5.9: Whatever it is desirable to know is a form of the mind, for the mind is what it is desirable to know. The mind protects him (who knows this) by becoming that (which it is desirable to know). 1.5.10: Whatever is unknown is a form of the vital force, for the vital force is what is unknown. The vital force protects him (who knows this) by becoming that (which is unknown). 1.5.11: The earth is the body of that organ of speech, and this fire is its luminous organ. And as far as the organ of speech extends, so far extends the earth and so far does this fire. 1.5.12: Heaven is the body of this mind, and that sun is its luminous organ. And as far as the mind extends, so far extends heaven, and so far does that sun. The two were united, and from that the vital force emanated. It is the Supreme Lord. It is without a rival. A second being is indeed a rival. He who knows it as such has no rival. 1.5.13: Water is the body of this vital force, and that moon is its luminous organ. And as far as the vital force extends, so far extends water, and so far does that moon. These are all equal, and all infinite. He who meditates upon these as finite wins a finite world, but he who meditates upon these as infinite wins an infinite world. 1.5.14: This Prajapati (Hiranyagarbha) has sixteen digits and is represented by the year. The nights (and days) are his fifteen digits, and the constant one is his sixteenth digit. He (as the moon) is filled as well as wasted by the nights (and days). Through this sixteenth digit he permeates all these living beings on the new-moon night and rises the next morning. Therefore on this night one should not take the life of living beings, not even of a chameleon, in adoration of this deity alone. 1.5.15: That Prajapati who has sixteen digits and is represented by the year is indeed this man who knows as above. Wealth constitutes his fifteen digits, and the body his sixteenth digit. He is filled as well as wasted by wealth. This body stands for a nave, and wealth is the felloe. Therefore if a man loses everything, but he himself lives, people say that he has only lost his outfit. 1.5.16: There are indeed three worlds, the world of men, the world of the Manes and the world of the gods. This world of men is to be won through the son alone, and by no other rite; the world of the Manes through rites; and the world of the gods through meditation. The world of the gods is the best of the worlds. Therefore they praise meditation. 1.5.17: Now therefore the entrusting: When a man thinks he will die, he says to his son, 'You are Brahman, you are the sacrifice, and you are the world'. The son replies, 'I am Brahman, I am the sacrifice, and I am the world.' (The father thinks 'Whatever is studied is all unified in the word "Brahman". Whatever sacrifices there are, are all unified in the word "sacrifice". And whatever worlds there are, are all unified in the world "world". All this (the duties of a householder) is indeed this much. He, being all this, will protect me from (the ties of) this world.' Therefor they speak of an educated son as being conducive to the world. Hence (a father) teaches his son. When a father who knows as above departs from this world, he penetrates his son together with the organ of speech, the mind and the vital force. Should anything be left undone by him through any slip the son exonerates him from all that. Therefore he is called a son. The father lives in this world through the son. Divine and immortal speech, mind and vital force permeate him. 1.5.18: The divine organ of speech from the earth and fire permeates him. That is the divine organ of speech through which whatever he says is fulfilled. 1.5.19: The divine mind from heaven and the sun permeates him. That is the divine mind through which he only becomes happy and never mourns. 1.5.20: The divine vital force from water and the moon permeates him. That is the divine vital force which, when it moves or does not move, feels no pain nor is injured. He who knows as above becomes the self of all beings. As is this deity (Hiranyagarbha), so is he. As all beings take care of this deity, so do they take care of him. Howsoever these beings may grieve, that grief of theirs is connected with them. But only merit goes to him. No demerit ever goes to the gods. 1.5.21: Now a consideration of the vow: Prajapati projected the organs. These, on being projected, quarreled with one another. The organ of speech took a vow, 'I will go on speaking'. The eye: 'I will see'. The ear: 'I will hear'. And so did the other organs according to their functions. Death captured them in the form of fatigue—it overtook the, and having overtaken them it controlled them. Therefore the organ of speech invariably gets tired, and so do the eye and the ear. But death did not overtake this vital force in the body. The organs resolved to know it. 'This is the greatest among us that, when it moves or does not move, feels no pain nor is injured. Well, let us all be of its form.' They all assumed its form. Therefore they are called by this name of 'Prāna'. That family in which a man is born who knows as above, is indeed named after him. And he who competes with one who knows as above shrivels, and after shriveling dies at the end. This is with reference to the body. 1.5.22: Now with reference to the gods: Fire took a vow, 'I will go on burning.' The sun: 'I will give heat'. The moon: 'I will shine'. And so did the other gods according to their functions. As is the vital force in the body among these organs, so is Vayu (air) among these gods. Other gods sink, but not air. Air is the deity that never sets.

1.5.23: Now there is this verse; 'The gods observed the vow of that from which the sun rises and in which he sets. It is (followed) to-day, and it will be (followed) to-morrow.' The sun indeed rises from the vital force and also sets in it. What these (gods) observed then, they observe to this day. Therefore a man should observe a single vow—do the functions of the Prāna and Apana (respiration and excretion), lest the evil of death (fatigue) should overtake him. And if he observes it, he should seek to finish it. Through it he attains identity with this deity, or lives in the same world with it.

1.6.1: This (universe) indeed consists of three things: name, form and action. Of those names, speech (sound in general) is the Uktha (source), for all names spring from it. It is their Saman (common feature), for it is common to all names. It is their Brahman (self), for it sustains all names. 1.6.2: Now of forms the eye (anything visible) is the Uktha (source), for all forms spring from it. It is their Saman (common feature), for it is common to all forms. It is their Brahman (self), for it sustains all forms. 1.6.3: And of actions the body (activity) is the Uktha (source), for all actions spring from it. It is their Saman (common feature), for it is common to all actions. It is their Brahman (self), for it sustains all actions. These three together are one—this body, and the body, although one, is these three. This immortal entity is covered by truth (the five elements): The vital force is the immortal entity, and name and form and truth; (so) this vital force is covered by them.

9. Gargya-Ajatasatru Dialogue

2.1.1: Om. There was a man of the Garga family called Proud Balaki, who was a speaker. He said to Ajatasatru, the king of Banares, 'I will tell you about Brahman'. Ajatasatru said, 'For this proposal I give you a thousand (cows). People indeed rush saying "Janaka, Janaka". (I too have some of his qualities.)' 2.1.2: Gargya said, 'That being who is in the sun, I meditate upon as Brahman'. Ajatasatru said, 'Please don't talk about him. I meditate upon him as all-surpassing, as the head of all beings and as resplendent. He who meditates upon him as such becomes all-surpassing, the head of all beings and resplendent. 2.1.3: Gargya said, 'that being who is in the moon, I meditate upon as Brahman'. Ajatasatru said, "Please don't talk about him. I meditate upon him as the great, white-robed, radiant Soma.' He who meditates upon him as such has abundant Soma pressed in his principal and auxiliary sacrifices every day, and his food never gets short. 2.1.4: Gargya said, 'That being who is in lightning, I meditate upon as Brahman'. Ajatasatru said, "Please don't talk about him. I meditate upon him as powerful'. He who meditates upon him as such becomes powerful, and his progeny too becomes powerful. 2.1.5: Gargya said, 'This being who is in the ether, I meditate upon as Brahman'. Ajatasatru said, "Please don't talk about him. I meditate upon him as full and unmoving'. He who meditates upon him as such is filled with progeny and cattle, and his progeny is never extinct from this world. 2.1.6: Gargya said, 'This being who is in air, I meditate upon as Brahman'. Ajatasatru said, "Please don't talk about him. I meditate upon him as the Lord, as irresistible, and as the unvanquished army.' He who meditates upon him as such ever becomes victorious and invincible, and conquers his enemies. 2.1.7: Gargya said, 'This being who is in fire, I meditate upon as Brahman'. Ajatasatru said, "Please don't talk about him. I meditate upon him as forbearing'. He who meditates upon him as such becomes forbearing, and his progeny too becomes forbearing. 2.1.8: Gargya said, 'This being who is in water, I meditate upon as Brahman'. Ajatasatru said, "Please don't talk about him. I meditate upon him as agreeable'. He who meditates upon him as such has only agreeable things coming to him, and not contrary ones; also from him are born children who are agreeable. 2.1.9: Gargya said, 'This being who is in a looking-glass, I meditate upon as Brahman'. Ajatasatru said:

"Please don't talk about him. I meditate upon him as shining'. He who meditates upon him as such becomes shining, and his progeny too becomes shining. He also outshines all those with whom he comes in contact. 2.1.10: Gargya said, 'This sound that issues behind a man as he walks, I meditate upon as Brahman'. Ajatasatru said, "Please don't talk about him. I meditate upon him as life'. He who meditates upon him as such attains his full term of life in this world, and life does not depart from him before the completion of that term. 2.1.11: Gargya said, 'This being who is in the quarters, I meditate upon as Brahman'. Ajatasatru said, "Please don't talk about him. I meditate upon him as second and as non-separating'. He who meditates upon him as such gets companions, and his followers never depart from him. 2.1.12: Gargya said, 'This being who identifies himself with the shadow, I meditate upon as Brahman'. Ajatasatru said, "Please don't talk about him. I meditate upon him as death'. He who meditates upon him as such attains his full term of life in this world, and death does not overtake him before the completion of that term. 2.1.13: Gargya said, 'This being who is in the self, I meditate upon as Brahman'. Ajatasatru said, "Please don't talk about him. I meditate upon him as self-possessed.' He who meditates upon him as such becomes self-possessed, and his progeny too becomes self-possessed. Gargya remained silent. 2.1.14: Ajatasatru said, 'is this all?' 'This is all'. 'By knowing this much **one cannot know (Brahman)**'. Gargya said, 'I approach you as a student'.

Ajatasatru teaches Gargya

2.1.15: Ajatasatru said, 'It is contrary to usage that a Brāhmana should approach a Kshatriya thinking, "he will teach me about Brahman". However I will instruct you'. Taking Gargya by the hand he rose. They came to a sleeping man. (Ajatasatru) addressed him by these names, Great, White-robed, radiant, Soma'. The man did not get up. (The King) pushed him with the hand till he awoke. Then he got up. 2.1.16: Ajatasatru said, 'When this being full of consciousness (identified with the mind) was thus asleep, where was it, and whence did it thus come?' Gargya did not know that. 2.1.17: Ajatasatru said, 'When this being full of consciousness is thus asleep, it absorbs at the time the functions of the organs through its own consciousness, and lies in the Ākāsha (Supreme Self) that is in the heart. When this being absorbs them, it is called Svapiti. Then the nose is absorbed, the organ of speech is absorbed, the eye is absorbed, the ear is absorbed, and the mind is absorbed'. 2.1.18: When it thus remains in the dream state, these are its achievements: It then becomes an emperor, as it were, or a noble Brāhmana, as it were, or attains states high or low, as it were. As an emperor, taking his citizens, moves about as he pleases in his own territory, so does it, thus taking the organs, move about as it pleases in its own body. 2.1.19: Again when it becomes fast asleep—when it does not know anything—it comes back along the seventy-two thousand nerves called Hita, which extend from the heart to the pericardium (the whole body), and remains in the body. As a baby, or an emperor, or a noble Brāhmana lives, having attained the acme of bliss, so does it remain. 2.1.20: As a spider moves along the thread (it produces), and as from a fire tiny sparks fly in all directions, so from this Self emanate all organs, all worlds, all gods and all beings. Its secret name (Upanishad) is 'the Truth of Truth'. The vital force is truth, and It is the Truth of that.

2.2.1: He who knows the calf with its abode, its special resort, its post and its tether kills his seven envious kinsmen: the vital force in the body is indeed the calf; this body is its abode, the head its special resort, strength its post, and food its tether. 2.2.2: These seven gods that prevent decay worship it: Through these pink lines in the eye Rudra attends on it; through the water that is in the eye, Parjanya; through the pupil, the sun; through the dark portion, fire; through the white portion, Indra; through the lower eye-lid the earth attends on it; and through the upper eye-lid, heaven. He who knows it as such never has any decrease of food. 2.2.3: Regarding this there is the following pithy verse: 'there is a bowl that has its opening below and bulges at the top; various kinds of knowledge have been put in it; seven sages sit by its side, and the organ of speech, which has communication with the Vedas, is the eighth'. The 'bowl that has its opening below and bulges at the top' is the head of ours, for it is the bowl that has its opening below and bulges at the top. 'various kinds of knowledge have been put in it', refers to the organs; these indeed represent various kinds of knowledge. 'Seven sages sit by its side', refers to the organs; they indeed are the sages. 'The organ of speech, which has communication with the Vedas, is the eighth', because the organ of speech is the eighth and communicates with the Vedas. 2.2.4: These two (ears) are Gautama and Bharadvaja: this one is Gautama, and this one is Bharadvaja: These two (eyes) are Visvamitra and Jamadagni: this one is Visvamitra, and this one Jamadagni. These two (nostrils) are Vasistha, and Kashyapa: this one is Vasistha, and this one Kashyapa: the tongue is Atri, for through the tongue food is eaten. He who knows it as such becomes the eater of all, and everything becomes his food.

2.3.1: Brahman has but two forms—gross and subtle, mortal and immortal, limited and unlimited, defined and undefined. 2.3.2: The gross (form) is that which is other than air and the ether. It is mortal, it is limited, and it is defined. The essence of that which is gross, mortal, limited and defined is the sun that shines, for it is the essence of the defined. 2.3.3: Now the subtle—it is air and the ether. It is immortal, it is unlimited, and it is undefined. The essence of that which is subtle, immortal, unlimited and undefined is the being that is in the sun, for that is the essence of the undefined. This is with reference to the gods. 2.3.4: Now with reference to the body: the gross form is but this—what is other than (the corporeal) air and the ether that is in the body. It is mortal, it is limited and it is defined. The essence of that which is gross, mortal, limited and defined is the eye, for it is the essence of the defined. 2.3.5: Now the subtle—it is (the corporeal) air and the ether that is in the body. It is immortal, it is unlimited, and it is undefined. The essence of that which is subtle, immortal, unlimited and undefined is this being that is in the right eye, for this is the essence of the undefined. 2.3.6: The form of that 'being' is as follows: like a cloth dyed with turmeric, or like grey sheep's wool, or like the (scarlet) insect called Indragopa, or like a tongue of fire, or like a white lotus, or like a flash of lightning. He who knows it as such attains splendor like a flash of lightning. Now therefore the description (of Brahman): 'Not this, not this'. Because there is no other and more appropriate description than this 'Not this'. Now Its name: 'The Truth of truth'. The vital force is truth, and It is the Truth of that.

10. Yajnavalkya and his wife maitreyi

2.4.1: 'Maitreyi, my dear', said Yajnavalkya, 'I am going to renounce this life. Allow me to finish between you and Katyayani'. 2.4.2: Thereupon Maitreyi said, 'Sir, if indeed this whole earth full of wealth be mine, shall I be immortal through that?' 'No', replied Yajnavalkya, 'your life will be just like that of people who have plenty of things, but there is no hope of immortality through wealth.' 2.4.3: Then Maitreyi said, 'What shall I do with that which will not make me immortal? Tell me, sir, of that alone which you know (to be the only means of immortality).' 2.4.4: Yajnavalkya said, 'My dear, you have been my beloved (even before), and you say what is in my mind. Come, take your seat, I will explain it to you. As I explain it, meditate (on its meaning). **2.4.5: He said: 'It is not for the sake of the husband, my dear, that he is loved, but for one's own Self sake that he is loved. It is not for the sake of the wife, my dear, that she is loved, but for one's own Self sake that she is loved.** It is not for the sake of the sons, my dear, that they are loved, but for one's own sake that they are loved. It is not for the sake of wealth, my dear, that it is loved, but for one's own sake that it is loved. It is not for the sake of the Brāhmana, my dear, that he is loved, but for one's own sake that he is loved. It is not for the sake of the Kshatriya, my dear, that he is loved, but for one's own sake that he is loved. It is not for the sake of worlds, my dear, that they are loved, but for one's own sake that they are loved. It is not for the sake of the gods, my dear, that they are loved, but for one's own sake that they are loved. It is not for the sake of beings, my dear, that they are loved, but for one's own sake that they are loved. It is not for the sake of all, my dear, that all is loved, but for one's own sake that it is loved. The Self, my dear Maitreyi, should be realized—should be heard of, reflected on and meditated upon. By the realization of the Self, my dear, through hearing, reflection and meditation, all this is known.

2.4.6: Perception of oneness of the Self in every being is the highest spiritual perfection. Sage **Yajnavalkya** said: A wife does not love her husband because of his or her physical satisfaction. She loves her husband because she feels the oneness of her soul with his soul. She is merged in her husband and becomes one with him (BrU 2.04.05). The foundation of Vedic marriage is based on this noble and solid rock of soul culture and is unbreakable. Trying to develop any meaningful human relationship without a firm understanding of the spiritual basis of all relationships is like trying to water the leaves of a tree rather than the root.

When one perceives one's own higher Self in all people and all people in one's own higher Self, then one does not hate or injure anybody **(IsU 06).** Eternal peace belongs to those who perceive God existing within everybody as Spirit **(KaU 5.13).** One should love others, including the enemy, because all are your own self.

Husband and wife should try to improve and help develop each other with tender loving care as a cow purifies her calf by licking. Their words to each other should be sweet, as if dipped in honey (AV 3.30.01-02).

The Brāhmana ousts (slights) one who knows him as different from the Self. The Kshatriya ousts one who knows him as different from the Self. Worlds oust one who knows them as different from the Self. The gods oust one who knows them as different from the Self. Beings oust one who knows them as different from the Self. All ousts one who knows it as different from the Self. This Brāhmana, this Kshatriya, these worlds, these gods, these beings, and this all are this Self. 2.4.7: As, when a drum is beaten, one cannot distinguish its various particular notes, but they are included in the general note of the drum or in the general sound produced by different kinds of strokes. 2.4.8: As, when a conch is blown, one cannot distinguish its various particular notes, but they are included in the general note of the conch or in the general sound produced by different kinds of playing. 2.4.9: As, when a Vina is played, one cannot distinguish its various particular notes, but they are included in the general note of the Vina or in the general sound produced by different kinds of playing. 2.4.10: As from a fire kindled with wet faggot diverse kinds of smoke issue, even so, my dear, the Rig-Veda, Yajur-Veda, Sama-Veda, Atharvangirasa, history, mythology, arts, Upanishads, pithy verses, aphorisms, elucidations and explanations are (like) the breath of this infinite Reality. They are like the breath of this (Supreme Self). 2.4.11: As the ocean is the one goal of all sorts of water, as the skin is the one goal of all kinds of touch, as the nostrils are the one goal of all odors, as the tongue is the one goal of all savors, as the eye is the one goal of all colors, as the ear is the one goal of all sounds, as the Manas is the one goal of all deliberations, as the intellect is the one goal of all kinds of knowledge, as the hands are the one goal of all sort of work, as the organ of generation is the one goal of all kinds of enjoyment, as the anus is the one goal of all excretions, as the feet are the one goal of all kinds of walking, as the organ of speech is the one goal of all Vedas. 2.4.12: As a lump of salt dropped into water dissolves with (its component) water, and no one is able to pick it up, but from wheresoever one takes it, it tastes salt, even so, my dear, this great, endless, infinite Reality is but Pure Intelligence. (The Self) comes out (as a separate entity) from these elements, and (this separateness) is destroyed with them. After attaining (this oneness) it has no more consciousness. This is what I say, my dear. So said Yajnavalkya. 2.4.13: Maitreyi said, 'Just here you have thrown me into confusion, sir—by saying that after attaining (oneness) the self has no more consciousness'. Yajnavalkya said, 'Certainly, I am not saying anything confusing, my dear; this is quite sufficient for knowledge, O Maitreyi'. 2.4.14: Because when there is duality, as it were, then one smells something, one sees something, one hears something, one speaks something, one thinks something, one knows something. (But) when to the knower of Brahman everything has become the self, then what should one smell and through what, what should one see and through what, what should one hear and through what, what should one speak and through what, what should one think and through what, what should one know and through what? Through what should one know That owing to which all this is known—**through what, O Maitreyi, should one know the Knower**?

2.5.1: This earth is (like) honey to all beings, and all beings are (like) honey to this earth. (The same with) the shining immortal being who is in this earth, and the shining, immortal, corporeal being in the body. (These four) are but this Self. This (Self-knowledge) is (the means of) immortality; this (underlying unity) is Brahman; this (knowledge of Brahman) is (the means of becoming) all.

2.5.2: This water is (like) honey to all beings, and all beings are (like) honey to this water. (The same with) the shining immortal being who is in this water, and the shining, immortal being identified with the seed in the body. (These four) are but this Self. This (Self-knowledge) is (the means of) immortality; this (underlying unity) is Brahman; this (knowledge of Brahman) is (the means of becoming) all. 2.5.3: This fire is (like) honey to all beings, and all beings are (like) honey to this fire. (The same with) the shining immortal being who is in this fire, and the shining, immortal being identified with the organ of speech in the body. (These four) are but this Self. This (Self-knowledge) is (the means of) immortality; this (underlying unity) is Brahman; this (knowledge of Brahman) is (the means of becoming) all. 2.5.4: This air is (like) honey to all beings, and all beings are (like) honey to this air. (The same with) the shining immortal being who is in this air, and the shining, immortal being who is the vital force in the body. (These four) are but this Self. This (Self-knowledge) is (the means of) immortality; this (underlying unity) is Brahman; this (knowledge of Brahman) is (the means of becoming) all. 2.5.5: This sun is (like) honey to all beings, and all beings are (like) honey to this sun. (The same with) the shining immortal being who is in this sun, and the shining, immortal being identified with the eye in the body. (These four) are but this Self. This (Self-knowledge) is (the means of) immortality; this (underlying unity) is Brahman; this (knowledge of Brahman) is (the means of becoming) all. 2.5.6: These quarters is (like) honey to all beings, and all beings are (like) honey to these quarters. (The same with) the shining immortal being who is these quarters, and the shining, immortal being identified with the ear and with the time of hearing in the body. (These four) are but this Self. This (Self-knowledge) is (the means of) immortality; this (underlying unity) is Brahman; this (knowledge of Brahman) is (the means of becoming) all. 2.5.7: This moon is (like) honey to all beings, and all beings are (like) honey to this moon. (The same with) the shining immortal being who is in this moon, and the shining, immortal being identified with the mind in the body. (These four) are but this Self. This (Self-knowledge) is (the means of) immortality; this (underlying unity) is Brahman; this (knowledge of Brahman) is (the means of becoming) all. 2.5.8: This lightning is (like) honey to all beings, and all beings are (like) honey to this lightning. (The same with) the shining immortal being who is in this lightning, and the shining, immortal being identified with light in the body. (These four) are but this Self. This (Self-knowledge) is (the means of) immortality; this (underlying unity) is Brahman; this (knowledge of Brahman) is (the means of becoming) all. 2.5.9: This cloud is (like) honey to all beings, and all beings are (like) honey to this cloud. (The same with) the shining immortal being who is in this cloud, and the shining, immortal being identified with sound and voice in the body. (These four) are but this Self. This (Self-knowledge) is (the means of) immortality; this (underlying unity) is Brahman; this (knowledge of Brahman) is (the means of becoming) all. 2.5.10: This ether is (like) honey to all beings, and all beings are (like) honey to this ether. (The same with) the shining immortal being who is in this ether, and the shining, immortal being identified with the ether in the heart, in the body. (These four) are but this Self. This (Self-knowledge) is (the means of) immortality; this (underlying unity) is Brahman; this (knowledge of Brahman) is (the means of becoming) all. 2.5.11: This righteousness (Dharma) is (like) honey to all beings, and all beings are (like) honey to this righteousness. (The same with) the shining immortal being who is in this righteousness, and the shining, immortal being identified with righteousness in the body. (These four) are but this Self. This (Self-knowledge) is (the means of) immortality; this (underlying unity) is Brahman; this (knowledge of Brahman) is (the means of becoming) all. 2.5.12: This truth is (like) honey to all beings, and all beings are (like) honey to this truth. (The same with) the shining immortal being who is in this truth, and the shining, immortal being identified with truth in the body. (These four) are but this Self. This (Self-knowledge) is (the means of) immortality; this (underlying unity) is Brahman; this (knowledge of Brahman) is (the means of becoming) all. 2.5.13: This human species is (like) honey to all beings, and all beings are (like) honey to this human species. (The same with) the shining immortal being who is in this human species, and the shining, immortal being identified with the human species in the body. (These four) are but this Self. This (Self knowledge) is (the means of) immortality; this (underlying unity) is Brahman; this (knowledge of Brahman) is (the means of becoming) all. 2.5.14: This (cosmic) body is (like) honey to all beings, and all beings are (like) honey to this (cosmic) body. (The same with) the shining immortal being who is in this (cosmic) body, and the shining, immortal being who is this (individual) self. (These four) are but this Self. This (Self-knowledge) is (the means of) immortality; this (underlying unity) is Brahman; this (knowledge of Brahman) is (the means of becoming) all. 2.5.15: This Self, already mentioned, is the ruler of all beings, and the king of all beings. Just as all the spokes are fixed in the nave and the felloe of a chariot-wheel, so are all beings, all gods, all worlds, all organs and all these (individual) selves fixed in this Self.

11. Meditation taught through a horse's mouth

2.5.16: This is that meditation on things mutually helpful which Dadhyac, versed in the Atharva-Veda, taught the Asvins. Perceiving this the Rishi (Mantra) said, 'O Asvins in human form, that terrible deed called Damsa which you committed out of greed, I will disclose as a cloud does rain—(how you learnt) the meditation on things mutually helpful that Dadhyac, versed in the Atharva-Veda, taught you through a horse's head. 2.5.17: This is that meditation on things mutually helpful which Dadhyac, versed in the Atharva-Veda, taught the Asvins. Perceiving this the Rishi said, 'O Asvins, you set a horse's head on (the shoulders of) Dadhyac, versed in the Atharva-Veda. O terrible ones, to keep his word, he taught you the (ritualistic) meditation on things mutually helpful connected with the sun, as also the secret (spiritual) meditation on them.' 2.5.18: This is that meditation on things mutually helpful which Dadhyac, versed in the Atharva-Veda, taught the Asvins. Perceiving this the Rishi said, 'He made bodies with two feet and bodies with four feet. That supreme Being first entered the bodies as a bird (the subtle body).' On account of his dwelling in all bodies, He is called the Purusha. There is nothing that is not covered by Him, nothing that is not pervaded by Him. 2.5.19: This is that meditation on things mutually helpful which Dadhyac, versed in the Atharva-Veda, taught the Asvins. Perceiving this the Rishi said, '(He) transformed Himself in accordance with each form; that form of His was for the sake of making Him known. The Lord on account of Maya (notions superimposed by ignorance) is perceived as manifold, for to Him are yoked ten organs, nay, hundreds of them. He is the organs; He is ten and thousands—many and infinite. That Brahman is without prior or posterior, without interior or exterior. This self, the perceiver of everything, is Brahman. This is the teaching.

2.6.1: Now the line of teachers: Pautimasya (received it) from Gaupavana. Gaupavana from another Pautimasya. This Pautimasya from another Gaupavana. This Gaupavana from Kausika. Kausika from Kaundinya. Kaundinya from Sandilya. Sandilya from Kausika and Gautama. Gautama—2.6.2: From Agnivesya. Agnivesya from Sandilya and Anabhimlata. Anabhimlata from another of that name. He from a third Anabhimlata. This Anabhimlata from Gautama. Gautama from Saitava and Pracinayogya. They from Parasarya. Parasarya from Bharadvaja. He from Bharadvaja and Gautama. Gautama from another Bharadvaja. He from another Parasarya. Parasarya from Baijavapayana. He from Kausikayani. Kausikayani—2.6.3: From Ghrtakausika. Ghrtakausika from Parasaryayana. He from Parasarya. Parasarya from Jatukarnya. Jatukarnya from Asurayana and Yaska. Asurayana from Traivani. Traivani from Aupajandhani. He from Asuri. Asuri from Bharadvaja. Bharadvaja from Atreya. Atreya from Manti. Manti from Gautama. Gautama from another Gautama. He from Vatsya. Vatsya from Sandilya. Sandilya from Kaisorya Kapya. He from Kumaraharita. Kumaraharita from Galava. Galava from Vidarbhi-kaundinya. He from Vatsanapat Babhrava. He from Pathin Saubhara. He from Ayasya Angirasa. He from Abhuti Tvastra. He from Visvarupa Tvastra. He from the Asvins. They from Dadhyac Atharvana. He from Atharvan Daiva. He from Mrityu Pradhvamsana. He from Pradhvamsana. Pradhvamsana from Ekarsi. Ekarsi from Viprachitti. Viprachitti from Vyasri. Vyasti from Sanaru. Sanaru from Sanatana. Sanatana from Sanaga. Sanaga from Paramesthin (Viraj). He from Brahman (Hiranyabarbha). Brahman is self-born. Salutation to Brahman.

12. Yajnavalkya: The best Vedic Scholar

3.1.1: Om. Janaka, Emperor of Videha, performed a sacrifice in which gifts were freely distributed. Vedic scholars from Kuru and Panchala were assembled there. Emperor Janaka of Videha had a desire to know, 'Which is the most erudite of these Vedic scholars?' He had a thousand cows confined in a pen, and on the horns of each cow were fixed ten Padas (of gold). 3.1.2: He said to them, 'Revered Brahmans, let him who is the best Vedic scholar among you drive these cows (home).' None of the Brahmans dared. Then Yajnavalkya said to a pupil of his, 'Dear Samarians, please drive these cows (home).' He drove them. The Brahmans were enraged. 'How does he dare to call himself the best Vedic scholar among us?' there was a Hot of Emperor Janaka of Videha named Asvala. He now asked Yajnavalkya, 'Yajnavalkya, are you indeed the best Vedic scholar among us?' Yajnavalkya replied, 'I bow to the best Vedic scholar, I just want the cows'. Thereupon the Hot Asvala determined to interrogate him. 3.1.3: 'Yajnavalkya', said he, 'since all this is overtaken by death, and swayed by it, by what means does the sacrificer go beyond the clutches of death?' 'Through the organ of speech—through fire, which is the (real) priest called Hot. The sacrificer's organ of speech is the Hotr. This organ of speech is fire; this fire is the Hotr; this (fire) is liberation; this (liberation) is emancipation'. 3.1.4: 'Yajnavalkya', said he, 'since all this is overtaken by day and night, and swayed by them, by what means does the sacrificer go beyond the clutches of day and night?' 'Through the eye—through the sun, which is the (real) priest called Adhvaryu. The eye of the sacrificer is the Adhvaryu. This eye is the sun; this sun is the Adhvaryu; this (sun) is liberation; this (liberation) is emancipation'. 3.1.5: 'Yajnavalkya', said he, 'since all this is overtaken by the bright and dark fortnights, and swayed by them, by what means does the sacrificer go beyond the bright and dark fortnights /' 'Through the vital force—through air, which is the (real) priest called Udgatir. The vital force of the sacrificer is the Udgatir. This vital force is air, and it is the Udgatir; this (air) is liberation; this (liberation) is emancipation.' 3.1.6: 'Yajnavalkya', said he, 'since the sky is, as it were, without a support, through what support does the sacrificer go to heaven?' 'Through the mind—through the moon, which is the (real) priest called Brahman. The mind of the sacrificer is the Brahman. This mind is the moon; the moon is the Brahman; this (moon) is liberation; this (liberation) is emancipation'. So far about the ways of emancipation; now about the meditations based on resemblance. 3.1.7: 'Yajnavalkya', said he, 'with how many kinds of Rik will the Hotr do his part in this sacrifice to-day?' 'With three kinds'. 'Which are those three?' 'The preliminary, the sacrificial, and the eulogistic hymns as the third'. 'What does he win through them?' 'All this that is living'. 3.1.8: 'Yajnavalkya', said he, 'how many kinds of oblations will the Adhvaryu offer in this sacrifice to-day?' 'Three'. 'Which are those three?' 'Those that blaze up on being offered, those that make a great noise, when offered, and those that sink on being offered'. 'What does he win through them?' 'Through those that blaze up on being offered he wins the world of the gods, for this world shines, as it were. Through those that make a great noise, when offered, he wins the world of the manes, for this world is full of uproar. And through those that sink on being offered, he wins the human world, for this world is lower.'

3.1.9: 'Yajnavalkya', said he, 'through how many gods does this Brahman from the right protect the sacrifice to-day?' 'Through one'. 'Which is that one?' 'The mind. The mind is indeed infinite, and infinite are the Visvadevas. Through this meditation he wins an infinite world'. 3.1.10: 'Yajnavalkya', said he, 'how many classes of hymns the Udgatir chant in this sacrifice today?' 'Three classes'. 'Which are those three?' 'The preliminary, the sacrificial, and the eulogistic hymns as the third'. 'Which are those that have reference to the body?' 'The Prana is the preliminary hymn, the Apana is the sacrificial hymn, and the Vyana is the eulogistic hymn'. 'What does he win through them?' 'Through the preliminary hymns he wins the earth, through the sacrificial hymns he wins the sky, and through the eulogistic hymns he wins heaven'. Thereupon the Hotr Asvala kept silent.

3.2.1: Then Artabhaga, of the line of Jaratkaru, asked him. 'Yajnavalkya', said he, 'how many are the Grahas, and how many are the Atigrahas?' 'There are eight Grahas and eight Atigrahas'. 'Which are those eight Grahas and eight Atigrahas?' 3.2.2: The Prāna (nose) indeed is the Graha; it is controlled by the Atigraha, the Apana (odor), for one smells odors through the Apana (the air breathed in). 3.2.3: The organ of speech indeed is the graha; it is controlled by the Atigraha, name, for one utters names through the organ of speech. 3.2.4: The tongue indeed is the Graha; it is controlled by the Atigraha, taste, for one knows tastes through the tongue. 3.2.5: The eye indeed is the Graha; it is controlled by the Atigraha, color, for one sees colors through the eye. 3.2.6: The ear indeed is the Graha; it is controlled by the Atigraha, sound, for one hears sounds through the ear. 3.2.7: The mind indeed is the Graha; it is controlled by the Atigraha, desire, for one wishes desires through the mind. 3.2.8: The hands indeed is the Graha; it is controlled by the Atigraha, work, for one does work through the hands. 3.2.9: The skin indeed is the Graha; it is controlled by the Atigraha, touch, for one feels touch through the skin. These are the eight Grahas and eight Atigrahas. 3.2.10: 'Yajnavalkya', said he, 'since all this is the food of death, who is that god whose food is death?' 'Fire is death; it is the food of water. (One who knows thus) conquers further death'. 3.2.11: 'Yajnavalkya', said he, 'when the (liberated) man dies, do his organs go up from him, or do they not?' 'No', replied Yajnavalkya, '(They) merge in Him only. The body swells, is inflated, and in that state lies dead.' 3.2.12: 'Yajnavalkya', said he, 'when this man dies, what is it that does not leave him?' 'Name. The name indeed is infinite, and infinite are the Visvadevas. He (who knows thus) wins thereby a really infinite world'. 3.2.13: 'Yajnavalkya', said he, 'when the vocal organ of a man who dies is merged in fire, the nose in air, the eye in the sun, the mind in the moon, the ear in the quarters, the body in the earth, the ether of the heart in the external ether, the hair on the body in herbs, that on the head in trees, and the blood and the seed are deposited in water, where is then the man?' 'Give me your hand, dear Artabhaga, we will decide this between ourselves, we cannot do it in a crowded place.' They went out and talked it over. What they mentioned there was only work, and what they praised there was also work alone. (Therefore) one indeed becomes good through good work and evil through evil work. Thereupon Artabhaga, of the line of Jaratkaru, kept silent.

3.3.1: Then Bhujyu, the grandson of Lahya, asked him. 'Yajnavalkya', said he, 'we traveled in Madra as students, and we came to the house of Patanchala of the line of Kapi. His daughter was possessed by a Gandharva. We asked him, "Who are you?" He said, "I am Sudhanvan, of the line of Angiras". When we asked him about the limits of the world, we said to him, "Where were the descendants of Pariksit?" And I ask you, Yajnavalkya, where were the descendants of Pariksit? (Tell me) where were the descendants of Pariksit?' 3.3.2: Yajnavalkya said, 'The Gandharva evidently told you that they went where the performers of the horse sacrifice go'. 'And where do the performers of the horse sacrifice go?' 'Thirty-two times the space covered by the sun's chariot in a day makes this world; around it, covering twice the area, is the earth; around the earth, covering twice the area, is the ocean. Now, as is the edge of a razor, or the wing of a fly, so is there just that much opening at the junction (of the two halves of the cosmic shell). (Through that they go out.) Fire, in the form of a falcon, delivered them to the air; the air, putting them in itself, took them where the (previous) performers of the horse sacrifice were'. Thus did the Gandharva praise the air. Therefore the air is the diversity of individuals, and the air is the aggregate. He who knows it as such conquers further death. Thereupon Bhujyu, the grandson of Lahya, kept silent.

3.4.1: Then Usata, the son of Chakra, asked him. 'Yajnavalkya', said he, 'explain to me the Brahman that is immediate and direct—the self that is within all.' 'This is your self that is within all'. 'Which is within all, Yajnavalkya?' 'That which breathes through the Prāna is your self that is within all. That which moves downwards through the Apana is your self that is within all. That which pervades through the Vyana is your self that is within all. That which goes out through the Udana is your self that is within all. This is your self that is within all.' 3.4.2: Usata, the son of Chakra, said, 'You have indicated it as one may say that a cow is such and such, or a horse is such and such. Explain to me the Brahman that is immediate and direct—the self that is within all'. 'This is your self that is within all'. 'Which is within all, Yajnavalkya?' 'You cannot see that which is the witness of vision; you cannot hear that which is the hearer of hearing; you cannot think that which is the thinker of thought; you cannot know that which is the knower of knowledge. This is your self that is within all; everything else but this is perishable.' Thereupon Usata, the son of Chakra, kept silent.

3.5.1: Then Kahola, the son of Kusitaka, asked him, 'Yajnavalkya', said he, 'explain to me the Brahman that is immediate and direct—the self that is within all'. 'This is your self that is within all'. 'Which is within all, Yajnavalkya?' 'That which transcends hunger and thirst, grief, delusion, decay and death. Knowing this very Self the Brāhmanas renounce the desire for sons, for wealth and for the worlds, and lead a mendicant's life. That which is the desire for sons is the desire for wealth, and that which is the desire for wealth is the desire for worlds, for both these are but desires. Therefore the knower of Brahman, having known all about scholarship, should try to live upon that strength which comes of knowledge; having known all about this strength and scholarship, he becomes meditative; having known all about both meditativeness and its opposite, he becomes a knower of Brahman. How does that knower of b behave? Howsoever he may behave, he is just such. Except this, everything is perishable.' Thereupon Kahola, the son of Kusitaka, kept silent.

3.6.1: Then Gargi, the daughter of Vacaknu, asked him, 'Yajnavalkya', she said, 'if all this is pervaded by water, by what is water pervaded?' 'By air, O Gargi'. 'By what is air pervaded?' 'By the sky, O Gargi'. 'By what is the sky pervaded?' 'By the world of the Gandharvas, O Gargi'. 'By what is the world of the Gandharvas pervaded?' 'By the sun, O Gargi.' 'By what is the sun pervaded?' 'By the moon, O Gargi.' 'By what is the moon pervaded?' 'By the stars, O Gargi'. 'By what are the stars pervaded?' 'By the world of the gods, O Gargi'. 'By what is the world of the gods pervaded?' 'By the world of Indra, O Gargi'. By what is the world of Indra pervaded?' 'By the world of Viraj, O Gargi'. 'By what is the world of Viraj pervaded?' 'By the world of Hiranyagarbha, O Gargi'. 'By what is the world of Hiranyagarbha pervaded?' He said, 'Do not, O Gargi, push your inquiry too far, lest your head should fall off. You are questioning about a deity that should not be reasoned about. Do not, O Gargi, push your inquiry too far.' Thereupon Gargi, the daughter of Vacaknu, kept silent.

3.7.1: Then Uddalaka, the son of Aruna, asked him. 'Yajnavalkya', said, 'in Madra we lived in the house of Patanchala Kapya (descendant of Kapi), studying the scriptures on sacrifices. His wife was possessed by a Gandharva. We asked him who he was. He said, "Kabandha, the son of Atharvan". He said to Patanchala Kapya and those who studied the scriptures on sacrifices, "Hapya, do you know that Sutra by which this life, the next life and all beings are held together?" Patanchala Kapya said, "I do not know it, sir". The Gandharva said to him and the students, "Kapya, do you know that Internal Ruler who controls this and the next life and all beings from within?" Patanchala Kapya said, "I do not know Him, sir". The Gandharva said to him and the students, "He who knows that Sutra and that Internal Ruler as above indeed knows Brahman, knows the worlds, knows the gods, knows the Vedas, knows beings, knows the self, and knows everything". He explained it all to them. I know it. If you, Yajnavalkya, do not know that Sutra and that Internal Ruler, and still take away the cows that belong only to the knowers of Brahman, your head shall fall off'. 'I know, O Gautama, that Sutra and that Internal Ruler'. 'Any one can say, "I know, I know". Tell us what you know.' 3.7.2: He said, 'Vayu, O Gautama, is that Sutra. Through this Sutra or Vayu this and the next life and all beings are held together. Therefore, O Gautama, when a man dies, they say that his limbs have been loosened, for they are held together, O Gautama, by the Sutra or Vayu.' 'Quite so, Yajnavalkya. Now describe the Internal Ruler.' 3.7.3: He who inhabits the earth, but is within it, whom the earth does not know, whose body is the earth, and who controls the earth from within, is the Internal Ruler, your own immortal self. 3.7.4: He who inhabits water, but is within it, whom water does not know, whose body is water, and who controls water from within, is the Internal Ruler, your own immortal self. 3.7.5: He who inhabits fire, but is within it, whom fire does not know, whose body is fire, and who controls fire from within, is the Internal Ruler, your own immortal self. 3.7.6: He who inhabits the sky, but is within it, whom the sky does not know, whose body is the sky, and who controls the sky from within, is the Internal Ruler, your own immortal self. 3.7.7: He who inhabits air, but is within it, whom air does not know, whose body is air, and who controls air from within, is the Internal Ruler, your own immortal self. 3.7.8: He who inhabits heaven, but is within it, whom heaven does not know, whose body is heaven, and who controls heaven from within, is the Internal Ruler, your own immortal self. 3.7.9: He who inhabits the sun, but is within it, whom the sun does not know, whose body is the sun, and who controls the sun from within, is the Internal Ruler, your own immortal self. 3.7.10: He who inhabits the quarters, but is within it, whom the quarters does not know, whose body is the quarters, and who controls the quarters from within, is the Internal Ruler, your own immortal self. 3.7.11: He who inhabits the moon and stars, but is within it, whom the moon and stars does not know, whose body is the moon and stars, and who controls the moon and stars from within, is the Internal Ruler, your own immortal self. 3.7.12: He who inhabits the ether, but is within it, whom the ether does not know, whose body is the ether, and who controls the ether from within, is the Internal Ruler, your own immortal self. 3.7.13: He who inhabits darkness, but is within it, whom darkness does not know, whose body is darkness, and who controls darkness from within, is the Internal Ruler, your own immortal self. 3.7.14: He who inhabits light, but is within it, whom light does not know, whose body is light, and who controls light from within, is the Internal Ruler, your own immortal self. This much with reference to the gods. Now with reference to the beings. 3.7.15: He who inhabits all beings, but is within it, whom no being knows, whose body is all beings, and who controls all beings from within, is the Internal Ruler, your own immortal self. This much with reference to the beings. Now with reference to the body. 3.7.16: He who inhabits the nose, but is within it, whom the nose does not know, whose body is the nose, and who controls the nose from within, is the Internal Ruler, your own immortal self. 3.7.17: He who inhabits the organ of speech, but is within it, whom the organ of speech does not know, whose body is the organ of speech, and who controls the organ of speech from within, is the Internal Ruler, your own immortal self. 3.7.18: He who inhabits the eye, but is within it, whom the eye does not know, whose body is the eye, and who controls the eye from within, is the Internal Ruler, your own immortal self. 3.7.19: He who inhabits the ear, but is within it, whom the ear does not know, whose body is the ear, and who controls the ear from within, is the Internal Ruler, your own immortal self. 3.7.20: He who inhabits the mind (Manas), but is within it, whom the mind does not know, whose body is the mind, and who controls the mind from within, is the Internal Ruler, your own immortal self. 3.7.21: He who inhabits the skin, but is within it, whom the skin does not know, whose body is the skin, and who controls the skin from within, is the Internal Ruler, your own immortal self. 3.7.22: He who inhabits the intellect, but is within it, whom the intellect does not know, whose body is the intellect, and who controls the intellect from within, is the Internal Ruler, your own immortal self. 3.7.23: He who inhabits the organ of generation, but is within it, whom the organ of generation does not know, whose body is the organ of generation, and who controls the organ of generation from within, is the Internal Ruler, your own immortal self. He is never seen, but is the Witness; He is never heard, but is the Hearer; He is never thought, but is the Thinker; He is never known, but is the Knower. There is no other witness but Him, no other hearer but Him, no other thinker but Him, no other knower but Him. He is the Internal Ruler, your own immortal self. Everything else but Him is mortal.' Thereupon Uddalaka, the son of Aruna, kept silent.

3.8.1: Then the daughter of Vachaknu said, 'Revered Brahmans, I shall ask him two questions, Should he answer me those, none of you can ever beat him in describing Brahman.' 'Ask, O Gargi'. 3.8.2: She said, 'I (shall ask) you (two questions). As a man of Banaras or the King of Videha, scion of a warlike dynasty, might string his unstrung bow and appear close by, carrying in his hand two bamboo-tipped arrows highly painful to the enemy, even so, O Yajnavalkya, do I confront you with two questions. Answer me those'. 'Ask, O Gargi'. 3.8.3: She said, 'By what, O Yajnavalkya, is that pervaded which is above heaven and below the earth, which is this heaven and earth as well as between them, and which they say was, is and will be?' 3.8.4: He said, 'That, O Gargi, which is above heaven and below the earth, which is this heaven and earth as well as between them, and which they say was, is and will be, is pervaded by the Unmanifested ether.' 3.8.5: She said, 'I bow to you, Yajnavalkya, who have fully answered this question of mine. Now be ready for the other question.' 'Ask, O Gargi". 3.8.6: She said, 'By what, O Yajnavalkya, is that pervaded which is above heaven and below the earth, which is this heaven and earth as well as between them, and which they say was, is and will be?' 3.8.7: He said, 'That, O Gargi, which is above heaven and below the earth, which is this heaven and earth as well as between them, and which they say was, is and will be, is pervaded by the Unmanifested ether alone.' 'By what is the un-manifest ether pervaded?' 3.8.8: He said: O Gargi, the knowers of Brahman say, this Immutable (Brahman) is that. It is neither gross nor minute, neither short nor long, neither red color nor oiliness, neither shadow nor darkness, neither air nor ether, unattached, neither savor nor odor, without eyes or ears, without the vocal organ or mind, non-luminous, without the vital force or mouth, not a measure, and without interior or exterior. It does not eat anything, nor is It eaten by anybody. 3.8.9: Under the mighty rule of this Immutable, O Gargi, the sun and moon are held in their positions; under the mighty rule of this Immutable, O Gargi, heaven and earth maintain their positions; under the mighty rule of this Immutable, O Gargi, moments, Muhurtas, days and nights, fortnights, months, seasons and years are held in their respective places; under the mighty rule of this Immutable one.

O Gargi, some rivers flow eastward from the White Mountains, others flowing westward continue in that direction, and still others keep to their respective courses; under the mighty rule of this Immutable, O Gargi, men praise those that give, the gods depend on the sacrificer, and the manes on independent offerings (Darvihoma). 3.8.10: He, O Gargi, who in this world, without knowing this Immutable, offers oblations in the fire, performs sacrifices and undergoes austerities even for many thousand years, finds all such acts but perishable; he, O Gargi, who departs from this world without knowing this Immutable, is miserable. But he, O Gargi, who departs from this world after knowing this Immutable, is a knower of Brahman. 3.8.11: This Immutable, O Gargi, is never seen but is the Witness; It is never heard, but is the Hearer; It is never thought, but is the Thinker; It is never known, but is the Knower. There is no other witness but This, no other hearer but This, no other thinker but This, no other knower but This. By this Immutable, O Gargi, is the (Unmanifested) ether pervaded. 3.8.12: She said, 'Revered Brahmans, you should consider yourselves fortunate if you can get off from him through salutations. Never shall any of you beat him in describing Brahman'. Then the daughter of Vachaknu kept silent.

3.9.1: Then Vidagdha, the son of Sakala, asked him. 'How many gods are there, Yajnavalkya?' Yajnavalkya decided it through this (group of Mantras known as) Nivid (saying), 'As many as are indicated in the Nivid of the Visvadevas—three hundred and three, and three thousand and three'. 'Very well', said Sakalya, 'how many gods exactly are there, Yajnavalkya?' 'Thirty-three'. 'Very well', said the other, 'how many gods exactly are there, Yajnavalkya?' 'six'. 'Very well', said Sakalya, 'how many gods exactly are there, Yajnavalkya?' 'Three'. 'Very well', said the other, 'how many gods exactly are there, Yajnavalkya?' 'Two'. 'Very well', said Sakalya, 'how many gods exactly are there, Yajnavalkya?' 'One and a half'. 'Very well', said Sakalya, 'how many gods exactly are there, Yajnavalkya?' 'One'. 'Very well', said Sakalya, 'which are those three hundred and three and three thousand and three?' 3.9.2: Yajnavalkya said, 'these are but the manifestation of them, but there are only thirty-three gods.' 'Which are those thirty-three?' 'The eight Vasus, the eleven Rudras and the twelve Adityas—these are thirty-one and Indra and Prajapati make up the thirty-three'. 3.9.3: 'Which are the Vasus /' 'Fire, the earth, air, the sky, the sun, heaven, the moon and the stars—these are the Vasus, for in these all this is placed; therefore they are called Vasus.' 3.9.4: 'Which are the Rudras?' 'The ten organs in the human body, with the mind as the eleventh. When they depart from this mortal body, they make (one's relatives) weep. Because they then make them weep, therefore they are called Rudras.' 3.9.5: 'Which are the Adityas?' 'The twelve months (are parts) of a year; these are the Adityas, for they go taking all this with them. Because they go taking all this with them, therefore they are called Adityas.' 3.9.6: 'Which is Indra, and which is Prajapati?' 'The cloud itself is Indra, and the sacrifice is Prajapati'. 'Which is the cloud?' 'Thunder (strength).' 'Which is the sacrifice?' 'Animals'. 3.9.7: 'Which are the six (gods)?' 'Fire, the earth, air, the sky, the sun, and heaven—these are the six. Because all those (gods) are (comprised in) these six.' 3.9.8: 'Which are the three gods?' 'These three worlds alone, because in these all those gods are comprised.' 'Which are the two gods?' 'Matter and the vital force.' 'Which are the one and a half?' 'This (air) that blows.' 3.9.9: 'Regarding this some say, 'Since the air blows as one substance, how can it be one and a half?' 'It is one and a half because through its presence all this attains surpassing glory'. 'Which is the one god?' 'The vital force (Hiranyagarbha); it is Brahman, which is called Tyat (that).' 3.9.10: 'He who knows that being whose abode is the earth, whose instrument of vision is fire, whose light is the Manas, and who is the ultimate resort of the entire body and organs, knows truly, O Yajnavalkya'. 'I do know that being of whom you speak—who is the ultimate resort of the entire body and organs. It is the very being who is identified with the body. Go on, Sakalya.' 'Who is his deity (cause)?' 'Nectar (chyle)', said he. 3.9.11: 'He who knows that being whose abode is lust, whose instrument of vision is the intellect, whose light is the Manas, and who is the ultimate resort of the entire body and organs, knows truly, O Yajnavalkya'. 'I do know that being of whom you speak—who is the ultimate resort of the entire body and organs. It is the very being who is identified with lust. Go on, Sakalya'. 'Who is his deity?' 'Women', said he. 3.9.12: 'He who knows that being whose abode is colors, whose instrument of vision is the eye, whose light is the Manas, and who is the ultimate resort of the entire body and organs, knows truly, O Yajnavalkya'. 'I do know that being of whom you speak—who is the ultimate resort of the entire body and organs. It is the very being who is in the sun. Go on Sakalya'. 'Who is his deity?' 'Truth (the eye),' said he. 3.9.13: 'He who knows that being whose abode is the ether, whose instrument of vision is the ear, whose light is the Manas, and who is the ultimate resort of the entire body and organs, knows truly, O Yajnavalkya'. 'I do know that being of whom you speak—who is the ultimate resort of the entire body and organs. It is the very being who is identified with the ear and with the time of hearing. Go on, Sakalya'. 'Who is his deity?' 'The quarters', said he. 3.9.14: 'He who knows that being whose abode is darkness, whose instrument of vision is the intellect, whose light is the Manas, and who is the ultimate resort of the entire body and organs, knows truly, O Yajnavalkya'. 'I do know that being of whom you speak—who is the ultimate resort of the entire body and organs. It is the very being who is identified with shadow (ignorance). Go on, Sakalya'. 'Who is his deity?' 'Death', said he. 3.9.15: 'He who knows that being whose abode is (particular) colors, whose instrument of vision is the eye, whose light is the Manas, and who is the ultimate resort of the entire body and organs, knows truly, O Yajnavalkya'. 'I do know that being of whom you speak—who is the ultimate resort of the entire body and organs. It is the very being who is in a looking-glass. Go on, Sakalya'. 'Who is his deity?' 'The vital force', said he. 3.9.16: 'He who knows that being whose abode is water, whose instrument of vision is the intellect, whose light is the Manas, and who is the ultimate resort of the entire body and organs, knows truly, O Yajnavalkya'. 'I do know that being of whom you speak—who is the ultimate resort of the entire body and organs. It is the very being who is in water. Go on, Sakalya'. 'Who is his deity?' 'Varuna (rain)', said he. 3.9.17: 'He who knows that being whose abode is the seed, whose instrument of vision is the intellect, whose light is the Manas, and who is the ultimate resort of the entire body and organs, knows truly, O Yajnavalkya'. 'I do know that being of whom you speak—who is the ultimate resort of the entire body and organs. It is the very being who is identified with the son. Go on, Sakalya'. 'Who is his deity?' 'Prajapati (the father)', said he. 3.9.18: 'Sakalya', said Yajnavalkya, 'have these Vedic scholars made you their instrument for burning charcoals?' 3.9.19: 'Yajnavalkya', said Sakalya, 'is it because you know Brahman that you have thus flouted these Vedic scholars of Kuru and Panchala?' 'I know the quarters

Brihadāranyaka Upanishad

with their deities and supports'. 'If you know the quarters with their deities and supports -3.9.20: 'What deity are you identified with in the east?' 'With the deity, sun'. 'On what does the sun rest?' 'On the eye'. 'On what does the eye rest?' 'On colors, for one sees colors with the eye'. 'On what do colors rest?' 'On the heart (mind)', said Yajnavalkya, 'for one knows colors through the heart; it is on the heart that colors rest'. 'It is just so, Yajnavalkya'. 3.9.21: 'What deity are you identified with in the south?' 'With the deity, Yama (the god of justice)'. On what does Yama rest?' 'On the sacrifice'. 'On what does the sacrifice rest?' 'On the remuneration (of the priests).' 'On what does the remuneration rest?' 'On faith, because whenever a man has faith, he gives remuneration to the priests; therefore it is on faith that the remuneration rests'. 'On what does faith rest?' 'On the heart', said Yajnavalkya, 'for one knows faith through the heart; therefore it is on the heart that faith rests'. 'It is just so, Yajnavalkya'. 3.9.22: 'What deity are you identified with in the west?' 'With the deity, Varuna (the god of rain)'. 'On what does Varuna rest?' 'On water'. 'On what does water rest?' 'On the seed'. 'On what does the seed rest?' 'On the heart. Therefore do they say of a new-born child closely resembles (his father), that he has sprung from (his father's) heart, as it were—that he has been made out of (his father's) heart, as it were. Therefore it is on the heart that the seed rests'. 'It is just so, Yajnavalkya'. 3.9.23: 'What deity are you identified with in the north?' 'With the deity, Soma (the moon and the creeper)' 'On what does Soma rest?' 'On initiation'. 'On what does initiation rest?' 'On truth. Therefore do they say to one initiated, "Speak the truth"; for it is on truth that initiation rests'. 'On what does truth rest?' 'On the heart', said Yajnavalkya, 'for one knows truth through the heart; therefore it is on the heart that truth rests'. 'It is just so, Yajnavalkya'. 3.9.24: 'What deity are you identified with in the fixed direction (above)?' 'With the deity, fire'. 'On what does fire rest?' 'On speech'. 'On what does speech rest?' 'On the heart'. 'On what does the heart rest?' 3.9.25: 'You ghost', said Yajnavalkya, 'when you think the heart is elsewhere than in us, (then the body is dead). Should it be elsewhere than in us, dogs would eat this body, or birds tear it to pieces'. 3.9.26: On what do the body and the heart rest?' 'On the Prāna'. 'On what does the Prāna rest?' 'On the Apana.' 'On what does the Apana rest?' 'On the Vyana.' 'On what does the Vyana rest?' 'On the Udana'. 'On what does the Udana rest?' 'On the Samana'. This self is That which has been described as 'Not this, not this'. It is imperceptible, for it is never perceived; undecaying, for It never decays; unattached, for It is never attached; unfettered—It never feels pain, and never suffers injury. 'These are the eight abodes, the eight instruments of vision, the eight deities and the eight beings. I ask you of that Being who is to be known only from the Upanishads, who definitely projects those beings and withdraws them into Himself, and who is at the same time transcendent. If you cannot clearly tell me of Him, your head shall fall off'. Sakalya did not know Him; his head fell off; and robbers snatched away his bones, mistaking them for something else. 3.9.27: Then he said, 'Revered Brāhmanas, whichsoever amongst you wishes may interrogate me or all of you may. Or I shall question whichsoever amongst you wishes, or all of you'. The Brāhmanas did not dare. 3.9.28 (1): He asked them through these verses: As a large tree, so indeed is a man. (This is) true. His hair is its leaves, his skin its outer bark. 3.9.28 (2): It is from his skin that blood flows, and from the bark sap. Therefore when a man is wounded, blood flows, as sap from a tree is injured. 3.9.28 (3): His flesh is its inner bark, and his tendons its innermost layer of bark; both are tough. His bones lie under, as does its wood; his marrow is comparable to its pith. 3.9.28 (4): If a tree, after it is felled, springs again from its root in a newer form, from what root indeed does man spring forth after he is cut off by death? 3.9.28 (5): Do not say, 'From the seed' (for) it is produced in a living man. A tree springs also from the seed; after it is dead it certainly springs again (from the seed as well). 3.9.28 (6): If someone pulls out a tree with its root, it no more sprouts. From what root does a man spring forth after he is cut off by death? 3.9.28 (7): If you think he is ever born, I say, no, he is again born. Now who should again bring him forth? --- Knowledge, Bliss, Brahman, the supreme goal of the dispenser of wealth as well as of him who has realized Brahman and lives in It.

4.1.1: Om. Janaka, Emperor of Videha, took his seat, when there came Yajnavalkya. Janaka said to him, 'Yajnavalkya, what has brought you here? To have some animals, or to hear some subtle questions asked?' 'Both, O Emperor', said Yajnavalkya. 4.1.2: 'Let me hear what any one of your teachers may have told you'. 'Jitvan, the son of Silina, has told me that the organ of speech (fire) is Brahman'. 'As one who has a mother, a father and a teacher should say, so has the son of Silina said this—that the organ of speech is Brahman, for what can a person have who cannot speak? But did he tell you about its abode (body) and support?' 'No, he did not'. 'This Brahman is only one-footed, O Emperor'. 'Then you tell us, Yajnavalkya'. 'The organ of speech is its abode, and the ether (the Undifferentiated) its support. It should be meditated upon as intelligence'. 'What is intelligence, Yajnavalkya?' 'The organ of speech itself, O Emperor', said Yajnavalkya, 'through the organ of speech, O Emperor, friend is known; The Rig-Veda, Yajur-Veda, Sama-Veda, Atharvangirasa, (Vedic) history, mythology, arts, Upanishads, verses, aphorisms, elucidations and explanations, (the effects of) sacrifices, (of) offering oblations in the fire and (of) giving food and drink, this world and the next, and all beings are known through the organ of speech alone,

O Emperor. The organ of speech, O Emperor, is the supreme Brahman. The organ of speech never leaves him who, knowing thus, meditates upon it, all beings eagerly come to him, and being a god, he attains the gods.' 'I give you a thousand cows with a bull like an elephant', said Emperor Janaka. Yajnavalkya replied, 'My father was of opinion that one should not accept (wealth) from a disciple without fully instructing him'.

4.1.3: 'Let me hear whatever any one may have told you'. 'Udanka, the son of Sulba, has told me that the vital force (Vayu) is Brahman'. 'As one who has a mother, a father and a teacher should say, so has the son of Sulba said this—that the vital force is Brahman, for what can a person have who does not live? But did he tell you about its abode (body) and support?' 'No, he did not'. 'This Brahman is only one-footed, O Emperor'. 'Then you tell us, Yajnavalkya'. 'The vital force is its abode, and the ether (the Undifferentiated) its support. It should be meditated upon as dear'. 'What is dearness, Yajnavalkya?' The vital force itself, O Emperor', said Yajnavalkya; 'for the sake of the vital force, O Emperor, a man performs sacrifices for one for whom they should not be performed, and accepts gifts one from whom they should not be accepted, and it is for the sake of the vital force, O Emperor, that one runs the risk of one's life in any quarter one may go to. The vital force, O Emperor, is the Supreme Brahman. The vital force never leaves him who, knowing thus, meditates upon it, all beings eagerly come to him, and being a god, he attains the gods'. 'I give you a thousand cows with a bull like an elephant', said Emperor Janaka. **Yajnavalkya replied, 'My father was of opinion that one should not accept (wealth) from a disciple without fully instructing him'.**

4.1.4: 'Let me hear whatever any one may have told you'. 'Barku, the son of Vrsna, has told me that the eye (sun) is Brahman'. 'As one who has a mother, a father and a teacher should say, so has the son of Vrsna said this—that the eye is Brahman. For what can a person have who cannot see? But did he tell you about its abode (body) and support?' 'No, he did not'. 'This Brahman is only one-footed, O Emperor'. 'Then you tell us, Yajnavalkya'. 'The eye is its abode, and the ether (the Undifferentiated) its support. It should be meditated upon as truth'. 'What is truth, Yajnavalkya?' ''The eye itself, O Emperor', said Yajnavalkya; if a person, O Emperor, says to one who has seen with his eyes, "Have you seen?" and the latter answers, "Yes, I have", then it is true. The eye, O Emperor, is the Supreme Brahman. The eye never leaves him who, knowing thus, meditates upon it; all beings eagerly come to him; and being a god, he attains the gods'. 'I give you a thousand cows with a bull like an elephant', said Emperor Janaka. Yajnavalkya replied, 'My father was of opinion that one should not accept (wealth) from a disciple without fully instructing him'. 4.1.5: 'Let me hear whatever any one may have told you'.

'Gardabhivipita, of the line of Bharadvaja, has told me that the ear (the quarters) is Brahman'. 'As one who has a mother, a father and a teacher should say, so has the descendant of Bharadvaja said this—that the ear is Brahman. For what can a person have who cannot hear? But did he tell you about its abode (body) and support?' 'No, he did not'. 'This Brahman is only one-footed, O Emperor'. 'Then you tell us, Yajnavalkya'. 'The ear is its abode, and the ether (the Undifferentiated) its support. It should be meditated upon as infinite'. 'What is infinity, Yajnavalkya?' 'The quarters themselves, O Emperor', said Yajnavalkya; 'therefore, O Emperor, to whatever direction one may go, one never reaches its end. (Hence) the quarters are infinite. The quarters, O Emperor, are the ear, and the ear, O Emperor, is the Supreme Brahman. The ear never leaves him who, knowing thus, meditates upon it; all beings eagerly come to him; and being a god, he attains the gods'. 'I give you a thousand cows with a bull like an elephant', said Emperor Janaka. Yajnavalkya replied, 'My father was of opinion that one should not accept (wealth) from a disciple without fully instructing him'. 4.1.6: 'Let me hear whatever any one may have told you'. 'Satyakama, the son of Jabala, has told me that the Manas (here, the moon) is Brahman'. 'As one who has a mother, a father and a teacher should say, so has the son of Jabala said this—that the Manas is Brahman. For what can a person have without the Manas? But did he tell you about its abode (body) and support?' 'No, he did not'. 'This Brahman is only one-footed, O Emperor'. 'Then you tell us, Yajnavalkya'. 'The Manas is its abode, and the ether (the Undifferentiated) its support. It should be meditated upon as bliss'. 'What is bliss, Yajnavalkya?' 'The manas itself, O Emperor', said Yajnavalkya; 'with the Manas, O Emperor, a man (fancies and) woos a woman. A son resembling him is born of her, and he is the cause of bliss. The Manas, O Emperor, is the Supreme Brahman. The Manas never leaves him who, knowing thus, meditates upon it; all beings eagerly come to him; and being a god, he attains the gods'. 'I give you a thousand cows with a bull like an elephant', said Emperor Janaka. Yajnavalkya replied, 'My father was of opinion that one should not accept (wealth) from a disciple without fully instructing him'. 4.1.7: 'Let me hear whatever any one may have told you'. 'Vidagdha, the son of Sakala, has told me that the heart (mind, here, Prajapati) is Brahman'. 'As one who has a mother, a father and a teacher should say, so has the son of Sakala said this—that the heart is Brahman. For what can a person have without the heart? But did he tell you about its abode (body) and support?' 'No, he did not'. 'This Brahman is only one-footed, O Emperor'. 'Then you tell us, Yajnavalkya'. 'The heart is its abode, and the ether (the Undifferentiated) its support. It should be meditated upon as stability'. 'What is stability, Yajnavalkya?' 'The heart itself, O Emperor', said Yajnavalkya; 'the heart, O Emperor, is the abode of all beings, and the heart, O Emperor, is the support of all beings; on the heart, O Emperor, all beings rest; the heart, O Emperor, is the Supreme Brahman. The heart never leaves him who, knowing thus, meditates upon it; all beings eagerly come to him; and being a god, he attains the gods'. 'I give you a thousand cows with a bull like an elephant', said Emperor Janaka. Yajnavalkya replied, 'My father was of opinion that one should not accept (wealth) from a disciple without fully instructing him'.

4.2.1: Janaka, Emperor of Videha, rose from his lounge and approaching Yajnavalkya said, 'Salutations to you, Yajnavalkya, please instruct me'. Yajnavalkya replied, 'As one wishing to go a long distance, O Emperor, should secure a chariot or a boat, so have you fully equipped your mind with so many secret names (of Brahman). You are likewise respected and wealthy, and you have studied the Vedas and heard the Upanishads; (but) where will you go when you are separated from this body?' 'I do not know, sir, where I shall go'. 'Then I will tell you where you will go'. 'Tell me, sir'. 4.2.2: This being who is in the right eye is named Indha. Though he is Indha, he is indirectly called Indra, for the gods have a fondness, as it were, for indirect names, and hate to be called directly. 4.2.3: The human form that is in the left eye is his wife, Viraj (matter). The space that is within the heart is their place of union. Their food is the lump of blood (the finest essence of what we eat) in the heart. Their wrap is the net-like structure in the heart. Their road for moving is the nerve that goes upward from the heart; it is like a hair split into a thousand parts. In this body there are nerves called Hita, which are placed in the heart. Through these the essence of our food passes as it moves on. Therefore the subtle body has finer food than the gross body. 4.2.4: Of the sage (who is identified with the vital force), the east is the eastern vital force, the south the southern vital force, the west the western vital force, the north the northern vital force, the direction above the upper vital force, the direction below the nether vital force, and all the quarters the different vital forces. This self is That which has been described as 'Not this, Not this', 'It is imperceptible, for It is never perceived; undecaying, for It never decays; unattached, for It is never attached; unfettered—It never feels pain, and never suffers injury. You have attained That which is free from fear, O Janaka', said Yajnavalkya. 'Revered Yajnavalkya', said Emperor Janaka, 'may That which is free from fear be yours, for you have made That which is free from fear known to us. Salutations to you! Here is this empire of Videha, as well as myself at your service!'

4.3.1: Yajnavalkya went to Janaka, Emperor of Videha. He thought he would not say anything. Now Janaka and Yajnavalkya had once talked on the Agnihotra, and Yajnavalkya had offered him a boon. He had begged the liberty of asking any questions he liked; and Yajnavalkya had granted him the boon. So it was the e who first asked him. 4.3.2: 'Yajnavalkya, what serves as the light for a man?' 'The light of the sun, O Emperor', said Yajnavalkya; 'it is through the light of the sun that he sits, goes out, works and returns'. 'It is just so, Yajnavalkya'. 4.3.3: 'When the sun has set, Yajnavalkya, what exactly serves as the light for a man?' 'The moon serves as his light. It is through the light of the moon that he sits, goes out, works and returns'. 'It is just so, Yajnavalkya'. 4.3.4: 'When the sun and the moon have set, Yajnavalkya, what exactly serves as the light for a man?' 'The fire serves as his light. It is through the fire that he sits, goes out, works and returns'. 'It is just so, Yajnavalkya'. 4.3.5: When the sun and the moon have both set, and the fire has gone out, Yajnavalkya, what exactly serves as the light for a man?' 'Speech (sound) serves as his light. It is through the light of speech that he sits, goes out, works and returns. Therefore, O Emperor, even when one's own hand is not clearly visible, if a sound is uttered, one manages to go there.' 'It is just so, Yajnavalkya'. 4.3.6: When the sun and the moon have both set, the fire has gone out, and speech has stopped, Yajnavalkya, what exactly serves as the light for a man?' 'The self serves as his light. It is through the light of the self that he sits, goes out, works and returns.' 'It is just so, Yajnavalkya'. 4.3.7: 'Which is the self?' 'This infinite entity (Purusha) that is identified with the intellect and is in the midst of the organs, the (self-effulgent) light within the heart (intellect). Assuming the likeness (of the intellect), it moves between the two worlds; it thinks, as it were, and shakes, as it were. Being identified with dream, it transcends this world—the forms of death (ignorance etc.).' 4.3.8: That man, when he is born, or attains a body, is connected with evils (the body and organs); and when he dies, or leaves the body, he discards those evils. 4.3.9: That man only two abodes, this and the next world. The dream state, which is the third, is at the junction (of the two). Staying at that junction, he surveys the two abodes, this and the next world. Whatever outfit he may have for the next world, providing himself with that he sees both evils (sufferings) and joys. When he dreams, he takes away a little of (the impressions of) this all-embracing world (the waking state), himself puts the body aside and himself creates (a dream body in its place), revealing his own luster by his own light—and dreams. In this state the man himself becomes the light. 4.3.10: There are no chariots, nor animals to be yoked to them, nor roads there, but he creates the chariots, the animals and the roads. There are no pleasures, joys, or delights there, but he creates the pleasures, joys and delights. There are no pools, tanks, or rivers there, but he creates the pools, tanks and rivers. For he is the agent. 4.3.11: Regarding this there are the following pithy verses: 'The radiant infinite being (Purusha) who moves alone, puts the body aside in the dream state, and remaining awake himself and taking the shining functions of the organs with him, watches those that are asleep. Again he comes to the waking state.

4.3.12: 'The radiant infinite being who is immortal and moves alone, preserves the unclean nest (the body) with the help of the vital force, and roams out of the nest. Himself immortal, he goes wherever he likes. 4.3.13: 'In the dream world, the shining one, attaining higher and lower states, puts forth innumerable forms. He seems to be enjoying himself in the company of women, or laughing, or even seeing frightful things. 4.3.14: 'All see his sport, but none sees him'. They say, 'Do not wake him up suddenly'. If he does not find the right organ, the body becomes difficult to doctor. Others, however, say that the dream state of a man is nothing but the waking state, because he sees in dream only those things that he sees in the waking state. (This is wrong) In the dream state the man himself becomes the light. 'I give you a thousand (cows), sir. Please instruct me further about liberation'. 4.3.15: After enjoying himself and roaming, and merely seeing (the result of) good and evil (in dream), he (stays) in a state of profound sleep, and comes back in the inverse order to his former condition, the dream state. He is untouched by whatever he sees in that state, for this infinite being is unattached. 'It is just so, Yajnavalkya. I give you a thousand (cows), sir. Please instruct me further about liberation itself.' 4.3.16: After enjoying himself and roaming in the dream state, and merely seeing (the results of) good and evil, he comes back in the inverse order to his former condition, the waking state. He is untouched by whatever he sees in that state, for this infinite being is unattached. 'It is just so, Yajnavalkya. I give you a thousand (cows), sir. Please instruct me further about liberation itself.' 4.3.17: After enjoying himself and roaming in the waking state, and merely seeing (the result of) good and evil, he comes back in the inverse order to his former condition, the dream state (or that of profound sleep). 4.3.18: As a great fish swims alternately to both the banks (of a river), eastern and western, so does this infinite being move to both these states, the dream and waking states. 4.3.19: As a hawk or a falcon flying in the sky becomes tired, and stretching its wings, is bound for its nest, so does this infinite being run for this state, where, falling asleep, he craves no desire and sees no dream. 4.3.20: In him are those nerves called Hita, which are as fine as a hair split into a thousand parts, and filled with white, blue, brown, green and red (serums). (They are the seat of the subtle body, in which impressions are stored). Now when (he feels) as if he were being killed or overpowered, or being pursued by an elephant, or falling into a pit, (in short) conjures up at the time through ignorance whatever terrible things he has experienced in the waking state, (that is the dream state). And when (he becomes) a god, as it were, or a king, as it were, thinks, 'This (universe) is myself, who am all', that is his highest state. 4.3.21: That is his form—beyond desires, free from evils and fearless. As a man, fully embraced by his beloved wife, does not know anything at all, either external or internal, so does this infinite being (self), fully embraced by the Supreme Self, not know anything at all, either external or internal. That is his form—in which all objects of desire have been attained and are but the self, and which is free from desire and devoid of grief. 4.3.22: In this state a father is no father, a mother no mother, worlds no worlds, the gods no gods, the Vedas no Vedas. In this state a thief is no thief, the killer of a noble Brāhmana no killer, a Chandala no Chandala, a Pulkasa no Pulkasa, a monk no monk, a hermit no hermit. (This form of his) is untouched by good work and untouched by evil work, for he is then beyond all the woes of his heart (intellect). 4.3.23: That it does not see in that state is because, though seeing then, it does not see; for the vision of the witness can never be lost, because it is imperishable. But there is not that second thing separate from it which it can see. 4.3.24: That it does not smell in that state is because, though smelling then, it does not smell; for the smeller's function of smelling can never be lost, because it is imperishable. But there is not that second thing separate from it which it can smell. 4.3.25: That it does not taste in that state is because, though tasting then, it does not taste; for the taster's function of tasting can never be lost, because it is imperishable. But there is not that second thing separate from it which it can taste. 4.3.26: That it does not speak in that state is because, though speaking then, it does not speak; for the speaker's function of speaking can never be lost, because it is imperishable. But there is not that second thing separate from it which it can speak. 4.3.27: That it does not hear in that state is because, though hearing then, it does not hear; for the listener's function of hearing can never be lost, because it is imperishable. But there is not that second thing separate from it which it can hear. 4.3.28: That it does not think in that state is because, though thinking then, it does not think; for the thinker's function of thinking can never be lost, because it is imperishable. But there is not that second thing separate from it which it can think. 4.3.29: That it does not touch in that state is because, though touching then, it does not touch; for the toucher's function of touching can never be lost, because it is imperishable. But there is not that second thing separate from it which it can touch. 4.3.30: That it does not know in that state is because, though knowing then, it does not know; for the knower's function of knowing can never be lost, because it is imperishable. But there is not that second thing separate from it which it can know. 4.3.31: When there is something else, as it were, then one can see something, one can smell something, one can taste something, one can speak something, one can hear something, one can think something, one can touch something, or one can know something. 4.3.32: It becomes (transparent) like water, one, the witness, and without a second. This is the sphere or state of Brahman, O Emperor. Thus did Yajnavalkya instruct Janaka: This is its supreme attainment, this is its supreme glory, this is its highest world, this is its supreme bliss. On a particle of this very bliss other beings live. 4.3.33: He who is perfect of physique and prosperous among men, the ruler of others, and most lavishly supplied with all human enjoyments, represents greatest joy among men. This human joy multiplied a hundred times makes one unit of joy for the manes who have won that world of theirs. The joy of these manes who have won that world multiplied a hundred times makes one unit joy in the world of the celestial minstrels. This joy in the world of the celestial minstrels multiplied a hundred times makes one unit of joy for the gods by action—those who have attained their godhead by their actions. This joy of the gods by action multiplied a hundred times makes one unit of joy for the gods by birth, as also of one who is versed in the Vedas, sinless and free from desire. This joy of the gods by birth multiplied a hundred times makes one unit of joy in the world of Prajapati (Viraj), as well as one who is versed in the Vedas, sinless and free from desire. This joy in the world of Prajapati multiplied a hundred times makes one unit of joy in the world of Brahman (Hiranyagarbha), as well as of one who is versed in the Vedas, sinless and free from desire. This indeed is the supreme bliss. This is the state of Brahman, O Emperor, said Yajnavalkya. 'I give you a thousand (cows), sir. Please instruct me further about liberation itself'. At this Yajnavalkya was afraid that the intelligent Emperor was constraining him to finish with all his conclusions. 4.3.34: After enjoying himself and roaming in the dream state, and merely seeing the effects of merits and demerits, he comes back, in the inverse order, to his former condition, the waking state. 4.3.35: Just as a cart, heavily loaded, goes on rumbling, so does the self that is in the body, being presided over by the Supreme Self, go making noises, when breathing becomes difficult. 4.3.36: When this (body) becomes thin—is emaciated through old age or disease—then, as a mango, or a fig, or a fruit of the Peepul tree is detached from its stalk, so does this infinite being, completely detaching himself from the parts of the body, again go, in the same way that he came, to particular bodies, for the unfoldment of his vital force.

4.3.37: Just as when a king is coming, the Ugras set against particular offences, the Sutas and the leaders of the village wait for him with varieties of food and drink and mansions ready, saying, 'Here he comes, here he comes', so for the person who knows about the results of his work, all the elements wait saying, 'Here comes Brahman, here he comes'. 4.3.38: Just as when the king wishes to depart, the Ugras set against particular offences, the Sutas and the leaders of the village approach him, so do all the organs approach the departing man at the time of death, when breathing becomes difficult.

4.4.1: When this self becomes weak and senseless, as it were, the organs come to it. Completely withdrawing these particles of light, it comes to the heart. When the presiding deity of the eye turns back from all sides, the man fails to notice color. 4.4.2: (The eye) becomes united (with the subtle body); then people say, 'He does not see'. (The nose) becomes united; then they say, 'He does not smell'. (The tongue) becomes united; then they say, 'He does not taste'. (The vocal Organ) becomes united; then they say, 'He does not speak'. (The ear) becomes united; then they say, 'He does not hear'. (The Manas) becomes united; then they say, 'He does not think'. (The skin) becomes united; then they say, 'He does not touch'. (The intellect) becomes united; then they say, 'He does not know'. The top of the heart brightens. Through that brightened top the self departs, either through the eye, or through the head, or through any other part of the body. When it departs, the vital force follows; when the vital force departs, all the organs follow. Then the self has particular consciousness, and goes to the body which is related to that consciousness. It is followed by knowledge, work and past experience. **4.4.3: Just as a leech supported on a straw goes to the end of it, takes hold of another support and contracts itself, so does the self throw this body aside—make it senseless—take hold of another support, and contract itself.** 4.4.4: **Just as a goldsmith takes apart a little quantity of gold and fashions another—a newer and better—form, so does the self throw this body away, or make it senseless, and make another—a newer and better—form** suited to the manes or the celestial minstrels, or the gods, or Viraj, or Hiranyagarbha, or other beings.

Just as a person puts on new garments after discarding the old ones, similarly the living entity or the individual soul acquires other new bodies after casting away the old bodies. (BG 2.22)

4.4.5: That self is indeed Brahman, as also identified with the intellect, the Manas and the vital force, with the eyes and ears, with earth, water, air and the ether, with fire, and what is other than fire, with desire and the absence of desire, with anger and the absence of anger, with righteousness and unrighteousness, with everything —-identified, in fact, with this (what is perceived) and with that (what is inferred). As it does and acts, so it becomes; by doing good it becomes good, and by doing evil it becomes evil—it becomes virtuous through good acts and vicious through evil acts. Others, however, say, 'The self is identified with desire alone. What it desires, it resolves; what it resolves, it works out; and what it works out, it attains.'

4.4.6: Regarding this there is the following pithy verse: 'Being attached he, together with the work, attains that result to which his subtle body or mind is attached. Exhausting the results of whatever work he did in this life, he returns from that world to this for (fresh) work'. Thus does the man who desires (transmigrate). But the man who does not desire (never transmigrates). Of him who is without desires, who is free from desires, the objects of whose desire have been attained, and to whom all objects of desire are but the Self—the organs do not depart. Being but Brahman, he is merged in Brahman. **4.4.7: Regarding this there is this pithy verse: 'When all the desires that dwell in his heart (mind) are gone, then he, having been mortal, becomes immortal, and attains Brahman in this very body'. Just as the lifeless Slough of a snake is cast off and lies in the ant-hill, so does this body lie.** (Also see KaU 6.14)Then the self becomes disembodied and immortal, (becomes) the Prāna (Supreme Self), Brahman, the Light. 'I give you a thousand (cows), sir', said Janaka, Emperor of Videha.

All desires cannot---and need not---be eliminated, but first selfish desires and motives must be eliminated for spiritual progress. All our actions by thought, word and deed, including desires, should be directed to glorify God and for the good of humanity.

4.4.8: Regarding this there are the following pithy verses: the subtle, extensive, ancient way has touched (been reached by) me. (Nay) I have realized it myself. Through that sages—the knowers of Brahman—(also) go to the heavenly sphere (liberation) after the fall of this body, being freed (even while living). 4.4.9: Some speak of it as white, others as blue, grey, green, or red. This path is realized by a Brāhmana (knower of Brahman). Any other knower of Brahman who has done good deeds and is identified with the Supreme Light, (also) treads this path. 4.4.10: Into blinding darkness (ignorance) enter those who worship ignorance (rites). Into greater darkness, as it were, than that enter those who are devoted to knowledge (the ceremonial portion of the Vedas). 4.4.11: Miserable are those worlds enveloped by (that) blinding darkness (ignorance). To them, after death, go those people who are ignorant and unwise. 4.4.12: If a man knows the Self as 'I am this', then desiring what and for whose sake will he suffer in the wake of the body? 4.4.13: He who has realized and intimately known the Self that has entered this perilous and inaccessible place (the body), is the maker of the universe, for he is the maker of all, (all is) his Self, and he again is indeed the Self (of all). 4.4.14: Being in this very body we have somehow known that (Brahman). If not, (I should have been) ignorant, (and) great destruction (would have taken place). Those who know It become immortal, while others attain misery alone. 4.4.15: When a man after (receiving instructions from a teacher) directly realizes this effulgent Self, the Lord of all that has been and will be, he no longer wishes to hide himself from it. 4.4.16: Below which the year with its days rotates, upon that immortal Light of all lights the gods meditate as longevity. 4.4.17: That in which the five groups of five and the (subtle) ether are placed, that very Atman I regard as the immortal Brahman. Knowing (Brahman) I am immortal. 4.4.18: Those who have known the Vital Force of the vital force, the Eye of the eye, the Ear of the ear, and the Mind of the mind, have realized the ancient, primordial Brahman. 4.4.19: Through the mind alone (It) is to be realized. There is no difference whatsoever in It. He goes from death to death, who sees difference, as it were, in It. 4.4.20: It should be realized in one form only, (for) It is unknowable and eternal. The Self is taintless, beyond the (subtle) ether, birthless, infinite and constant. 4.4.21: The intelligent aspirant after Brahman, knowing about this alone, should attain intuitive knowledge. (He) should not think of too many words, for it is particularly fatiguing to the organ of speech. 4.4.22: That great, birthless Self which is identified with the intellect and is in the midst of the organs, lies in the ether that is within the heart. It is the controller of all, the lord of all, the ruler of all. It does not grow better through good work nor worse through bad work. It is the lord of all, It is the ruler of all beings, It is the protector of all beings. It is the bank that serves as the boundary to keep the different worlds apart. The Brāhmanas seek to know It through the study of the Vedas, sacrifices, charity, and austerity consisting in a dispassionate enjoyment of sense-objects. Knowing It alone, one becomes a sage. Desiring this world (the Self) alone, monks renounce their homes. This is (the reason for it); The ancient sages, it is said, did not desire children (thinking), 'What shall we achieve through children, we who have attained this Self, this world (result).' They, it is said, renounced their desire for sons, for wealth and for the worlds, and lived a mendicant's life. That which is the desire for sons is the desire for wealth, and that which is the desire for wealth is the desire for worlds, for both these are but desires. This self is That which has been described as 'Not this, Not this'. It is imperceptible, for It is never perceived; undecaying, for It never decays; unattached, for It is never attached; unfettered—It never feels pain, and never suffers injury. (it is but proper) that the sage is never overtaken by these two thoughts, 'I did an evil act for this', 'I did a good act for this'. He conquers both of them. Things done or not done do not trouble him.

4.4.23: This has been expressed by the following hymn: This is the eternal glory of a knower of Brahman: it neither increases nor decreases through work. (Therefore) one should know the nature of that alone. Knowing it one is not touched by evil action. Therefore he who knows it as such becomes self-controlled, calm, withdrawn into himself, enduring and concentrated, and sees the self in his own self (body); he sees all as the Self. Evil does not overtake him, but he transcends all evil. Evil does not trouble him, (but) he consumes all evil. He becomes sinless, taintless, free from doubts, and a Brāhmana (knower of Brahman). This is the world of Brahman, O Emperor, and you have attained it—said Yajnavalkya. 'I give you sir, the empire of Videha, and myself too with it, to wait upon you'. 4.4.24: That great, birthless Self is the eater of food and the giver of wealth (the fruits of one's work). He who knows It as such receives wealth (as fruits). 4.4.25: That great, birthless Self is undecaying, immortal, undying, fearless and Brahman (infinite). Brahman is indeed fearless. He who knows It as such certainly becomes the fearless Brahman.

12a. Knowledge is the best wealth

4.5.1: Now **Yajnavalkya** had two wives, **Maitreyi and Katyayani.** Of these Maitreyi used to discuss Brahman, (while) Katyayani had then only an essentially feminine outlook. One day Yajnavalkya, with a view to embracing life—4.5.2: 'O Maitreyi, my dear', said Yajnavalkya, 'I am going to renounce this life for monasticism. Allow me to finish between you and Katyayani'. 4.5.3: Thereupon Maitreyi said, 'Sir, if indeed this whole earth full of wealth be mine, shall I be immortal through that, or not?' 'No', replied Yajnavalkya, 'your life will be just like that of people who possess plenty of things, but there is no hope of immortality through wealth.' 4.5.4: Then Maitreyi said, 'What shall I do with that which will not make me immortal? Tell me, sir, of that alone which you know (to be the only means of immortality).' 4.5.5: Yajnavalkya said, 'My dear, you have been my beloved (even before), and you have magnified what is after my heart. If you wish, my dear, I will explain it to you. As I explain it, meditate (upon its meaning). **4.5.6: He said: 'It is not for the sake of the husband, my dear, that he is loved, but for one's own sake that he is loved. It is not for the sake of the wife, my dear, that she is loved, but for one's own sake that she is loved.** It is not for the sake of the sons, my dear, that they are loved, but for one's own sake that they are loved. It is not for the sake of wealth, my dear, that it is loved, but for one's own sake that it is loved. It is not for the sake of the Brāhmana, my dear, that he is loved, but for one's own sake that he is loved. It is not for the sake of the Kshatriya, my dear, that he is loved, but for one's own sake that he is loved. It is not for the sake of worlds, my dear, that they are loved, but for one's own sake that they are loved. It is not for the sake of the gods, my dear, that they are loved, but for one's own sake that they are loved. It is not for the sake of beings, my dear, that they are loved, but for one's own sake that they are loved. It is not for the sake of all, my dear, that all is loved, but for one's own sake that it is loved. The Self, my dear Maitreyi, should be realized—should be heard of, reflected on and meditated upon. When the Self, my dear, is realized by being heard of, reflected on and meditated upon, all this is known. 4.5.7: The Brāhmana ousts (slights) one who knows him as different from the Self. The Kshatriya ousts one who knows him as different from the Self. Worlds oust one who knows them as different from the Self. The gods oust one who knows them as different from the Self. The Vedas oust one who knows them as different from the Self. Beings oust one who knows them as different from the Self. All ousts one who knows it as different from the Self. This Brāhmana, this Kshatriya, these worlds, these gods, these Vedas, these beings and these all -- are this Self. 4.5.8: As, when a drum is beaten, one cannot distinguish its various particular notes, but they are included in the general note of the drum or in the general sound produced by different kinds of strokes. 4.5.9: As, when a conch is blown, one cannot distinguish its various particular notes, but they are included in the general note of the conch or in the general sound produced by different kinds of playing. 4.5.10: As, when a Vina is played, one cannot distinguish its various particular notes, but they are included in the general note of the Vina or in the general sound produced by different kinds of playing. 4.5.11: As from a fire kindled with wet faggot diverse kinds of smoke issue, even so, my dear, the Rig-Veda, Yajur-Veda, Sama-Veda, Atharvangirasa, history, mythology, arts, Upanishads, pithy verses, aphorisms, elucidations, explanations, sacrifices, oblations in the fire, food, drink, this world, the next world and all beings are (like) the breath of this infinite Reality. They are like the breath of this (Supreme Self). 4.5.12: As the ocean is the one goal of all sorts of water, as the skin is the one goal of all kinds of touch, as the nostrils are the one goal of all odors, as the tongue is the one goal of all savors, as the eye is the one goal of all colors , as the ear is the one goal of all sounds, as the Manas is the one goal of all deliberations, as the intellect is the one goal of all kinds of knowledge, as the hands are the one goal of all sort of work, as the organ of generation is the one goal of all kinds of enjoyment, as the anus is the one goal of all excretions, as the feet are the one goal of all kinds of walking, as the organ of speech is the one goal of all Vedas. 4.5.13: As a lump of salt is without interior or exterior, entire, and purely saline in taste, even so is the Self without interior or exterior, entire, and Pure Intelligence alone. (The Self) comes out (as a separate entity) from these elements, and (this separateness) is destroyed with them. After attaining (this oneness) it has no more consciousness. This is what I say, my dear. So said Yajnavalkya. 4.5.14: Maitreyi said, 'Just here you have led me into the midst of confusion, sir, I do not at all comprehend this'. He said, 'Certainly, I am not saying anything confusing. This self is indeed immutable and indestructible, my dear'. 4.5.15:

Because when there is duality, as it were, then one sees something, one smells something, one tastes something, one speaks something, one hears something, one thinks something, one touches something, one knows something. (But) when to the knower of Brahman everything has become the Self, then what should one see and through what, what should one smell and through what, what should one taste and through what, what should one speak and through what, what should one hear and through what, what should one think and through what, what should one touch and through what, what should one know and through what? Through what should one know that owing to which all this is known? This self is That which has been described as 'Not this, Not this'. It is imperceptible, for It is never perceived; undecaying, for It never decays; unattached, for It is never attached; unfettered—it never feels pain, and never suffers injury. Through what, O Maitreyi, should one know the Knower? So you have got the instruction, Maitreyi. This much indeed is (the means of) immortality, my dear. Saying this Yajnavalkya left.

4.6.1: Now the line of teachers: Pautimasya (received it) from Gaupavana. Gaupavana from another Pautimasya. This Pautimasya from another Gaupavana. This Gaupavana from Kausika. Kausika from Kaundinya. Kaundinya from Sandilya. Sandilya from Kausika and Gautama. 4.6.2: Gautama from Agnivesya. Agnivesya from Sandilya and Anabhimlata. Anabhinlata from another of that name. He from a third Anabhimlata. This Anabhimlata from Gautama. Gautama from Saitava and Pracinayogya. They from Parasarya. Parasarya from Bharadvaja. He from Bharadvaja and Gautama. Gautama from another Bharatvaja. He from another Parasarya. Parasarya from Baijavapayana. He from Kausikayani. Kausikayani from Ghrtakausika. Ghrtakausika from Parasaryayana. He from Parasarya. Parasarya from Jatukarnya. Jatukarnya from Asurayana and Yaska. Asurayana from Traivani. Traivani from Aupajandhani. He from Asuri. Asuri from Bharadvaja. Bharadvaja from Atreya. Atreya from Manti. Manti from Gautama. Gautama from another Gautama. He from Vatsya. Vatsya from Sandilya. Sandilya from Kaisorya Kapya. He from Kumaraharita. Kumaraharita from Galava. Galava from Vidarbhi-kaundinya. He from Vatsanapat Babhrava. He from Pathin Saubhara. He from Ayasya Angirasa. He from Abhuti Tvastra. He from Visvarupa Tvastra. He from the Asvins. They from Dadhyac Atharvana. He from Atharvan Daiva. He from Mrtyu Pradhvamsana. He from Pradhvamsana. Pradhvamsana from Ekarsi. Ekarsi from Viprachitti. Viprachitti from Vyasri. Vyasti from Sanaru. Sanaru from Sanatana. Sanatana from Sanaga. Sanaga from Paramesthin (Viraj). He from Brahman (Hiranyabarbha). Brahman is self-born. Salutation to Brahman.

5.1.1: Om. That (Brahman) is infinite, and this (universe) is infinite. The infinite proceeds from the infinite. (Then) taking the infinitude of the infinite universe, it remains as the infinite (Brahman) alone. Om is the ether-Brahman—the eternal ether. 'The ether containing air,' says the son of Kauravyayani. It is the Veda, (so) the Brahmans (knowers of Brahman) know; (for) through it one knows what is to be known. 5.2.1: Three classes of Prajapati's sons lived a life of continence with their father, Prajapati (Viraj)—the gods, men and Asuras. The gods, on the completion of their term, said, 'Please instruct us'. He told them the syllable 'Da' (and asked), 'have you understood?' (They) said, 'We have. You tell us: Control yourselves'. (He) said, 'Yes, you have understood'. 5.2.2: Then the men said to him, 'Please instruct us'. He told them the same syllable 'Da' (and asked), 'Have you understood?' (They) said, 'We have. You tell us: Give'. (He) said, 'Yes, you have understood'. 5.2.3: Then the Asuras said to him, 'Please instruct us'. He told them the same syllable 'Da' (and asked), 'Have you understood?' (They) said, 'We have. You tell us: Have compassion'. (He) said, 'Yes, you have understood'. That very thing is repeated by the heavenly voice, the cloud, as Da.

13. Three 'Da'

'Control yourselves', 'Give', and 'have compassion'. Therefore one should learn these three—self-control, charity and compassion.

5.3.1: This is Prajapati - this heart (intellect). It is Brahman, it is everything. 'Hridaya' (heart) has three syllables. 'Hr' is one syllable. To him who knows as above, his own people and others bring (presents). 'Da' is another syllable. To him who knows as above, his own people and others give (their powers). 'Ya' is another syllable. He who knows as above goes to heaven.

5.4.1: That (intellect-Brahman) was but this—Satya (gross and subtle) alone. He who knows this great, adorable, first-born (being) as the Satya-Brahman, conquers these worlds, and his (enemy) is thus conquered and becomes non-existent—he who knows this great, adorable, first-born (being) thus, as the Satya-Brahman, for Satya is indeed Brahman.

5.5.1: This (universe) was but water (liquid oblations connected with sacrifices) in the beginning. That water produced Satya. Satya is Brahman. Brahman (produced) Prajapati, and Prajapati the gods. Those gods meditate upon Satya alone. This (name) 'Satya' consists of three syllables: 'Sacrifice' is one syllable, 'Ti' is another syllable, and "Ya' is the third syllable. The first and last syllables are truth. In the middle is untruth. This untruth is enclosed on either side by truth. (Hence) there is a preponderance of truth. One who knows as above is never hurt by untruth. 5.5.2: That which is Satya is that sun—the being who is in that orb and the being who is in the right eye. These two rest on each other. The former rests on the latter through the rays, and the latter rests on the former through the function of the eyes. When a man is about to leave the body, he sees the solar orb as clear. The rays no more come to him. 5.5.3: Of this being who is in the solar orb, the syllable 'Bhur' is the head, for there is one head, and there is this one syllable; the word 'Bhuvar' is the arms, for there are two arms, and there are these two syllables; the word 'Svar' is the feet, for there are two feet, and there are these two syllables. His secret name is 'Ahar'. He who knows as above destroys and shuns evil. 5.5.4: Of this being who is in the right eye, the syllable 'Bhur' is the head, for there is one head, and there is this one syllable; the word 'Bhuvar' is the arms, for there are two arms, and there are these two syllables; the word 'Svar' is the feet, for there are two feet, and there are these two syllables. His secret name is 'Aham'. He who knows as above destroys and shuns evil.

5.6.1: This being identified with the mind and resplendent (is realized by the Yogins) within the heart like a grain of rice or barley. He is the lord of all, the ruler of all, and governs whatever there is.

5.7.1: They say lightning is Brahman. It is called lightning (Vidyut) because it scatters (darkness). He who knows it as such—that lightning is Brahman—scatters evils (that are ranged against) him, for lightning is indeed Brahman.

5.8.1: One should meditate upon speech (the Vedas) as a cow (as it were). She has four teats—the sounds "Svaha', 'Vasat', 'Hanta' and 'Svadha'. The gods live on two of her teats—the sounds 'Svaha' and 'Vasat', men on the sound 'Hanta', and the manes on the sound 'Svadha'. Her bull is the vital force, and her calf the mind.

5.9.1: This fire that is within a man and digests the food that is eaten, is Vaisvanara. It emits this sound that one hears by stopping the ears thus. When a man is about to leave the body, he no more hears this sound.

5.10.1: When a man departs from this world, he reaches the air, which makes an opening there for him like the hole of a chariot-wheel. He goes upwards through that and reaches the sun, who makes an opening there for him like the hole of a tabor. He goes upwards through that and reaches the moon, who makes an opening there for him like the hole of a drum. He goes upwards through that and reaches a world free from grief and from cold. He lives there for eternal years.

5.11.1: This indeed is excellent austerity that a man suffers when he is ill. He who knows as above wins an excellent world. This indeed is excellent austerity that a man after death is carried to the forest. He who knows as above wins an excellent world. This indeed is excellent austerity that a man after death is placed in the fire. He who knows as above wins an excellent world.

5.12.1: Some say that food is Brahman. It is not so, for food rots without the vital force. Others say that the vital force is Brahman. It is not so, for the vital force dries up without food. But these two deities being united attain their highest. So Pratrda said to his father, 'What good indeed can I do to one who knows like this, and what evil indeed can I do to him either?' The father, with a gesture of the hand, said, 'O, no, Pratrda, for who would attain his highest by being identified with them?' Then he said to him this: 'It is "Vi". Food is "vi", for all these creatures rest on food. It is "Ram". The vital force is "Ram", for all these creatures delight if there is the vital force'. On him who knows as above all creatures rest, and in him all creatures delight.

5.13.1: (One should meditate upon the vital force as) the Uktha (a hymn of praise). The vital force is the Uktha, for it raises this universe. From him who knows as above rises a son who is a knower of the vital force, and he achieves union with and abode in the same world as the Uktha. 5.13.2: (One should meditate upon the vital force as) the Yajus. The vital force is the Yajus, for all these beings are joined with one another if there is the vital force. All beings are joined for the eminence of him who knows as above, and he achieves union with and abode in the same world as the Yajus (vital force). 5.13.3: (One should meditate upon the vital force as) the Saman. The vital force is the Saman, for all these beings are united if there is the vital force. For him who knows as above all beings are united, and they succeed in bringing about his eminence, and he achieves union with abode in the same world as the Saman. 5.13.4: (One should meditate upon the vital force as) the Ksatra. The vital force is the Ksatra, for it is indeed the Ksatra. The vital force protects the body from wounds. He who knows as above attains this Ksatra (vital force) that has no other protector, and achieves union with and abode in the same world as the Ksatra.

5.14.1: 'Bhumi' (the earth), 'Antariksa' (sky) and 'Dyaus' (heaven) make eight syllables, and the first foot of the Gayatri has eight syllables. So the above three worlds constitute the first foot of the Gayatri. He who knows the first foot of the Gayatri to be such wins as much as there is in those three worlds. 5.14.2: 'Reah', 'Yajumsi' and 'Samani' make eight syllables, and the second foot of the Gayatri has eight syllables. So the above three Vedas constitute the second foot of the Gayatri. He who knows the second foot of the Gayatri to be such wins as much as that treasury of knowledge, the three Vedas, has to confer. 5.14.3:

'Prana', 'Apana' and 'Vyana' make eight syllables, and the third foot of the Gayatri has eight syllables. So the above three forms of vital force constitute the third foot of the Gayatri. He who knows the third foot of the Gayatri to be such wins all the living beings that are in the universe. Now it's Turiya, apparently visible, supra-mundane foot is indeed this—the sun that shines. 'Turiya' means the fourth. 'Apparently visible foot', because he is seen, as it were. 'Supra-mundane', because he shines on the whole universe as its overlord. He who knows the fourth foot of the Gayatri to be such shines in the same way with splendor and fame. 5.14.4: That Gayatri rests on this fourth, apparently visible, supra-mundane foot. That again rests on truth. The eye is truth, for the eye is indeed truth. Therefore if even today two persons come disputing, one saying, 'I saw it', and another, 'I heard of it', we believe him only who says, 'I saw it'. That truth rests on strength. The vital force is strength. (Hence) truth rests on the vital force. Therefore they say strength is more powerful than truth. Thus the Gayatri rests on the vital force within the body. That Gayatri saved the Gayas. The organs are the Gayas; so it saved the organs. Now, because it saved the organs, therefore it is called the Gayatri. The Savitri that the teacher communicates to the pupil is no other than this. It saves the organs of him to whom it is communicated. 5.14.5: Some communicate (to the pupil) the Savitri that is Anustubh (saying), 'speech is Anustubh; we shall impart that to him'. One should not do like that. One should communicate that Savitri which is the Gayatri. Even if a man who knows as above accepts too much as gift, as it were, it is not (enough) for even one foot of the Gayatri. 5.14.6: He who accepts these three worlds replete (with wealth), will be receiving (the results of knowing) only the first foot of the Gayatri. He who accepts as much as this treasury of knowledge, the Vedas (has to confer), will receive (the results of knowing) only its second foot. And he who accepts as much as (is covered by) all living beings, will receive (the results of knowing) only its third foot. With its fourth, apparently visible, supra-mundane foot—the sun that shines—is not to be counter balanced by any gift received. Indeed how could anyone accept so much as gift? 5.14.7: Its salutation: 'O Gayatri, thou art one-footed, two-footed, there-footed and four-footed, and thou art without any feet, for thou art unattainable. Salutation to thee, the fourth, apparently visible, supra-mundane foot! May the enemy never attain his object!' (Should the knower of the Gayatri) bear hatred towards anybody, (he should) either (use this Mantra): 'Such and such—way his desired object never flourish!'—in which case that object of the person against whom he thus salutes the Gayatri, never flourishes—or (he may say), 'May I attain that (cherished object) of his!' 5.14.8: On this Janaka, Emperor of Videha, is said to have told Budila, the son of Asvatarasva, 'Well, you gave yourself out as a knower of the Gayatri; then why, alas, are you carrying (me) as an elephant?' He replied, 'Because I did not know its mouth, O Emperor'. 'Fire is its mouth. Even if they put a large quantity of fuel into the fire, it is all burnt up. Similarly, even if one who knows as above commits a great many sins, he consumes them all and becomes pure, cleansed, undecaying and immortal'.

5.15.1: The face (nature) of Satya (Brahman) is hidden (as it were) with a golden vessel. O Pusan (nourisher of the world—the sun), remove it, so that I, whose reality is Satya, may see (the face). O Pusan, O solitary Rishi (seer or traveler), O Yama (controller), O Surya (sun), O son of Prajapati (God or Hiranyagarbha), take away thy rays, curb thy brightness. I wish to behold that most benignant form of yours. I myself am that person; and I am immortal. (When my body falls) may my vital force return to the air (cosmic force), and this body too, reduced to ashes, (go to the earth)! O fire, who art the syllable 'Om', O Deity of deliberations, recollect, recollect all that I have done, O Deity of deliberations, recollect, recollect all that I have done. O Fire, lead us along the good way towards our riches (deserts). O Lord, thou knowest everybody's mental states; remove the wily evil from us. We utter repeated salutations to thee.

6.1.1: Om. He who knows that which is the oldest and greatest, becomes the oldest and greatest among his relatives. The vital force is indeed the oldest and greatest. He who knows it to be such becomes the oldest and greatest among his relatives as well as among those of whom he wants to be such. 6.1.2: He who knows the Vasistha (that which best helps to dwell or cover) becomes the Vasistha among his relatives. The organ of speech is indeed the Vasistha. He who knows it as such becomes the Vasistha among his relatives as well as among those of whom he wants to be such. 6.1.3: He who knows Pratistha (that which has steadiness) lives steadily in difficult as well as smooth places and times. The eye indeed is Pratistha, for through the eye one lives steadily in difficult as well as smooth places and times. He who knows it as such lives steadily in difficult as well as smooth places and times. 6.1.4: He who knows Sampad (prosperity) attains whatever object he desires. The ear indeed is Sampad, for all these Vedas are acquired when one has the ear (intact). He who knows it to be such attains whatever object he desires. 6.1.5: He who knows the abode becomes the abode of his relatives as well as of (other) people. The Manas indeed is the abode. He who knows it to be such becomes the abode of his relatives as well as of (other) people. 6.1.6: He who knows Prajati (that which has the attribute of generation) is enriched with children and animals. The seed (organ) has this attribute. He who knows it to be such is enriched with children and animals. 6.1.7: These organs, disputing over their respective greatness, went to Brahman and said to him, 'Which of us is the Vasistha?' He said, 'That one of you will be the Vasistha, who departing from among yourselves, people consider this body far more wretched'. 6.1.8: The organ of speech went out. After staying a whole year out it came back and said, 'How did you manage to live without me?' They said, 'We lived just as dumb people do, without speaking through the organ of speech, but living through the vital force, seeing through the eye, hearing through the ear, knowing through the mind and having children through the organ of generation.' So the organ of speech entered. 6.1.9: The eye went out. After staying a whole year out it came back and said, 'How did you manage to live without me?' They said, 'We lived just as blind people do, without seeing through the eye, but living through the vital force, speaking through the organ of speech, hearing through the ear, knowing through the mind and having children through the organ of generation.' So the eye entered. 6.1.10: The ear went out. After staying a whole year out it came back and said, 'How did you manage to live without me?' They said, 'We lived just as deaf people do, without hearing through the ear, but living through the vital force, speaking through the organ of speech, seeing through the eye, knowing through the mind and having children through the organ of generation.' So the ear entered. 6.1.11: The mind went out. After staying a whole year out it came back and said, 'How did you manage to live without me?' They said, 'We lived just as idiots do, without knowing through the mind, but living through the vital force, speaking through the organ of speech, seeing through the eye, hearing through the ear and having children through the organ of generation.' So the mind entered. 6.1.12: The organ of generation went out. After staying a whole year out it came back and said, 'How did you manage to live without me?' They said, 'We lived just as eunuchs do, without having children through the organ of generation, but living through the vital force, speaking through the organ of speech, seeing through the eye, hearing through the ear and knowing through the mind.' So the organ of generation entered. 6.1.13: Then as the vital force was about to go out, it uprooted those organs just as a great, fine horse from Sind pulls out the pegs to which his feet are tied. They said, 'Please do not go out, sir, we cannot live without you'. 'Then give me tribute.' 'All right'. 6.1.14: The organ of speech said, 'That attribute of the Vasistha which I have is yours'. The eye: 'That attribute of steadiness which I have is yours'. The ear: 'That attribute of prosperity which I have is yours'. The mind: 'That attribute of abode which I have is yours'. The organ of generation: 'That attribute of generation which I have is yours'. (The vital force said:) 'Then what will be my food and my dress?' (The organs said:) 'Whatever is (known as) food, including dogs, worms, insects and moths, is your food, and water your dress'. He who knows the food of the vital force to be such, never happens to eat anything that is not food, or to accept anything that is not food. Therefore wise men who are versed in the Vedas sip a little water just before and after eating. They regard it as removing the nakedness of the vital force.

6.2.1: Svetaketu, the grandson of Aruna, came to the assembly of the Panchalas. He approached Pravahana, the son of Jivala, who was being waited on (by his servants). Seeing him the King addressed him, 'Boy!' He replied, 'Yes, sir'. 'Have you been taught by your father?' He said, 'Yes'. 6.2.2: 'Do you know how these people diverge after death?' 'No', said he. 'Do you know how they return to this world?' 'No', said he. 'Do you know how the other world is never filled by so many people dying thus again and again?' 'No', said he. 'Do you know after how many oblations are offered water (the liquid offerings) rises up possessed of a human voice (or under the name of man) and speaks?' 'No', said he. 'Do you know the means of access to the way of the gods, or that to the way of the manes—doing which people attain either the way of the gods or the way of the manes? We have heard the words of the Mantra: 'I have heard of two routes for men, leading to the manes and the gods. Going along them all this is united. They lie between the father and the mother (earth and heaven)."' He said, 'I know not one of them'. 6.2.3: Then the King invited him to stay. The boy, disregarding the invitation to stay, hurried away. He came to his father and said to him, 'Well, did you not tell me before that you had (fully) instructed me?' 'How (did you get hurt), my sagacious child?' 'That wretch of a Kshatriya asked me five questions, and I knew not one of them.' 'Which are they?' 'These', and he quoted their first words. 6.2.4: The father said, 'My child, believe me, whatever I knew I told you every bit of it. But come, let us go there and live as students'. 'You go alone, please'. At this Gautama came to where King Pravahana, the son of Jivala, was giving audience. The King gave him a seat, had water brought for him, and made him the reverential offering. Then he said, 'We will give revered Gautama, a boon'. 6.2.5: Aruni said, 'You have promised me this boon. Please tell me what you spoke to my boy about'. 6.2.6: The King said, 'This comes under heavenly boons, Gautama. Please ask some human boon'. 6.2.7: Aruni said, 'You know that I already have gold, cattle and horses, maid-servants, retinue, and dress. Be not ungenerous towards me alone regarding this plentiful, infinite and inexhaustible (wealth).' 'Then you must seek it according to form, Gautama'. 'I approach you (as a student)'. The ancients used to approach a teacher simply through declaration. Aruni lived as a student by merely announcing that he was at his service. 6.2.8: The King said: Please do not take offence with us, Gautama, as your paternal grandfathers did not (with ours). Before this, this learning never rested with a Brāhmana. But I shall teach it to you; for who can refuse you when you speak like this? 6.2.9: That word (heaven), O Gautama, is fire, the sun is its fuel, the rays its smoke, the day its flame, the four quarters its cinder, and the intermediate quarters its sparks. In this fire the gods offer faith (liquid oblations in subtle form). Out of that offering King Moon is born (a body is made in the moon for the sacrificer). 6.2.10: Parjanya (the god of the rain), O Gautama, is fire, the year is its fuel, the clouds its smoke, lightning its flame, thunder its cinder, and the rumblings its sparks. In this fire the gods offer King Moon. Out of that offering rain is produced. 6.2.11: This world, O Gautama, is fire, the earth is its fuel, fire its smoke, the night its flame, the moon its cinder, and stars its sparks. In this fire the gods offer rain. Out of that offering food is produced. 6.2.12: Man, O Gautama, is fire, the open mouth is its fuel, the vital force its smoke, speech its flame, the eye its cinder, and the ear its sparks. In this fire the gods offer food. Out of that offering the seed is produced. 6.2.13: Woman, O Gautama, is fire. In this fire the gods offer the seed. Out of that offering a man is born. He lives as long as he is destined to live. Then, when he dies - 6.2.14: They carry him to be offered in the fire. The fire becomes his fire, the fuel his fuel, the smoke his smoke, the flame his flame, the cinder his cinder, and the sparks his sparks. In this fire the gods offer the man. Out of that offering the man emerges radiant.

6.2.15: Those who know this as such, and those others who meditate with faith upon the Satya-Brahman in the forest, reach the deity identified with the flame, from him the deity of the day, from him the deity of the fortnight in which the moon waxes, from him the deities of the six months in which the sun travels northward, from them the deity identified with the world of the gods, from him the sun, and from the sun the deity of lightning. (Then) a being created from the mind (of Hiranyagarbha) comes and conducts them to the worlds of Hiranyagarbha. They attain perfection and live in those worlds of Hiranyagarbha for a great many years. They no more return to this world. 6.2.16: While those who conquer the worlds through sacrifices, charity and austerity, reach the deity of smoke, from him the deity of the night, from him the deity of the fortnight in which the moon wanes, from him the deities of the six months in which the sun travels southward, from them the deity of the world of the manes, and from him the moon. Reaching the moon they become food. There the gods enjoy them as the priests drink the shining Soma juice (gradually, saying, as it were), 'Flourish, dwindle'. And when their past work is exhausted, they reach (become like) this ether, from the ether air, from air rain, and from rain the earth. Reaching the earth they become food. Then they are again offered in the fire of man, thence in the fire of woman, whence they are born (and perform rites) with a view to going to other worlds. Thus do they rotate. While those others who do not know these two ways become insects and moths, and these frequently biting things (gnats and mosquitoes).

6.3.1: He who wishes to attain greatness (should perform) on an auspicious day in a fortnight in which the moon waxes, and under a male constellation, during the northward march of the sun, (a sacrifice in the following manner): He should undertake for twelve days a vow connected with the Upasads (i.e. live on milk), collect in a cup of bowl made of fig wood all herbs and their grains, sweep and plaster (the ground), purify the offerings in the prescribed manner, interpose the Mantha (paste made of those things), and offer oblations with the following Mantras: 'O Fire, to all those gods under you, who spitefully frustrate men's desires, I offer their share. May they, being satisfied, satisfy me with all objects of desire! Svaha. To that all-procuring deity who turns out spiteful under your protection, thinking she is the support of all, I offer this stream of clarified butter. Svaha'. 6.3.2: Offering oblations in the fire saying, 'Svaha to the oldest, Svaha to the greatest', he dips the remnant adhering to the ladle into the paste. Offering oblations in the fire saying, 'Svaha to the vital force, Svaha to the Vasistha', he drips the remnant, etc. Offering oblations saying, 'Svaha to the organ of speech, Svaha to that which has steadiness', he drips, etc. Offering oblations saying, Svaha to the eye, Svaha to prosperity', he drips etc. Offering oblations saying, 'Svaha to the ear, Svaha to the abode', he drips, etc. Offering oblations saying, 'Svaha to the Manas, Svaha to Prajati', he drips, etc. Offering oblations saying, 'Svaha to the organ of generation', he drips, etc. 6.3.3: Offering an oblation in the fire saying, 'Svaha to fire', he drips the remnant adhering to the ladle into the paste. Offering and oblation saying, 'Svaha to the moon,' he drips, etc. Offering an oblation saying, 'Svaha to the earth', he drips, etc. Offering an oblation saying, 'Svaha to the sky', he drips, etc. Offering an oblation saying, 'Svaha to heaven', he drips, etc. Offering an oblation saying, 'Svaha to the earth, sky and heaven', he drips, etc. Offering an oblation saying, 'Svaha to the Brāhmana', he drips, etc. Offering an oblation saying, 'Svaha to the Kshatriya', he drips, etc. Offering an oblation saying, 'Svaha to the past', he drips, etc. Offering an oblation saying, 'Svaha to the future', he drips, etc. Offering an oblation saying, 'Svaha to the whole', he drips, etc. Offering an oblation saying, 'Svaha to all', he drips, etc. Offering an oblation saying, 'Svaha to Prajapati', he drips, etc. 6.3.4: Then he touches the paste saying, 'You move (as the vital force), you burn (as fire), you are infinite (as Brahman), you are still (as the sky). You combine everything in yourself. You are the sound 'Him', and are uttered as 'Him' (in the sacrifice by the Prastotr). You are the Udgītha and are chanted (by the Udgatr). You are recited (by the Adhvaryu) and recited back (by the Agnidhra). You are fully ablaze in a humid (cloud). You are omnipresent, and master. You are food (as the moon), and light (as fire). You are death, and you are that in which all things merge'. 6.3.5: Then he takes it up saying, 'You know all (as the vital force); we too are aware of your greatness. The vital force is the king, the lord, the ruler. May it make me king, lord and ruler!' 6.3.6: Then he drinks it saying, 'The radiant sun is adorable. The winds are blowing sweetly, the rivers are shedding honey, may the herbs be sweet unto us! Svaha to the earth. Glory we meditate upon; May the nights and days be charming, and the dust of the earth be sweet, may heaven, our father, be gracious! Svaha to the sky. May he direct our intellect; May the Soma creeper be sweet unto us, may the sun be kind, may the quarters be helpful to us! Svaha to heaven'. Then he repeats the whole Gayatri and the whole Madhumati, and says at the end, 'May I be all this! Svaha to the earth, sky and heaven.' Then he drinks the whole remnant, washes his hands, and lies behind the fire with his head to the east. In the morning he salutes the sun saying, 'Thou art the one lotus of the quarters; may I be the one lotus of men!' Then he returns the way he went, sits behind the fire, and repeats the line of teachers. 6.3.7: Uddalaka, the son of Aruni, taught this to his pupil Yajnavalkya, the Vajasaneya, and said, 'Should one sprinkle it even on a dry stump, branches would grow and leaves sprout'. 6.3.8: The Yajnavalkya, the Vajasaneya, taught this to his pupil Madhuka, the son of Paingi and said, 'Should one sprinkle it even on a dry stump, branches would grow and leaves sprout'. 6.3.9: Madhuka, the son of Paingi, again taught this to his pupil Cula, the son of Bhagavitta, and said, 'Should one sprinkle it even on a dry stump, branches would grow and leaves sprout'. 6.3.10: Then Cula, the son of Bhagavitta, taught this to his pupil Janaki, the son of Ayasthuna, and said, 'Should one sprinkle it even on a dry stump, branches would grow and leaves sprout'. 6.3.11: Janaki, the son of Ayasthuna, again taught this to Satyakama, the son of Jabala, and said, 'Should one sprinkle it even on a dry stump, branches would grow and leaves sprout'. 6.3.12: And Satyakama, the son of Jabala, in his turn, taught this to his pupils and said, 'Should one sprinkle it even on a dry stump, branches would grow and leaves sprout'. One must not teach this to anyone but a son or a pupil. 6.3.13: Four things are made of fig wood: the ladle, the bowl, the fuel and the two mixing rods. The cultivated grains are ten in number: Rice, barley, sesame, beans, Anu, Priyangu, wheat, lentils, pulse and vetches. They should be crushed and soaked in curds, honey and clarified butter, and offered as an oblation.

6.4.1: The earth is the essence of all these beings, water the essence of the earth, herbs of water, flowers of herbs, fruits of flowers, man of fruits, and the seed of man. 6.4.2: Prajapati thought, 'Well, let me make an abode for it', and he created woman. 6.4.3: and 6.4.4: Knowing verily this, Uddalaka, the son of Aruna, Naka, the son of Mudgala, and Kumaraharita said, 'Many men -Brāhmanas only in name—who have union without knowing as above, depart from this world impotent and bereft of merits'. 6.4.5: and 6.4.6: If man sees his reflection in water, he should recite the following Mantra: '(May the gods grant) me luster, manhood, reputation, wealth and merits'. She (his wife) is indeed the goddess of beauty among women. Therefore he should approach this handsome woman and speak to her. 6.4.7: If she is not willing, he should buy her over; and if she is still unyielding, he should strike her with a stick or with the hand and proceed, uttering the following Mantra, 'I take away your reputation', etc. She is then actually discarded. 6.4.8: If she is willing, he should proceed, uttering the following Mantra: 'I transmit reputation into you', and they both become reputed. 6.4.9-12: If a man's wife has a lover whom he wishes to injure, he should put the fire in an unbaked earthen vessel, spread stalks of reed and Kusa grass in an inverse way, and offer the reed tips, soaked in clarified butter, in the fire in an inverse way, saying, 'Thou hast sacrificed in my kindled fire, I take away thy Prāna and Apana—such and such. Thou hast sacrificed in my kindled fire, I take away thy sons and animals—such and such. Thou hast sacrificed in my kindled fire, I take away thy Vedic rites and those done according to the Smriti—such and such. Thou hast sacrificed in my kindled fire, I take away thy hopes and expectations—such and such'. The man whom a Brāhmana with knowledge of this ceremony curses, departs from this world emasculated and shorn of his merits. Therefore one should not wish even to cut jokes with the wife of a Vedic scholar who knows this ceremony, for he who has such knowledge becomes an enemy. 6.4.13: If anybody's wife has the monthly sickness, she should drink of three days out of a cup (Kamsa). No Sudra man or woman should touch her. After three nights she should bathe, put on a new cloth, and be put to thresh rice. 6.4.14: He who wishes that his son should be born fair, study one Veda and attain a full term of life, should have rice cooked in milk, and he and his wife should eat it with clarified butter. Then they would be able to produce such a son. 6.4.15: He who wishes that his son should be born tawny or brown, study two Vedas and attain a full term of life, should have rice cooked in curd, and he and his wife should eat it with clarified butter. Then they would be able to produce such a son. 6.4.16: He who wishes that his son should be born dark with red eyes, study three Vedas and attain a full term of life, should have rice cooked in water and he and his wife should eat with clarified butter. Then they would be able to produce such a son. 6.4.17: He who wishes that a daughter should be born to him who would be a scholar and attain a full term of life, should have rice cooked with sesame, and he and his wife should eat it with clarified butter. Then they would be able to produce such a daughter. 6.4.18: and 6.4.19: In the very morning he purifies the clarified butter according to the mode of Sthalipaka, and offers Sthalipaka oblations again and again, saying, 'Svaha to fire, Svaha to Anumati, Svaha to the radiant sun who produces infallible results'. After offering, he takes up (the remnant of the cooked food), eats part of it and gives the rest to his wife. Then he washes his hands, fills the water-vessel and sprinkles her thrice with that water, saying. 'Get up from here, Visvavasu, and find out another young woman (who is) with her husband.' 6.4.20: He embraces her saying, 'I am the vital force, and you are speech; you are speech, and I am the vital force; I am Saman, and you are Rik; I am heaven, and you are the earth; come, let us strive together so that we may have a male child.'

6.4.21-24: When (the son) is born, he should bring in the fire, take him in his lap, put a mixture of curd and clarified butter in a cup, and offer oblations again and again with that, saying, 'Growing in this home of mine (as the son), may I maintain a thousand people! May (the goddess of fortune) never depart with children and animals from his line! Svaha. The vital force that is in me, I mentally transfer to you. Svaha. If I have done anything too much or too little in this ceremony, may the all-knowing beneficent fire make it just right for me—neither too much nor too little! Svaha.' 6.4.25: Then putting (his mouth) to the child's right ear, he should thrice repeat, 'Speech, speech'. Next mixing curd, honey and clarified butter, he feeds him with (a strip of) gold not obstructed (by anything), saying, 'I put the earth into you, I put the sky into you, I put heaven into you, I put the whole of the earth, sky and heaven into you'. 6.4.26: The he gives him a name, 'You are Veda (knowledge)'. That is his secret name. 6.4.27: Then he hands him to his mother to be suckled, saying, 'Offering Sarasvati, that breast of thine which is stored with results, is the sustainer of all, full of milk, the obtainer of wealth (one's deserts) and generous, and through which thou nourishest all who are worthy of it (the gods etc.)—transfer that here (to my wife, for my babe) to suck'. 6.4.28: Then he addressed the mother: 'You are the adorable Arundhati, the wife of Vasistha; you have brought forth a male child with the help of me, who am a man. Be the mother of many sons, for you have given us a son'. Of him who is born as the child of a Brāhmana with this particular knowledge, they say, 'You have exceeded your father, and you have exceeded your grandfather. You have reached the extreme limit of attainment through your splendor, fame and Brahmanical power.'

6.5.1: Now the line of teachers: The son of Pautimsa (received it) from the son of Katyayani. He from the son of gautami. The son of Gautami from the son of Bharadvaji. He from the son of Parasari. The son of Parasari from the son of Aupasvasti. He from the son of another Parasari. He from the son of Katyayani. The son of katyayani from the son of Kausiki. The son of Kausiki from the son of Alambi and the son of Vaiyaghrapadi. The son of Vaiyaghrapadi from the son of Kanvi and the son of Kapi. The son of Kapi—6.5.2: From the son of Atreyi. The son of Atreyi from the son of gautami. The son of Gautami from the son of Bharadvaji. He from the son of parasari. The son of Parasari from the son of Vatsi. The son of Vatsi from the son of another Parasari. The son of Parasari from the son of Varkaruni. He from the son of another Varkaruni. This one from the son of Artabhagi. He from the son of Saungi. The son of Saungi from the son of Samkrti. He from the son of Alambayani. He again from the son of Alambi. The son of Alambi from the son of jayanti. He from the son of Mandukayani. He in his turn from the son of Manduki. The son of manduki from the son of Sandili. The son of Sandili from the son of Rathitari. He from the son of Bhaluki. The son of Bhaluki from the two sons of Krauneiki. They from the son of Vaidabhrti. He from the son of Karsakeyi. He again from the son of Pracinayogi. He from the son of Samjivi. The son of Samjivi from Asurivasin, the son of Prasni. The son of Prasni from Asurayana. He from Asuri. 6.5.3: Asuri from Yajnavalkya. Yajnavalkya from Uddalaka. Uddalaka from Aruna. Aruna from Upavesi. Upavesi from Kusri. Kusri from Vajasravas. He from Jihvavat, the son of Badhyoga. He from Asita, the son of Varsagana. He from Harita Kasyapa. He from Silpa Kasyapa. This one from Kasyana, the son of Nidhruva. He from Vac. She from Ambhini. She from the sun. These white Yajuses received from the sun are explained by Yajnavalkya Vajasaneya. 6.5.4: The same up to the son of Samjivi. The son of Samjivi from Mandukayani. Mandukayani from mandavya. Mandavya from Kautsa. Kautsa from Mahitthi. He from Vamakaksayana. He from Sandilya. Sandilya from Vatsya. Vatsya from Kusri. Kusri from Yajnavacas, the son of rajastamba. He from Tura, the son of Kavasi. He from Prajapati (Hiranyagarbha). Prajapati through his relation to Brahman (the Vedas). Brahman is self-born. Salutation to Brahman.

Om! That (Brahman) is infinite, and this (universe) is infinite. The infinite proceeds from the infinite. (Then) taking the infinitude of the infinite (universe), It remains as the infinite (Brahman) alone.

Om! Shantih! Shantih! Shantih!!

Here ends the Brihadaranyakopanishad, as contained in the Sukla-Yajur-Veda.

Brihadaranyaka Upanishad

Commentary

by Swami Nirmalananda Giri

Correcting Our Ideas about Brahman

Now we come to the oldest Upanishadic dialogue between teacher and student. Gargya, the student, will speak the truth, but without exact perception. That is, his statements will be either partial, skewed, or not of dead-center accuracy. So I will not say much about what he says, but concentrate on what the teacher Ajatasatru will say in correcting his statements—which are not false, but imperfect and lacking. (All through this discourse Ajatasatru's disagreements with Gargya are only that Gargya aims much too low in his views of reality, whereas Ajatasatru keeps insisting on viewing Reality—Brahman—and not its manifestations or appearances.

It must also be kept in mind that when Ajatasatru speaks of "children" or "progeny" he is speaking of the progeny of the illumined mind. Just as the scriptures speak of "the mind-born sons of Brahma" so each has mind-born offspring, symbolically speaking. Thoughts, words, and deeds, are all our "children."

The pride of ignorance

"Gargya, son of Valaka, was a good talker, but exceedingly vain. Coming one day into the presence of Ajatasatru, king of Varanasi, he accosted him with boastful speech. Gargya said: 'I will teach you of Brahman.' Ajatasatru said: 'Indeed? Well, just for that kind proposal you should be rewarded with a thousand cows. People nowadays flock to King Janaka to speak and hear of Brahman; I am pleased that you have come to me instead.'" (Brihadaranyaka Upanishad 2:1:1)

The Sanskrit text actually says: "There was a man of the Garga family called Proud Balaki, who was eloquent." Shankara comments that he was "Proud' because of his very ignorance about the real Brahman." We see this a lot in every area of life, not just religion. As someone once said: "The problem with ignorance is that it picks up confidence as it goes along." It has been my observation that the more confidence some people possess, the more ignorant they are. When they speak with bullying assurance they should never be believed. This has saved me from a lot of potentially disastrous situations.

As has been the practice in nearly all ancient cultures, at that time cows were prized so highly as to even be a medium of exchange, often preferred to money. (It is interesting that the oldest money found in England are huge blocks of metal embossed with the figure of a cow to indicate that each one possesses the value of one cow.)

Janaka was, as a Brief Sanskrit Glossary says: "The royal sage (rajarishi) who was the king of Mithila and a liberated yogi, a highly sought-after teacher of philosophy in ancient India." So it was very pleasing to Ajatasatru that someone would approach him for philosophical discourse. However, Gargya came to teach and instead was taught—fortunate man! The fact that he was amenable to being taught indicates that his pride was really harmless, like the pride of a child. This is a trait of a sattwic mind.

Transcendent and transcending knowledge

"Gargya said: 'He who is the being in the sun and at the same time the being in the eye; he who, having entered the body through the eye, resides in the heart and is the doer and the experiencer—him I meditate upon as Brahman.' Ajatasatru said: 'Nay, nay! Do not speak thus of Brahman. That being I worship as transcendental, luminous, supreme. He who meditates upon Brahman as such goes beyond all created beings and becomes the glorious ruler of all." (Brihadaranyaka Upanishad 2:1:2)

It is certainly true that Brahman is all-pervading and therefore immanent in all creation, but It is much more, and those further attributes are the ones so necessary for the aspiring yogi to learn. That which Gargya said can be held by any devoted religious person in ignorance. But Ajatasatru's assertions are "the last word" in the matter, both as to the true nature of Brahman and that which he will himself become who comes to know this of Brahman by the direct experience possible only to adept yogis. Brahman is not confined to this present world-experience, and neither are we in our true nature. This must be realized if we would be free (mukta).

Beyond the mind

"Gargya said: 'The being who is in the moon and at the same time in the mind—him I meditate upon as Brahman.' Ajatasatru said: 'Nay, nay! Do not speak thus of Brahman. That being I worship as infinite, clad in purity, blissful, resplendent. He who meditates upon Brahman as such lacks nothing and is forever happy.'" (Brihadaranyaka Upanishad 2:1:3)

Brahman is certainly in the mind [manas], but cannot be grasped by the mind, for it is an instrument of illusory perception. The intellect [buddhi] can be so purified that it becomes a mirror-reflection of Spirit-Being—which is why the Gita emphasizes Buddhi Yoga. The buddhi can perceive Brahman "as infinite, clad in purity, blissful, resplendent." Such is the gateway to the fulfillment of all right desires and unbroken bliss.

Omnipotence

"Gargya said: 'The being who is in the lightning and at the same time in the heart—him I meditate upon as Brahman.' Ajatasatru said: 'Nay, nay! Do not speak thus of Brahman. That being I worship as power. He who meditates upon Brahman as such becomes powerful, and his children after him." (Brihadaranyaka Upanishad 2:1:4)

We see astounding phenomena in creation, but they are only appearances, however wondrous. Brahman is their source, but It is the Power that produces those phenomena, It is their foundation without which they could not occur. Brahman is unlimited Potential. And so are those who come to know Brahman.

Omnipresence

"Gargya said: 'The being who is in the sky and at the same time in the heart—him I meditate upon as Brahman.' Ajatasatru said: 'Nay, nay! Do not speak thus of Brahman. That being I worship as all-pervading, changeless. He who meditates upon Brahman as such is blessed with children and with cattle. The thread of his progeny shall never be cut." (Brihadaranyaka Upanishad 2:1:5)

Brahman is not just in a lot of places, Brahman is everywhere and within all things, for It IS all things. And this all-pervasiveness is eternal—has been so forever.

Invincible

"Gargya said: 'The being who is in the wind and who at the same time is the breath within—him I meditate upon as Brahman.' Ajatasatru said: 'Nay, nay! Do not speak thus of Brahman. That being I worship as the Lord, invincible and unconquerable. He who meditates upon Brahman as such becomes himself invincible and unconquerable." (Brihadaranyaka Upanishad 2:1:6)

Wind and breath wax, wane, and cease—Brahman never does. It cannot be even affected by anything, much less controlled.

Forbearing

"Gargya said: 'The being who is in the fire and at the same time in the heart—him I meditate upon as Brahman.' Ajatasatru said: 'Nay, nay! Do not speak thus of Brahman. That being I worship as forgiving [forbearing]. He who meditates upon Brahman as such becomes himself forgiving, and his children after him." (Brihadaranyaka Upanishad 2:1:7)

The idea here is that, being within all things, Brahman experiences all that happens to them. That is why Bishop James I. Wedgwood, an adherent of Advaita Vedanta, wrote the prayer he called *An Act of Union*: "Unto Thee, O Perfect One, the Lord and Lover of men, do we commend our life and hope. For Thou art the Heavenly Bread, the Life of the whole world; *Thou art in all places and endurest all things*, the Treasury of endless good and the Well of infinite compassion." Brahman is not just in many things, It is the Consciousness inside of all things as the Infinite Witness.

Harmony

"Gargya said: 'The being who is in the water and at the same time in the heart—him I meditate upon as Brahman.' Ajatasatru said: 'Nay, nay! Do not speak thus of Brahman. That being I worship as harmony. He who meditates upon Brahman as such knows only what is harmonious. Of him are born tranquil children." (Brihadaranyaka Upanishad 2:1:8) Water takes the form of any vessel into which it is poured. It is the softest of substances, and has no innate resistance. (Water pressure comes from restraining forms, not from water itself.) Thus it is a perfect symbol of harmony—or "agreeableness" as Madhavananda translates it. Ajatasatru points out that we should not exalt finite objects that exemplify worthy characteristics, but Brahman Which IS those traits, the substances and objects only being tiny reflections of Brahman. We must not mistake the mirror image for the actual object.

Self-effulgent

"Gargya said: 'The being who is in the mirror—him I meditate upon as Brahman.' Ajatasatru said: 'Nay, nay! Do not speak thus of Brahman. That being I worship as effulgent. He who meditates upon Brahman as such becomes himself effulgent, and his children after. He shines brighter than all who approach him." (Brihadaranyaka Upanishad 2:1:9)

The ancient Indians were far more sophisticated than is known in the West. Although I once read such an idea denounced as "Hindu Fundamentalism" and "Militant Hinduism," it is my serious belief that India has in the past attained levels of technology, medicine, and all aspects of culture that have been undreamed of elsewhere on earth. India truly has forgotten more than the modern world can possibly know. This verse is an instance of this.

We see our reflection in a mirror because light waves strike the surface of our bodies and clothing, and as they are deflected into the mirror we see an image there. But Brahman is *swayamprakash*, Its own illumination. That is why Christian mysticism speaks of Divinity as the "Light of light." Brahman is the source, the cause, not the effect. "He shining, everything shines." (Katha Upanishad 2:2:15)

Life itself

"Gargya said: 'The sound that follows a man as he walks—that I meditate upon as Brahman.' Ajatasatru said: 'Nay, nay! Do not speak thus of Brahman. That being I worship as the vital force. He who meditates upon Brahman as such reaches his full age in this world: breath does not leave him before his time." (Brihadaranyaka Upanishad 2:1:10)

Brahman is Life Itself, Existence Itself. All phenomena are simply echoes of Brahman. As just quoted: "He shining, everything shines." (Katha Upanishad 2:2:15)

My own Self

"Gargya said: 'The being who pervades space—him I meditate upon as Brahman.' Ajatasatru said: 'Nay, nay! Do not speak thus of Brahman. That being I worship as a second self, who can never be separated from me. He who meditates upon Brahman as such is never lonely, and his followers never forsake him." (Brihadaranyaka Upanishad 2:1:11)

Brahman is not outside us as any "thing." Rather, Brahman is our own Self. What is most important about this verse is that it indicates the important truth that Brahman is our *second* Self—not our Atman in the simplistic sense. For that would mean that we do not even exist—that as false Advaita says, when we attain realization we will cease to exist and only Brahman will remain. This is not the teaching of the Upanishads or the Gita. Brahman is the Self of our Self. First we must come to know our own individual Self, and then proceed to know the Supreme Self, Brahman. Brahman is at the core of our Self, inseparable from It. How this can be is beyond human intelligence, but not beyond our experience, our direct knowing. Buddhi Yoga is the key.

Divine will

"Gargya said: 'The being who dwells in the heart as intelligence—him I meditate upon as Brahman.' Ajatasatru said: 'Nay, nay! Do not speak thus of Brahman. That being I worship as the lord of will. He who meditates upon Brahman as such achieves self-control, and his children after him." (Brihadaranyaka Upanishad 2:1:13)

Intelligence or buddhi is centered in the subtle body known as the jnanamaya kosha, which corresponds to the air (vayu) element. But the subtlest body is the anandamaya kosha, which corresponds to the ether (akasha) element. That is the seat of will, the highest power of the individual. The only thing higher is the Self, and since it borders on the Self, the Self (whose Self is Brahman) is "the lord of will." We can see this in our daily life. We choose what we will or will not think about. Sometimes we even shove thoughts out of our mind, refusing to think on certain subjects or postponing thought till a later time. So the Self is the direct controller of the will. The will determines everything, and even unsophisticated philosophy considers free will the prime trait of a human being.

Insufficient

"Gargya ceased speaking. Ajatasatru, continuing, questioned him. Ajatasatru said: 'Is that all that you know of Brahman?' Gargya said: 'That is all that I know.' Ajatasatru said: 'By knowing only so much, one cannot profess to know Brahman.' Gargya said: 'Please, sir, accept me as a disciple, and teach me of Brahman." (Brihadaranyaka Upanishad 2:1:14)

A practical demonstration

"Ajatasatru said: 'I will teach you.' So saying, Ajatasatru took Gargya by the hand and rose. Then, as the two walked side by side, they came to a sleeping man. Ajatasatru said to the sleeper: 'O thou great one, clad in white raiment, O Soma, O king!' At first the man did not stir. Then, as Ajatasatru touched him, he awoke." (Brihadaranyaka Upanishad 2:1:15)

Occasionally in the Upanishads we find humor used to make a point, and this is one of them. Coming across a sleeping man, Ajatasatru addressed him as the divine Self: "O thou great one, clad in white raiment, O Soma, O king!" But it did no good, for the man was unconscious. It was pointless to address him at all. In the same way, all the positive affirming and philosophizing are worthless if the speaker and the hearers are spiritually asleep! Sleepers do not need high-sounding words about the Self: they need to awaken. So Ajatasatru shook him until he woke up. We need to be shaken up, to awaken and see with our real eyes and hear with our real ears. Otherwise nothing will really go on. The truth being spoken to us means nothing if we are not awake to hear it. Yoga is the great awakener. Other factors can disturb our sleep, get us to open our eyes a bit and then go back to sleep, and just mumble and turn over and sleep on. Yoga alone awakens. All the religion and piety mean absolutely nothing if we are not awake and clear in the mind. Ajatasatru now analyzes sleep, dream, and dreamless sleep.

The sleeper

"Ajatasatru said to Gargya: 'This man, who is a conscious, intelligent being—where was he when he was thus asleep, and how did he thus wake up?' Gargya was silent.

"When this man, who is a conscious, intelligent being, is thus in deep sleep, he enters into the ether within the lotus of the heart, having withdrawn into himself both his senses and his mind. When his senses and his mind are thus withdrawn, he is said to be absorbed in the [lower] self.

"In this state he knows nothing; he enters into the seventy-two thousand nerves [nadis] which go out from the lotus of the heart. Even as a young man, or an emperor, or the best of Brahmins, when he has experienced the ecstasy of love, straightway takes sweet repose, so does a man deep in sleep find rest.

"But when he sleeps, but also dreams, he lives in a world of his own. He may dream that he is a king, or that he is the best of Brahmins; he may dream that he is an angel, or that he is a beast. As an emperor, having obtained the objects of enjoyment, moves about at will in his dominions, so the sleeper, gathering up the impressions of sense, compounds them into dreams according to his desires." (Brihadaranyaka Upanishad 2:1:16-19)

In sleep we withdraw from the physical senses. In dream we are using the astral senses to create whatever our mind decides. In dreamless sleep we are centered in the causal body. We can even think in such a state without waking, though it is not common to do so. Yet, as Ajatasatru points out, we are always conscious, witnessing the dream and dreamless states just as we witness the waking state. Even more, when we awaken we often remember the dreams and even say: "I did not dream," showing that we remember dreamlessness as vividly as we do dreaming and waking. That witnessing conscious is our Self, pure being itself.

The source

The "bottom line" is that the Self is the source of our waking, dreaming, and dreamless sleep. It is the source of our entire life, determining every aspect. So Ajatasatru concludes with these words:

"As threads come out of the spider, as little sparks come out of the fire, so all the senses, all the worlds, all the gods, yes, all beings, issue forth from the Self. His secret name is Truth of the Truth." (Brihadaranyaka Upanishad 2:1:20)

The Self, and ultimately Brahman, is/are the origin and existence of all things. When we know that Self we know, possess, and control all. That and that alone is what it means to be a Master.

The Dearness of the Self

Now we come to the best-known dialogue of this Upanishad: the conversation between the great sage Yajnavalkya and Maitreyi his wife. Maitreyi and Gargi (whom we will meet later in this Upanishad) are evidence that in the time of the ancient sages women were among their number and were teachers of Brahman in their own right. True Hindu traditionalists such as the Arya Samajis make no distinction between male and female in the spiritual rituals (samskaras) received, all wearing the sacred thread (yajnopavita) and performing the Vedic rites. The most perfect and powerful fire sacrifice I have ever attended was that of the high school girls in the Arya Samaj girls' school in Baroda. I have never seen better "brahmins" than those intelligent and skilled young women. I hope they have retained the glorious wisdom they learned at that true gurukula under the direction of the venerable sage Pandit Anandapriya of the Arya Samaj.

The vital question

"Yajnavalkya said to his wife: 'Maitreyi, I am resolved to give up the world and begin the life of renunciation. I wish therefore to divide my property between you and my other wife, Katyayani.'

"Maitreyi said: 'My lord, if this whole earth belonged to me, with all its wealth, should I through its possession attain immortality?' Yajnavalkya said: 'No. Your life would be like that of the rich. None can possibly hope to attain immortality through wealth.'

"Maitreyi said: 'Then what need have I of wealth? Please, my lord, tell me what you know about the way to immortality.'

"Yajnavalkya said: 'Dear to me have you always been, Maitreyi, and now you ask to learn of that truth which is nearest my heart. Come, sit by me. I will explain it to you. Meditate on what I say." (Brihadaranyaka Upanishad 2:4:1-4)

What a beautiful picture! I cannot count the number of enslaved "spiritual" men who have rhapsodized to me about how "special" their wives were, that turned out to really be materialistic, anti-spiritual, manipulative harpies. Women have better sense; they rarely extol the duds they are married to—though both sexes are quite willing to use their spouse as justification for neglecting or abandoning spiritual life. After all, they have taken "vows" and taken "obligations" on themselves! God, for another life, has to go to the end of the line and wait.

But that is not what we see here. We see a real spiritual marriage in action. Both seek Reality. In those days the life of a samnyasi was one of perpetual wandering, so there is no thought of Maitreyi accompanying Yajnavalkya in his new stage of life. But we can be assured that her sadhana was no less intense than his, for she has been honored for centuries as one of the great illuminati of India, no less than her husband.

Yajnavalkya calls Maitreyi *priya*, which mean dear, beloved, and pleasing. And he does not mean it in the small-minded egocentric way we are so inured to. And lest she think so, he now begins one of the most quoted passages of the Upanishads.

For the sake of the Self

"It is not for the sake of the husband, my beloved, that the husband is dear, but for the sake of the Self.

"It is not for the sake of the wife, my beloved, that the wife is dear, but for the sake of the Self.

"It is not for the sake of the children, my beloved, that the children are dear, but for the sake of the Self.

"It is not for the sake of wealth, my beloved, that wealth is dear, but for the sake of the Self.

"It is not for the sake of the Brahmins, my beloved, that the Brahmins are held in reverence, but for the sake of the Self.

"It is not for the sake of the Kshatriyas, my beloved, that the Kshatriyas are held in honor, but for the sake of the Self.

"It is not for the sake of the higher worlds, my beloved, that the higher worlds are desired, but for the sake of the Self.

"It is not for the sake of the gods, my beloved, that the gods are worshipped, but for the sake of the Self.

"It is not for the sake of the creatures, my beloved, that the creatures are prized, but for the sake of the Self.

"It is not for the sake of itself, my beloved, that anything whatever is esteemed, but for the sake of the Self.

"The Self, Maitreyi, is to be known. Hear about it, reflect upon it, meditate upon it. By knowing the Self, my beloved, through hearing, reflection, and meditation, one comes to know all things." (Brihadaranyaka Upanishad 2:4:5)

The Self (Atman) is of the nature of bliss (ananda). When the things enumerated above are encountered a person feels a touch of the joy that is the Self. Actually, our response to them opens the barrier between us and the Self for a while, and like the light coming through the shutter of a camera we get a flash, a glimpse of the bliss of the Self. What we are really valuing is that touch of the Self, but in our ignorance we think those objects are the source. Therefore it really is because of—"for the sake of"—the Self that they are thought by us as dear.

The wise seek to know the Self through study, deep thought, and meditation upon the Self. And we are assured that "by knowing the Self through hearing, reflection, and meditation, one comes to know all things."

All are the Self

To know the Self is to know everything. To not know the Self is to know nothing. So the sage continues:

"Let the Brahmin ignore him who thinks that the Brahmin is different from the Self.

"Let the Kshatriya ignore him who thinks that the Kshatriya is different from the Self.

"Let the higher worlds ignore him who thinks that the higher worlds are different from the Self.

"Let the gods ignore him who thinks that the gods are different from the Self.

"Let all creatures ignore him who thinks that the creatures are different from the Self.

"Let all ignore him who thinks that anything whatever is different from the Self.

"The priest, the warrior, the higher worlds, the gods, the creatures, whatsoever things there be— these are the Self." (Brihadaranyaka Upanishad 2:4:6)

That is certainly clear. And so is this:

"As, when the drum is beaten, its various particular notes are not heard apart from the whole, but in the total sound all its notes are heard; as, when the conch shell is blown, its various particular notes are not heard apart from the whole, but in the total sound all its notes are heard; as, when the vina is played, its various particular notes are not heard apart from the whole, but in the total sound all its notes are heard—so, through the knowledge of the Self, Pure Intelligence, all things and beings are known. There is no existence apart from the Self." (Brihadaranyaka Upanishad 2:4:7-9)

The incredible spectacle of the endless creations of infinite elaboration springs only from Brahman and has no existence apart from Brahman. The same is true of our own continuing saga of lifetimes: it all emanates from the Self. The cosmic and individual dreams arise only from Consciousness. The dreams are illusion, yet wisdom (jnana) is inherent in them. So Yajnavalkya further says:

"As smoke and sparks arise from a lighted fire kindled with damp fuel, even so, Maitreyi, have been breathed forth from the Eternal all knowledge and all wisdom— what we know as the Rig Veda, the Yajur Veda, and the rest. They are the breath of the Eternal." (Brihadaranyaka Upanishad 2:4:10)

The all-pervading center

"As for water the one center is the ocean, as for touch the one center is the skin, as for smell the one center is the nose, as for taste the one center is the tongue, as for form the one center is the eyes, as for sound the one center is the ears, as for thought the one center is the mind, as for divine wisdom the one center is the heart—so for all beings the one center is the Self." (Brihadaranyaka Upanishad 2:4:11)

In the twenty-second chapter of Autobiography of a Yogi, Paramhansa Yogananda describes seeing with the "eye" of the Self: "Spiritual sight, x-ray like, penetrates into all matter; the divine eye is center everywhere, circumference nowhere. I realized anew, standing there in the sunny courtyard, that when man ceases to be a prodigal child of God, engrossed in a physical world indeed dream, baseless as a bubble, he re-inherits his eternal realms. If 'escapism' be a need of man, cramped in his narrow personality, can any escape compare with the majesty of omnipresence?"

"As a lump of salt when thrown into water melts away and the lump cannot be taken out, but wherever we taste the water it is salty, even so, O Maitreyi, the individual self, dissolved, is the Eternal—pure consciousness, infinite and transcendent. Individuality arises by identification of the Self, through ignorance, with the elements; and with the disappearance of consciousness of the many, in divine illumination, it disappears. Where there is consciousness of the Self, [seeming] individual separation is no more. This it is, O my beloved, that I wanted to tell you." (Brihadaranyaka Upanishad 2:4:12)

A doubt

"Maitreyi said: "Where there is consciousness of the Self, individual separation is no more." This that you say, my lord, confuses me.' Yajnavalkya said: 'My beloved, let nothing I have said confuse you. But meditate well the truth that I have spoken.

"As long as there is duality, one sees the other, one hears the other, one smells the other, one speaks to the other, one thinks of the other, one knows the other; but when for the illumined soul the all is dissolved in the Self, who is there to be seen by whom, who is there to be smelt by whom, who is there to be heard by whom, who is there to be spoken to by whom, who is there to be thought of by whom, who is there to be known by whom? Ah, Maitreyi, my beloved, the Intelligence which reveals all—by what shall it be revealed? By whom shall the Knower be known? The Self is described as Not This, Not That. It is incomprehensible, for it cannot be comprehended; undecaying, for it never decays; unattached, for it never attaches itself; unbound, for it is never bound. By whom, O my beloved, shall the Knower be known?

"This it is that I teach you, O Maitreyi. This is the truth of immortality.'

"So saying, Yajnavalkya entered upon the path of renunciation." (Brihadaranyaka Upanishad 2:4:13-14)

Yajnavalkya is not saying that the enlightened go into a kind of non-dual coma in which nothing is perceived. Rather, he says that those who have known Brahman, even though they still hear and see names and forms, they know that they are not seeing something "other," but are seeing only the Supreme Self. They do not just believe that, they see that to be so. Only the One remains, however many "things" might be seen in the cosmic dream.

Nothing "other" can reveal this Consciousness to us, for that is the Revealer, never the Revealed. For the vision of God takes place within, not without—though afterward we do see Divinity both within and without.

The machine does not run the operator, the operator runs the machine.

Because of Its transcendent nature, Brahman is described as *Neti Neti*—Not This, Not That. We can only say what Brahman is not, and when we come to the end, having negated everything, what remains, though unspeakable and inconceivable, is Brahman.

"By whom, O my beloved, shall the Knower be known?" Only to Itself—to our Self.

14. Each Soul is dear to the other

We have had a discourse on how it is the Self that makes all things dear or beloved to us. We often use the expression "sweet" to express our pleasure or delight in something, and so the Upanishad speaks of how all things are "honey' (madhu) because "Brahman is the soul in each; he indeed is the Self in all. He is all." The nature of Brahman is bliss (ananda), and Brahman is the soul, the Self of all. **Consequently all things are joy for the awakened and realized person.**

To avoid tedium from the type of repetition that is found in many Sanskrit texts (and in many Pali sutras of Buddhism), I will just give the first "honey" verse and the simply list all of the subjects covered, since except for the keyword each verse is absolutely identical.

"This earth is honey for all beings, and all beings are honey for this earth. The intelligent, immortal being, the soul of this earth, and the intelligent, immortal being, the soul in the individual being—each is dear to the other. (because there is no other) Brahman is the soul in each; he indeed is the Self in all. He is all." (Brihadaranyaka Upanishad 2:5:1)

Verses two to fourteen affirm the joyful nature of water, fire, air, the sun, space, the moon, lightning, thunder, ether, dharma, truth (satyam), humanity (manusham), and all things (sarvesham).

The Upanishad sums it all up with the following verses:

"This Self is the lord of all beings, the king of all beings. As the spokes are held together in the hub and in the felly of a wheel, just so all beings, all creatures, all gods, all worlds, all lives, are held together in the Self.

"He made bodies with two feet, he made bodies with four feet. He entered into all bodies, and because he dwells within the lotus of the heart, he is known as Purusha. There is nothing that is not surrounded by him, nothing that is not filled with him.

"He assumed all forms. He assumed all forms to reveal himself in all forms. He, the Lord, is revealed in forms through his Maya. He is tens, he is thousands—he is numberless.

"This Brahman is without cause, without effect, without inside or outside. This Brahman is the Self." (Brihadaranyaka Upanishad 2:5:15.18-19)

15. The Wisdom of the Wise (Yagnavalkya)

The next section of the Upanishad is a marvel of wisdom that opens with some humor.

I want those cows!

"Janaka, King of Videha, on a certain occasion performed a sacrifice and in connection therewith distributed costly gifts. Among those who attended the ceremony were the wise men of Kuru and of Panchala. King Janaka observed them and wanted to find out which was the wisest.

"Now it happened that the king kept a thousand cows enclosed in a pen, and between the horns of every one of them were fastened ten gold coins.

"Venerable Brahmins,' said King Janaka, 'let him who is the wisest among you take away these cows.'

"The Brahmins dared not stir, save Yajnavalkya alone.

"My learned son,' said Yajnavalkya to his disciple, 'drive home my cows.'

"Hurrah!" cried the lad, and made for them.

"The rest of the Brahmins were enraged. 'How dare he call himself the wisest!' they shouted. **At last, Aswala, priest to King Janaka,** accosted Yajnavalkya, saying:

"Yajnavalkya, are you quite sure you are the wisest among us?'

"I bow down,' replied Yajnavalkya, 'to the wisest. But I want those cows!'

"Then Aswala began to question him." (Brihadaranyaka Upanishad 3:1:2)

As already mentioned, Janaka is considered the prime example of a "worldly" person who attained perfect knowledge. He is also considered the prime example of one who possessed great wealth. "Rich as Janaka" is the Indian equivalent of the West's "rich as Midas."

It was the custom for those who attended spiritual events to be given rich gifts, and it was obvious to all those at the sacrifice that the thousand cows and ten thousand gold coins strung between their horns were meant to be given to the one who could best expound philosophy and answer all challenging questions. (It may be that the ten thousand padas of gold mentioned in the text were not coins of one pada each, but covers with large gold knobs that were affixed to the cows' horns.)

Those who attended the sacrifice were truly wise men, for they were also modest. When told that the cows and gold were for the wisest among them "they dared not stir."

Yajnavalkya, on the other hand, was tactful. He told a student to take the cows to his home rather than claim he was the wisest, though he was—and knew he was. When challenged by Aswala he said: "I bow down to the wisest, but I want those cows!" In this way he masked his wisdom with humor that appeared to be simple greed. Saints often do this, pretending to be ignorant or unaware, hiding their true status from the truly ignorant and unaware (who, blinded by their ego, are always fooled by the ruse). Swami Sivananda often did this, as I witnessed myself. Only the wise dare to be thought a fool.

Now there follows the questioning of Yajnavalkya.

How to overcome death

"**Aswala** said: 'Yajnavalkya, since everything connected with sacrificial rites is pervaded by death, and is subject to death, by what means can the worshiper overcome death?' Yajnavalkya said: 'By knowledge of the identity between the worshiper, the fire, and the ritual word. For the ritual word is indeed the worshiper, and the ritual word is the fire, and the fire, which is one with Brahman, is the worshiper. This knowledge leads to liberation; this knowledge leads one beyond death." (Brihadaranyaka Upanishad 3:1:3)

All relative things begin and end, are born and die in a manner of speaking. Everything that is connected with the fire sacrifice is perishable, including the fire itself—all are pervaded by death and subject to death. Obviously, then the sacrifice cannot lead to immortality. So how can we overcome ("go beyond" is the literal wording) death? The answer is simple: by knowing the non-dual Brahman which alone is immortal and immortality itself.

What "eats" death?

"Aswala held his peace. But **Artabhaga** asked: 'Yajnavalkya, everything is the food of death. Is there any power for which death is food?' Yajnavalkya said: 'Indeed, yes. Fire devours everything, and fire, again, is the food of water. Similarly, **there is a death to death**. The knower of the truth of Brahman overcomes death." (Brihadaranyaka Upanishad 3:2:10)

Those who know Brahman have "devoured" death just as the eater of food transmutes it into his own body and lives on it. So death itself is the gateway of immortality to the yogi.

The liberated at death

"Artabhaga said: 'Yajnavalkya, when such one gives up his body, do his perceptive faculties, along with his mind, go out of him, or do they not?' Yajnavalkya said: 'They do not. They merge in the final cause, the Self.

The body lies lifeless, inflated, and swollen." (Brihadaranyaka Upanishad 3:2:11)

In relative existence we possess five levels. Artabhaga is asking if all but the physical (material) levels or bodies go along with the liberated individual at the departure from the body. Yajnavalkya replies that the pranic (pranamaya) and sensory-mind (manomaya) bodies do not go along with the liberated person, but are resolved back into the universal energy from which they arose when he entered into relativity. We only take with us the buddhi (jnanamaya) and creative will (anandamaya) bodies which are causal in nature, the seats of intellect and intuition respectively. For the liberated are free forever of the physical and astral bodies, though they can take new ones on again if they elect to return to incarnation in the astral or physical worlds as avatar-saviors in those worlds.

The Atman-Self

"Artabhaga held his peace. Then **Ushasta** asked: 'Yajnavalkya, what is the ultimate, the immediate Brahman, Brahman himself alone, directly realized as such, the Self which dwells within all?' Yajnavalkya (pointing to his heart) said: 'This, thy Self, which is within all.' Ushasta said: 'Which self, O Yajnavalkya, is within all?' Yajnavalkya said: 'That which breathes in is thy Self, which is within all. That which breathes down is thy Self, which is within all. That which diffuses breath is thy Self, which is within all. That which breathes out is thy Self, which is within all. Again I reply: This, thy Self, which is within all.'" (Brihadaranyaka Upanishad 3:4:1)

Brahman is the Self within, the Self that enlivens and activates all through the functions of the five prāṇas. If we can trace back the prāṇas, especially through the breath, we will find the Self.

"Ushasta said: 'As one might say, in distinguishing a cow from a horse, that the cow is the animal that walks, and the horse is the animal that runs, exactly so simple, so clear, O wise one, has been your teaching about Brahman! But tell me, I ask again, who is the ultimate, the immediate Brahman, Brahman himself alone, directly realized as such, the Self which dwells within all?' Yajnavalkya said: 'This, thy Self, which is within all.' Ushasta said: 'Which self, O Yajnavalkya, is within all?' Yajnavalkya said: 'Thou canst not see the seer of the sight, thou canst not hear the hearer of the sound, thou canst not think the thinker of the thought, thou canst not know the knower of the known. Again I reply: This, thy Self, which is within all. Anything that is not the Self perishes.' Ushasta held his peace." (Brihadaranyaka Upanishad 3:4:2)

There is only one Self: the Self that cannot be seen, heard, thought, or known by the limited mind. It, being inside everything, is not an object of perception. If we take away all "things" only the Self remains, knowing Itself by Itself. Naturally this is not easy to grasp intellectually, because the Self is far beyond the intellect. Nevertheless, these truths can be known by the yogi.

"**Kahola** asked: 'Yajnavalkya, what is the ultimate, the immediate Brahman, Brahman himself alone, directly realized as such, the Self which dwells within all?' Yajnavalkya said: 'This, thy Self, which is within all.' Kohala said: 'Which self, O Yajnavalkya, is within all?' Yajnavalkya said: 'That which is beyond hunger, thirst, grief, delusion, decay, and death.

"Having realized this Self, the sages renounce the craving for progeny, wealth, and existence in the other worlds, and live the life of mendicants.

"The craving for progeny leads to the craving for wealth, and the craving for wealth to the craving for existence in the other worlds. Thus there are two cravings—craving for a life of enjoyment here, and craving for a life of greater enjoyment hereafter.

"Therefore should a sage, when he has fully attained the knowledge of the Self, desire to live with that knowledge as his only refuge. When he has fully attained that knowledge, and realized it as his only refuge, he should devote himself exclusively to contemplation of the Self.

"He alone is the true knower of Brahman who directs his mind towards the Self and shuns all other thoughts as distractions.

"How does such a knower of Brahman act and conduct himself? Whatever he may do or howsoever he may conduct himself, he is free from craving, and is forever established in the knowledge of Brahman. Anything that is not the Self perishes.'

"Kahola held his peace." (Brihadaranyaka Upanishad 3:5:1)

Those who know the Self turn from the nonsense and ties of the world and lead the life of a bhikshu, a monk. (Although in modern times either "sannyasi" or "sadhu" is used to designate a monk, in earlier centuries "bhikshu"—one who lives on alms—was also quite common usage.) Those without ties, but with good sense, knowing this, lead that life from the beginning of their quest. Those that learn of the Self after have tied themselves to the world and yet are wise, begin right away moving toward the life of renunciation and loosening those ties, anticipating the day when they will walk away into freedom. It is not unknown for a realized person to continue living "at home" but in total separation from any obligations that it might entail for others, and certainly utterly out of the "game" of home life. Such a one was Yogiraj Sri Shyama Charan Lahiri, as a study of his life, especially in Autobiography of a Yogi, will reveal. However, those who do not live exactly as he did are deluding themselves if they think they are like him.

Those who are Knowers consider that knowledge their only refuge, the only stable thing in their life, and live ever in meditation on the Self.

A lot of ignoramuses and skallawags claim to be enlightened and able to teach others the way of enlightenment, but Yajnvaklya tells us: "He alone is the true knower of Brahman who directs his mind towards the Self and shuns all other thoughts as distractions." And: "Whatever he may do or howsoever he may conduct himself, he is free from craving, and is forever established in the knowledge of Brahman." It is a pity that unlike Kahola they do not hold their peace.

The Sutratman, the "Thread" Self

In the Bhagavad Gita we read: "Nothing higher than Me exists. On Me all this universe is strung like pearls on a thread." (7:7) This concept is Upanishadic:

Uddalaka spoke: 'Yajnavalkya, we lived as students in Madra, in the house of Kapya, whose wife was once possessed by a Gandharva, a celestial singer. We asked the Gandharva who he was. He replied that he was Kabandha, and proceeded to question Kapya thus: "Dost thou know that thread whereon this life, the next life, and all beings are strung together?" Kapya did not know. The Gandharva continued: "Dost thou know that Inner Ruler who controls, from within, this life, the next life, and all beings?" Kapya did not know. The Gandharva then said: "He who knows that thread and that Inner Ruler knows Brahman, knows the worlds, knows the gods, knows the Vedas, knows the creatures, knows the Self—knows all things." I myself know these things that the Gandharva taught. Yajnavalkya, if thou, without knowing that thread and that Inner Ruler, take the cows that belong only to the wisest, accursed shalt thou be.' Yajnavalkya said: 'I know that thread and that Inner Ruler.' Uddalaka said: 'Anybody can say, "I know, I know." Tell us what you know.' (Brihadaranyaka Upanishad 3:7:1)

This questioning contains a lot of facts regarding the Self:

It is the connecting foundation of all beings.

It is the cohesive force that impels all beings through a succession of lives for their evolution.

It is the absolute Ruler and Controller of all lives and beings as their inmost essential nature.

To know the Self is to know all things, both the manifester and the manifested.

Now Yajnavalkya responds.

"Yajnavalkya said: 'The subtle principle of life is that thread whereon this life and the next life and all beings are strung. Hence, when a man dies, they say his limbs are loosed, for while he lives they are held together by that principle of life.' Uddalaka said: 'That is true, Yajnavalkya. Now speak of the Inner Ruler." (Brihadaranyaka Upanishad 3:7:2)

The Self is the principle of Life itself.

Present but separate

"Yajnavalkya said: 'He who dwells on earth, but is separate from the earth, whom the earth does not know, whose body the earth is, and who controls the earth from within—he, the Self, is the Inner Ruler, the Immortal.

"He who dwells in water but is separate from water, whom water does not know, whose body water is, and who controls water from within—he, the Self, is the Inner Ruler, the Immortal.

"He who dwells in fire but is separate from fire, whom fire does not know, whose body fire is, and who controls fire from within—he, the Self, is the Inner Ruler, the Immortal.

""He who dwells in the sky, in the air, in heaven, in the four quarters, in the sun, in the moon, in the stars, in ether, in darkness, in light, but is separate from them, whom none of them knows, whose body they are, and who controls them from within—he, the Self, is the Inner Ruler, the Immortal.

"He who dwells in all beings but is separate from all beings, whom no being knows, whose body all beings are, and who controls all beings from within—he, the Self, is the inner Ruler, the Immortal.

"He who dwells in odor, speech, sight, hearing, and touch, but is separate from them, whom odor, speech, sight, hearing, and touch do not know, whose body is odor, speech, sight, hearing, and touch are, and who controls them all from within—he, the Self, is the Inner Ruler, the Immortal.

"He who dwells in the mind, but is separate from the mind, whom the mind does not know, whose body the mind is, and who controls the mind from within—he, the Self, is the Inner Ruler, the Immortal.

"**He who dwells in the intellect, but is separate from the intellect, whom the intellect does not know,** whose body the intellect is, and who controls the intellect from within—he, the Self, is the Inner Ruler, the Immortal.

"Unseen, but the seer; unheard but the hearer, unthinkable, but the thinker; unknown, but the knower—there is no seer but he, there is no hearer but he, there is no other but he, there is no knower but he. He, the Self, is the Inner Ruler, the Immortal.

"Anything that is not the Self perishes.'

"Uddalaka held his peace." (Brihadaranyaka Upanishad 3:7:3-23)

If we have not figured this out already, nothing can be said that will give us the idea. But we do have the idea, and this is an affirmation intended to confirm us in our understanding.

16. Gargi and the Imperishable

Now we hear from the female sage, Gargi.

"Then arose Gargi, the daughter of Vachaknu, and addressed the sages: 'Revered Brahmins, I shall ask Yajnavalkya two questions. If he is able to answer them, no one among you can ever defeat him. He will be the great expounder of the truth of Brahman.' Yajnavalkya said: 'Ask, O Gargi.'

"Gargi said: 'Yajnavalkya, as the son of a warrior from Kashi or Videha might string his loosened bow and with two deadly arrows in his hand rise to give battle, even so have I risen to fight thee with two questions.' Yajnavalkya said: 'Ask, O Gargi.'

"Gargi said: 'Yajnavalkya, that of which they say that it is above heaven and below the earth, which is between heaven and earth as well, and which was, is, and shall be—tell me, in what is it **woven, warp and woof**?'

"Yajnavalkya said: 'That of which they say, O Gargi, that it is above heaven and below the earth, which is between heaven and earth as well, and which was, is, and shall be—that is woven, warp and woof, in the ether.'" (Brihadaranyaka Upanishad 3:8:1-4)

Ether (Akasha) is the subtlest element, so subtle that it is often indistinguishable from Consciousness. Without it nothing can exist. Yet there is more, so Gargi persists.

"Gargi said: 'Thou hast answered my first question. I bow to thee, O Yajnavalkya. Be ready now to answer my second question.' Yajnavalkya said: 'Ask, O Gargi.'

"Gargi said: 'In whom is that ether woven, warp and woof?'

"Yajnavalkya said: 'The seers, O Gargi, call him Akshara—the changeless Reality. He is neither gross nor fine, neither short nor long, neither hot nor cold, neither light nor dark, neither of the nature of air, nor of the nature of ether. He is without relations. He is without taste or smell, without eyes, ears, speech, mind, vigor, breath, mouth; he is without measure; he is without inside or outside. He enjoys nothing; nothing enjoys him." (Brihadaranyaka Upanishad 3:8:58)

"Akshara" means imperishable, indestructible, and immutable. It is sometimes a synonym for the Chidakasha, the Ether of Consciousness in which the element of ether rests. As Yajnavalkya makes clear, the Imperishable Brahman and the imperishable Self are No Thing, having not attributes or form whatsoever; yet It is infinite and omnipresent. "He enjoys nothing" because there is no second, no separate object for Brahman to be involved with or relate to. And "nothing enjoys him" because nothing can perceive Brahman. "Things" do not really exist. Brahman, on the other hand, is the sole Existence.

"At the command of that Akshara, O Gargi, sun and moon hold their courses. At the command of that Akshara, O Gargi, heaven and earth keep their positions. At the command of that Akshara, O Gargi, moments, hours, days and nights, fortnights and months, seasons and years— all follow their paths. At the command of that Akshara, O Gargi, rivers, issuing from the snowy mountains, flow on, some eastward, some westward, others in other directions.

"He, O Gargi, who in this world, without knowing this Akshara, offers oblations, performs sacrifices, practices austerities, even though for many thousands of years, gains little: his offerings and practices are perishable. He, O Gargi, who departs this life without knowing the Imperishable, is pitiable. But he, O Gargi, who departs this life knowing the Akshara, is wise.

"This Akshara, O Gargi, is unseen but is the seer, is unheard but is the hearer, is unthinkable but is the thinker, is unknown but is the knower. There is no seer but he, there is no hearer but he, there is no thinker but he, there is no knower but he. In Akshara, verily, O Gargi, the ether is woven, warp and woof.'

"Gargi said: 'Revered Brahmins, well may you feel blest if you get off with bowing before him! No one will defeat Yajnavalkya, expounder of the truth of Brahman.' Gargi held her peace." (Brihadaranyaka Upanishad 3:8:9-12)

Is it any wonder that men and women throughout the ages have devoted their entire lives to the pursuit of the knowledge of Brahman? What else is there?

"Yajnavalkya addressed the sages: 'Revered Brahmins, ask me questions if you will—any one of you in the assembly, or all of you. Or if any one of you so desires, I will question him. Or I will question all of you.' But the Brahmins held their peace." (Brihadaranyaka Upanishad 3:9:27) Let us hope they returned home and doubled and tripled their efforts to realize Brahman. And so may we, for that is the purpose of this section.

17. Janaka and Yajnavalkya - 1

We come now to the lengthiest dialogue in any of the Upanishads. Swami Prabhavananda ended his translation of the Upanishad at its conclusion, evidently feeling that anything following it would be of vastly inferior value.

Wealth or knowledge?

"On a certain occasion, Janaka, king of Videha, having seated himself to give audience, saw the sage Yajnavalkya among his visitors and accosted him. Janaka said: 'Yajnavalkya, what brings you here? Do you come for cattle, or for philosophy?' Yajnavalkya said: 'For both, Your Majesty.'" (Brihadaranyaka Upanishad 4:1:1)

The great sages, whether past or present, always have a sense of humor. And they are not interested in how they "look" to others. I have seen both of these principles more than once in Swami Sivananda and other great yogis in India.

Humorous though it be, this verse has a real message: the intelligent yogi is interested in the total picture, both material and spiritual. It is ignorance that postulates an incompatibility between material and spiritual life. It is ignorance that creates the problem, not matter or spirit. After all, matter is a manifestation of spirit. Both Janaka and Yajnavalkya were rich in material possessions and in wisdom.

In America we have had two men that were equally successful in finance and spirituality: J. C. Penney, founder of "Penney's" department store chain and James J. Lynn, whose many-branched multimillion dollar empire could not keep him from becoming one of this country's greatest yogis and the successor of Paramhansa Yogananda as president of Self-Realization Fellowship. In India I met men of fabulous wealth whose whole mind and heart were centered in spirit-consciousness while working tirelessly for the welfare of the people.

As Sri Ramakrishna said: "If you can weigh salt, you can weigh sugar."

Word-Brahman

"[Yajnavalkya said:] 'I wish to hear what your teachers may have taught you.'

"Janaka said: 'Jitwa taught me that the word [vak] is Brahman.'

"Yajnavalkya said: 'As one who in childhood was instructed adequately, first by his mother and then by his father, and after that was initiated into the sacred mysteries by a sage—as such an one should teach, so has Jitwa taught you the truth when he said that the word is Brahman. For what could a person achieve without the word? But did he tell you about the abode and support of this Word-Brahman?'

"Janaka said: 'No, he did not.'

"Yajnavalkya said: 'Then you have been only partly taught.'

"Janaka said: 'Do you, then, teach me, O Yajnavalkya.'

"Yajnavalkya said: 'The organ of speech is its abode, and ether, the primal cause of the universe, is its eternal support. Meditate upon the word as identical with knowledge.'

"Janaka said: 'What is knowledge, Yajnavalkya?'

"Yajnavalkya said: 'The word is knowledge, Your Majesty. For through the word a friend is known, and likewise all knowledge, spiritual or otherwise. Through the word is gained knowledge of this world and of the next. Through the word is obtained knowledge of all creatures. The word, Your Majesty, is the Supreme Brahman.'

"Janaka said: 'I give you a thousand cows with a bull as big as an elephant for teaching me.

"Yajnavalkya said: 'My father was of the opinion that one should not accept any reward from a disciple without fully instructing him.'" (Brihadaranyaka Upanishad 4:1:2)

The power of Word, both conceptualization and verbal expression of concepts, is the distinctive feature of the human being, although many other species on earth use sound for communication. There is great power is speech for many reasons, some intellectual and some esoteric. Yajnavalkya points out that it is not enough to appreciate the power of word, but we must know that which gives word it power, what is its "abode and support." He then tells us that it is the faculty of speech, the innate capacity of the human being for speech, that is the abode of word, for without the faculty of speech there could be no word expressed. Yet that is not the ultimate basis of the word. "Ether, the primal cause of the universe, is its eternal support." Here, again, the Chidakasha is meant. Sound arises out of the element of ether, and the consciousness behind intelligent sound is the Chidakasha, the Self of the nature of Consciousness. So it is this Consciousness that is the origin of the Word-Brahman, the Shabda Brahman, whose primary form is Om. That Word is to be meditated upon as Prajna ("knowledge"), the inmost consciousness.

"My father was of the opinion that one should not accept any reward from a disciple without fully instructing him." This tells us two things: Yajnavalkya possessed a spiritual lineage, a tradition with roots. Also he considered that partial knowledge was of little value.

Breath-Brahman

"[Yajnavalkya said:] 'I wish to know what anyone else may have taught you.'

"Janaka said: 'Udanka taught me that breath [prana] is Brahman. He did not tell me about its abode and support.'

"Yajnavalkya said: 'Prana is its abode and ether [akasha] its support. It should be meditated upon as dear. For life is indeed dear. The primal energy is Brahman." (Brihadaranyaka Upanishad 4:1:3)

When we breathe we live, and when we stop breathing, we die. That is why breath holds such a principal place in the practice of yoga. However, the breath is just the objectified physical manifestation of the inner movement of prāna, the primal life energy within the human being. Prāna is the force of life itself, but it, like the faculty of speech, has the Chidākāsha as its origin and support. The prāna is indeed dear, for it is the coin of life.

Sight-Brahman

Now we have another of the same-word passages:

"[Yajnavalkya said:] 'Tell me what more you have been taught.'

"Janaka said: 'Barku taught me that the eye is Brahman. But he did not teach me its abode and support.'

"Yajnavalkya said: 'Sight is its abode and ether its support. It should be meditated upon as truth. For it is by sight that objects are known. Sight is Brahman. What more have you learned?" (Brihadaranyaka Upanishad 4:1:4)

The word *chakshu* means both the physical eye and the faculty of sight. The eye is meaningless if one lacks the faculty of sight. And that, too, is rooted in the Chidakasha. Thus we see that all our faculties are but rays of the sun that is the Chidakasha.

The next few verses are going to follow this pattern: the teachers of Janaka will have named the material sense organ, and Yajnavalkya will explain that it is the faculty—and ultimately the Chidakasha— that is the attribute/power of Brahman.

Hearing-Brahman

"Janaka said: 'Gardabhivipati taught me that the ear [shrotra] is Brahman.' Yajnavalkya said: 'Hearing [shrotra] is its abode and ether its support. It should be meditated upon as limitless. For sound is carried by space, and space is limitless. Hearing is Brahman." (Brihadaranyaka Upanishad 4:1:5)

There is a yogic aspect to this, since sound in the form of subtle inner hearing is the quintessential element of meditation practice. This faculty is rooted in the ether element which is all-pervading and limitless. Thus through working with sound in meditation we can access the all-pervading and limitless Consciousness that is Brahman.

Mind-Brahman

"Janaka said: 'Satyakama taught me that the mind [manas] is Brahman.' Yajnavalkya said: 'The mind [manas] is its abode and ether its support. It should be meditated upon as happiness. For by the mind alone is happiness experienced. Mind is Brahman." (Brihadaranyaka Upanishad 4:1:6)

Here the lower, sensory mind is being spoken of whose basis is the higher mind, the intellect (buddhi). The important principle is the fact that happiness is only in the intelligent mind.

Heart-Brahman

"Janaka said: 'Vidagdha taught me that the heart [hridaya] is Brahman.' Yajnavalkya said: 'The heart [hridaya] is its abode and ether its support. It should be meditated upon as the resting-place. For all beings find rest in the heart. The heart is Brahman." (Brihadaranyaka Upanishad 4:1:7)

The "heart" is the faculty of consciousness in the human being, and that rests within the greater Consciousness of Brahman.

Further teaching

"Janaka (descending from his throne and humbly addressing the sage) said: 'I bow down to you. Yajnavalkya, please teach me.'

"Yajnavalkya said: 'Your Majesty, as a person wishing to make a long journey furnishes himself with a chariot or a boat, so have you equipped your mind with sacred wisdom. You are honorable and wealthy, and you have studied the Vedas and learned the Upanishads. Whither then shall you go when you leave this body?'

"Janaka said: 'I do not know, revered sir.'

"Yajnavalkya said: 'I will tell you where you will go.'

"Janaka said: 'Tell me, please.'

"Yajnavalkya said: 'Indha is the Self-identified with the physical self. Viraj, the physical world is his wife, the object of his enjoyment. The space within the heart is their place of union in dream, when the Self is identified with the subtle body, or mind. The Self in dreamless sleep is identified with the vital force. Beyond this is the Supreme Self—he that has been described as Not This, Not That. He is incomprehensible, for he cannot be comprehended; he is undecaying, for he never decays; he is unattached, for he does not attach himself; he is unfettered, for nothing can fetter him. He is never hurt. You have attained him who is free from fear, O Janaka, and free from birth and death.'

Janaka said: 'May that fearlessness come to you who teach us fearlessness. I bow down to you. Behold, this empire of Videha, and I myself, are at your service." (Brihadaranyaka Upanishad 4:2:1-4)

In reality, the liberated person does not "go" anywhere, but abides as the Self. Wherefore let us strive to know the Self and transcend all "coming" and "going."

18. Janaka and Yajnavalkya - 2

In this next conversation of Yajnavalkya and Janaka, the first seven verses are a complete unit, so to speak.

The light of human beings

"Once when Yajnavalkya came to the court of King Janaka, the King welcomed him with a question.

"Janaka said: 'Yajnavalkya, what serves as the light for man?'

"Yajnavalkya said: 'The light of the sun, Your Majesty; for by the light of the sun man sits, goes out, does his work, and returns home.'

"Janaka said: 'True indeed, Yajnavalkya.'

"But when the sun has set, what serves then as his light?' Yajnavalkya said: 'The moon is then his light.'

"Janaka said: 'When the sun has set, O Yajnavalkya, and the moon has set, what serves then as his light?' Yajnavalkya said: 'The fire is then his light.'

"Janaka said: 'When the sun has set, O Yajnavalkya, and the moon has set, and the fire has gone out, what serves then as his light?' Yajnavalkya said: 'Sound is then his light; for with sound alone as his light, man sits, goes out, does his work, and returns home. Even though he cannot see his own hand, yet when he hears a sound he moves towards it.' Janaka said: 'True indeed, O Yajnavalkya.'

"When the sun has set, and the moon has set, and the fire has gone out, and no sound is heard, what serves then as his light?' Yajnavalkya said: 'The Self indeed is his light; for by the light of the Self man sits, moves about, does his work, and when his work is done, rests.'

"Janaka said: 'Who is that Self?' Yajnavalkya said: 'The self-luminous being who dwells within the lotus of the heart, surrounded by the senses and sense organs, and who is the light of the intellect, is that Self. Becoming identified with the intellect, he moves to and fro, through birth and death, between this world and the next. Becoming identified with the intellect, the Self appears to be thinking, appears to be moving. While the mind is dreaming, the Self also appears to be dreaming, and to be beyond the next world as well as this." (Brihadaranyaka Upanishad 4:3:1-7)

This is all quite clear, but it is good note that it is identity with the intellect, the intelligence principle in our makeup that both enables and causes us to move between this world and another, for we think that we are engaging in the functions of the intellect, not realizing that it is but an instrument formed of the three gunas and is not us at all. So we say: "I slept; I woke up; I was dreaming," and so forth. Another important point is implied here. Notice that Yajnavalkya does not speak of identifying with the body, senses, emotions, etc. This is because the Upanishad is intended for the instruction of those who have evolved beyond that type of identity, whose center of awareness in the intellect, in the highest level of their being. Is this "elitist"? Absolutely! As Jesus said, "Give not that which is holy unto the dogs, neither cast ye your pearls before swine, lest they trample them under their feet, and turn again and rend you." (Matthew 7:6)

A third point is that the Self is not "beyond the next world as well as this." That is, It is not subject to coming and going, is neither within nor without any world. It transcends those kinds of designation.

The real "root of all evil"

"When man, the individual soul, is born, and assumes relationship with the body and sense organs, he becomes associated with the evils of the world. When at death he gives up the body, he leaves all evils behind." (Brihadaranyaka Upanishad 4:3:8)

Yajnavalkya does not say that false identity is the problem, rather that mere birth in a body creates unavoidable association with all the troubles and risks that every embodied being endures. We see this in the life of great avatars and masters: their lives were filled with troubles, and many of them died quite painfully. Why anyone would pray to them to remove troubles and disease is beyond comprehension. Why do the good suffer? *Because they are in a body*. This is a basic fact of life. That is why spiritually intelligent people understand that the real sacrifice made by masters of all ages was their incarnation—and everything went on from there. To endure the limitations and dangers of finite existence is a great, even a terrible, sacrifice they undergo at every moment. Being masters inwardly as well as outwardly, the sacrifice never overwhelms them, and they realized the implications of birth before they were even conceived. Since they are always in charge, they do not experience the mental anguish we do, but they go through the entire range of earthly miseries just like anyone else. With them everything is voluntary, for they have no karma to drag them into birth and through all that happens afterward. They walk through life, while we are pushed and pulled along. But for both

The human status

"There are two states for man—the state in this world, and the state in the next; there is also a third state, the state intermediate between these two, which can be likened to dream. While in the intermediate state, a man experiences both the other states, that in this world and that in the next; and the manner thereof is as follows: When he dies, he lives only in the subtle body, on which are left the impressions of his past deeds, and of these impressions he is aware, illumined as they are by the pure light of the Self. Thus it is that in the intermediate state he experiences the first state, or that of life in the world. Again, while in the intermediate state, he foresees both the evils and the blessings that will yet come to him, as these are determined by his conduct, good and bad, upon the earth, and by the character in which this conduct has resulted. Thus it is that in the intermediate state he experiences the second state, or that of life in the world to come." (Brihadaranyaka Upanishad 4:3:9)

We are either embodied in this world, or disembodied and living in the astral realm. But between the two is the dream state in which we experience both material and astral conditions. For example, we fall off a cliff and experience falling just as we would in the waking state. But when we hit the ground we do not die—it does not even hurt. That is how it is in the astral world. And that is why little children are so fearless and will go right into a life-threatening situation without hesitation—in the astral world it is not threatening at all. It may even be fun. One of Yogananda's monastic disciples once explained to a group of people that they should not be impatient with the intense reactions of children to pain and frustration. For in the astral world they get anything they want just by wanting, and they can go anywhere and do anything without pain. So when the situation is different in this world they are terrified and angry. They are also miserable in realizing that they are now in a world in which uncertainty is the only certainty. A friend of mine was once found by her father sitting in the midst of the floor crying bitterly. (She was two years old at the time.) When he asked her what was wrong, she complained that she could not fly. Luckily, he was a metaphysician, so he explained to her that although she could fly in the world she had come from, in this world people could not fly. "Then it's a dumb world!" she said. "I agree. So do your best not to come back," was his counsel.

When we leave our bodies we gain a great deal of understanding. We comprehend the life that has just ended and realize its deeper meanings. We analyze it, actually, and learn from it. Sometimes we have helpers in doing this. So even though we underwent things on earth with complete non-comprehension, now then see clearly their roots and their purpose. Those who do not know this often ask what good it is for infants and children to reap negative karmas and die young, for they cannot understand. Indeed, in this world they cannot understand, but the moment they are freed from the body they can and do understand. Also, it was their karma to suffer uncomprehendingly. It all works out to perfection, however it seems at the present moment. A religion that does not teach these facts to its adherents is unworthy of anyone's attention. And a religion that tells people that God wills it all—is doing it to them because He has "a plan"—is a barefaced liar that deserves only contempt. But of course, many people deserve a contemptible religion. That, too, is karma.

Dream

"In the intermediate state, there are no real chariots, nor horses, nor roads; but by the light of the Self he creates chariots and horses and roads. There are no real blessings, nor joys, nor pleasures; but he creates blessings and joys and pleasures. There are no real ponds, nor lakes, nor rivers; but he creates ponds and lakes and rivers. He is the creator of all these out of the impressions left by his past deeds." (Brihadaranyaka Upanishad 4:3:10)

Just see what an incredible power of creative intelligence we all have! Also, even dreams are a matter of karma. Paramhansa Yogananda said that we can work out karma in the dream state.

"Regarding the different states of consciousness, it is written: While one is in the state of dream, the golden, self-luminous being, the Self within, makes the body to sleep, though he himself remains forever awake and watches by his own light the impressions of deeds that have been left upon the mind. Thereafter, associating himself again with the consciousness of the organs of sense, the Self causes the body to awake." (Brihadaranyaka Upanishad 4:3:11)

In all states we are the self-luminous, untouched Witness. And all states are under our control.

"While one is in the state of dream, the golden, self-luminous being, the Self within, the Immortal One, keeps alive the house of flesh with the help of the vital force, but at the same time walks out of this house. The Eternal goes wherever he desires." (Brihadaranyaka Upanishad 4:3:12)

Here is clear teaching that in dream we sometimes leave the body and travel in either this world or the next. In that state:

"The self-luminous being assumes manifold forms, high and low, in the world of dreams. He seems to be enjoying the pleasure of love, or to be laughing with friends, or to be looking at terrifying spectacles." (Brihadaranyaka Upanishad 4:3:13)

This experience is common to all, from the least intelligent to the genius. Yet: "Everyone is aware of the experiences; no one sees the Experiencer." (Brihadaranyaka Upanishad 4:3:14) That is the riddle we must all solve.

"Some say that dreaming is but another form of waking, for what a man experiences while awake he experiences again in his dreams. Be that as it may, the Self, in dreams, shines by his own light.' Janaka said: 'Revered sir, I offer you a thousand cattle. Instruct me further for the sake of my liberation." (Brihadaranyaka Upanishad 4:3:15)

Free while bound

Even a tethered animal can move about as much as it likes within the bounds of the tether. It is the same with us. So we are never absolutely bound, but always experience a great deal of freedom, even if it is mostly psychological. A lot of what follows is obvious and even common knowledge, so no comment is needed.

"Yajnavalkya said: 'The Self, having in dreams tasted enjoyment, gone hither and thither, experienced both good and evil, attains to the state of dreamless sleep; then again he comes back to dreams. 'Whatever he may experience in dreams does not affect him, for the true nature of the Self remains forever unaffected.'

"Janaka said: 'So it is indeed, Yajnavalkya. I offer you another thousand cattle, revered sir. Speak on for the sake of my liberation.'

"Yajnavalkya said: 'The Self, having in dreams tasted enjoyment, gone hither and thither, experienced good and evil hastens back to the state of waking from which he started. Whatever he may experience in dreams does not affect him, for the true nature of the Self remains forever unaffected.'

"Janaka said: 'So it is indeed, Yajnavalkya. Another thousand cattle shall be yours, revered sir. Speak on for the sake of my liberation.'

"Yajnavalkya said: 'The Self, having in wakefulness enjoyed the pleasures of sense, gone hither and thither, experienced good and evil, hastens back again to his dreams.'

"As a large fish moves from one bank of a river to the other, so does the Self move between dreaming and waking.'

"As a hawk or a falcon flying in the sky becomes tired, and stretching its wings comes back to its nest, so does the Self hasten to that state where, deep in sleep, he desires no more desires, and dreams no more dreams." (Brihadaranyaka Upanishad 4:3:16-19)

The transcendent Self

There now follows one of the most thrilling and exalted passage of the Upanishads.

"Indeed, the Self, in his true nature, is free from craving, free from evil, free from fear. As a man in the embrace of his loving wife knows nothing that is without, nothing that is within, so man in union with the Self knows nothing that is without, nothing that is within, for in that state all desires are satisfied. The Self is his only desire; he is free from craving, he goes beyond sorrow.'

"Then father is no father, mother is no mother; worlds disappear, gods disappear, scriptures disappear; the thief is no more, the murderer is no more, castes are no more; no more is there monk or hermit. The Self is then untouched either by good or by evil, and the sorrows of the heart are turned into joy.'

"He does not see, nor smell, nor taste, nor speak, nor hear, nor think, nor touch, nor know; for there is nothing separate from him, there is no second. Yet he can see, for sight and he are one; yet he can smell, for smelling and he are one; yet he can taste, for taste and he are one; yet he can speak, for speech and he are one; yet he can hear, for hearing and he are one; yet he can think, for thinking and he are one; yet he can touch, for touching and he are one; yet he can know, for knowing and he are one. Eternal is the light of consciousness; immortal is the Self.'

"When there is another, then one sees another, smells another, tastes another, speaks to another, hears another, thinks of another, touches and knows another.'

"Pure like crystal water is that Self, the only seer, the One without a second. He is the kingdom of Brahman—man's highest goal, supreme treasure, greatest bliss. Creatures who live within the bounds of ignorance experience but a small portion of his infinite being." (Brihadaranyaka Upanishad 4:3:21-32)

For some reason Swami Prabhavananda omitted the next verse, perhaps because it had already appeared in the Taittiriya Upanishad in his translation. Here is Swami Madhavananda's translation:

"He who is perfect of physique and prosperous among men, the ruler of others, and most lavishly supplied with all human enjoyments, represents greatest joy among men. This human joy multiplied a hundred times makes one unit of joy for the manes who have won that world of theirs. The joy of these manes who have won that world multiplied a hundred times makes one unit joy in the world of the celestial minstrels. This joy in the world of the celestial minstrels multiplied a hundred times makes one unit of joy for the gods by action—those who have attained their godhead by their actions. This joy of the gods by action multiplied a hundred times makes one unit of joy for the gods by birth, as also of one who is versed in the Vedas, sinless and free from desire. This joy of the gods by birth multiplied a hundred times makes one unit of joy in the world of Prajapati (Viraj), as well as one who is versed in the Vedas, sinless and free from desire. This joy in the world of Prajapati multiplied a hundred times makes one unit of joy in the world of Brahman (Hiranyagarbha), as well as of one who is versed in the Vedas, sinless and free from desire. This indeed is the supreme bliss. This is the state of Brahman, O Emperor,' said Yajnavalkya." (Brihadaranyaka Upanishad 4:3:33)

KNOW THE SELF!

19. The Process of Reincarnation

The following verses alone in all the Upanishads describe to some degree the process of reincarnation.

Dreaming and waking

"Janaka said: 'You shall have still another thousand cattle. Speak on, revered sir, for the sake of my liberation.'

"Yajnavalkya said: 'The Self, having in dreams enjoyed the pleasures of sense, gone hither and thither, experienced good and evil, hastens back to the state of waking from which he started.'

"As a man passes from dream to wakefulness, so does he pass at death from this life to the next. When a man is about to die, the subtle body, mounted by the intelligent Self, groans—as a heavily laden cart groans under its burden.'

"When his body becomes thin through old age or disease, the dying man separates himself from his limbs, even as a mango or a fig or a banyan fruit separates itself from its stalk, and by the same way that he came he hastens to his new abode, and there assumes another body, in which to begin a new life." (Brihadaranyaka Upanishad 4:3:33-36)

Passing from life to life is only a shifting in a dream. When the stored-up life force (a form of karma) for a life is running out, just as the charge in a battery is expended and fails, so do the physical and grosser pranic bodies. And, just as the ripe fruit falls from the tree, so the subtle body separates itself from the material body and begins its process toward another earthly birth in a new body. In between births, the individual spends time in the astral regions, sometimes just wandering and frittering his time away, and sometimes in learning and evolving so his next life will be markedly better—and wiser—than the previous one. This time spent in this intermediate state can be anything from a matter of hours to centuries and even thousands of years. This is precisely determined by karma.

(By the way, it is nonsense to say that unevolved people reincarnate quickly and evolved people only come back in thousands of years. Both ends of the spectrum are similar: Very unevolved beings reincarnate very fast, and so do those that are highly evolved, for they are getting ready to graduate and are "cramming" for the final test.

Leaving the body

"When his body grows weak and he becomes apparently unconscious, the dying man gathers his senses about him and completely withdrawing their powers descends into his heart. No more does he see form or color without.

"He neither sees, nor smells, nor tastes. He does not speak, he does not hear. He does not think, he does not know. For all the organs, detaching themselves from his physical body, unite with his subtle body. Then the point of his heart, where the nerves join, is lighted by the light of the Self, and by that light he departs either through the eye, or through the gate of the skull, or through some other aperture of the body. When he thus departs, life departs; and when life departs, all the functions of the vital principle depart. The Self remains conscious, and, conscious, the dying man goes to his abode. The deeds of this life, and the impressions they leave behind, follow him." (Brihadaranyaka Upanishad 4:4:1-2)

He becomes apparently unconscious. This is important. The person may cease to perceive anything, but that is not being unconscious. We are never unconscious at any time, but we mistakenly call total absence of sensory perception unconsciousness. There is a vital point I want to mention here. The very last sense to fail is the sense of hearing. Sometimes it never fails. A lot of people give up and die because they hear the doctor say there is no hope or that they will soon be dead. So if you are around a dying, "unconscious" person please remember this. You can speak to them and help them either revive or go to higher worlds. That is why both Hindus and Buddhists read scriptures to the dying or recite mantras or sing mantras. In Pure Land Buddhism people sit by the dying and sing the mantra of Amida Buddha, continuing to do so for several hours after the person appears to be dead, knowing that sometimes they may have trouble getting out of the body or may be disoriented when they do.

Yogananda spoke of this to his students, one of whom was the famous opera singer Amelita Galli-Curci. So when her brother was dying she talked to him and called him back to life. When he became "conscious" he told her that he had heard doctor saying he would soon be dead, so he accepted it and began drifting away. Then he heard her voice calling to him from far off, and telling him to return. So he did! At one point he even saw Yogananda, about whom he knew virtually nothing but he recognized Yogananda when his sister showed a picture to him.

It is sometimes possible to revive a person by intoning Om in their right ear. Yogananda also recommended this.

Then the point of his heart, where the nerves join, is lighted by the light of the Self, and by that light he departs either through the eye, or through the gate of the skull, or through some other aperture of the body. This is the Light that so many people tell about seeing who have returned from near-death. There are many gates by which a person may leave the body, and they are all determined by the level of consciousness (bhava) in which he has habitually lived during his lifetime. (This is one of the major teachings of the Bhagavad Gita.) To leave through a center in the head is the best, and will determine what highly evolved world he will enter. Those who leave through the center at the top of the head, the Brahmarandhra, will not return to rebirth. Those who leave at lower centers in the body or spine will go to lesser worlds, and some of the lowest centers are literally gates to negative worlds we call "hells." Some even lead to rebirth in animal forms, though this is rare.

The Self remains conscious, and, conscious, the dying man goes to his abode. The deeds of this life, and the impressions they leave behind, follow him. Some of low evolution simply go to sleep and only wake a little before reincarnating, and some do not even awaken until they are born. But the people to which this Upanishad is addressed will certainly depart in full consciousness and will review their life and be aware of the psychic changes their previous actions have produced. And they will be aware of exactly why and how they eventually find themselves in an astral or causal realm that corresponds to those karmas and samskaras. It is all a matter of learning.

Astral birth

"As a leech, having reached the end of a blade of grass, takes hold of another blade and draws itself to it, so the Self, having left this body behind it unconscious, takes hold of another body and draws himself to it." (Brihadaranyaka Upanishad 4:4:3) Birth in the astral world is a conscious act. Only on earth or in the negative astral worlds do we mistakenly think that we are helpless and that we are not in charge. That is why the simile of a leech is used, and why the Sanskrit text literally says that we *make* another body for ourselves. And that happens in earthly rebirth, too. We choose where to whom we will be born, and we enter the womb of our chosen mother and, taking the material provided by both parents, make our next body-habitation in accordance with our karma and samskara—this is how powerful and intelligent we all are! Yogananda said in his Gita commentary that the individual consciously guides the growth of his body in the womb. (That was the first sentence of Yogananda's teaching that I read, sitting in a public library in the fall of 1960.)

"As a goldsmith, taking an old gold ornament, molds it into another, newer and more beautiful, so the Self, having given up the body and left it unconscious, takes on a newer and better form, either that of the fathers, or that of the celestial singers, or that of the gods, or that of other beings, heavenly or earthly." (Brihadaranyaka Upanishad 4:4:4)

In the higher worlds, the individual creates a body that is appropriate to the world in which he shall be living until he takes rebirth—also voluntarily. This experience will train him for even more efficiently making his body when he returns to earth.

Sometimes in the subtle worlds an individual takes on a body that is higher than his present evolutionary status and practices living on that level. This prepares him for a higher level on earth, as well. This is mentioned as taking place even for animals in the forty-third chapter of Yogananda's autobiography, "The Resurrection of Sri Yutkeshwar."

Misidentification

"The Self is verily Brahman. Through ignorance it identifies itself with what is alien to it, and appears to consist of intellect, understanding, life, sight, hearing, earth, water, air, ether, fire, desire and the absence of desire, anger and the absence of anger, righteousness and the absence of righteousness. It appears to be all things—now one, now another.

"As a man acts, so does he become. A man of good deeds becomes good, a man of evil deeds becomes evil. A man becomes pure through pure deeds, impure through impure deeds.

"**As a man's desire is, so is his destiny**. For as his desire is, so is his will; as his will is, so is his deed; and as his deed is, so is his reward, whether good or bad." (Brihadaranyaka Upanishad 4:4:5)

Lest in all this we forget that it is really the dream-life of the individual spirit, Yajnavalkya reminds Janaka of this. For in all these changes, the Self is unchanging, in all these births and deaths the Self remains birthless and deathless. The fact that we so easily forget this truth is evidence of how good we are at fooling ourselves! We are always masters of the situation.

Desire

"A man acts according to the desires to which he clings. After death he goes to the next world bearing in his mind the subtle impressions of his deeds; and after reaping there the harvest of his deeds, he returns again to this world of action. Thus he who has desires continues subject to rebirth.

"But he in whom desire is stilled suffers no rebirth. After death, having attained to the highest, desiring only the Self, he goes to no other world. Realizing Brahman, he becomes Brahman."

(Brihadaranyaka Upanishad 4:4:6)

It is ignorance that causes our mistaken identification, but the power behind rebirth is desire. Once we cut off desire, rebirth is finished. Desireless, we transcend all worlds and know ourselves as Eternal Brahman.

"When all the desires which once entered into his heart have been driven out by divine knowledge, the mortal, attaining to Brahman, becomes immortal.

""As the slough of a snake lies cast off on an anthill, so lies the body of a man at death; while he, freed from the body, becomes one with the immortal spirit, Brahman, the Light Eternal.'

"Janaka said: 'Sir, again I give You a thousand cows. Speak on, that I may be liberated.'" (Brihadaranyaka Upanishad 4:4:7)

All glory to those that have freed themselves by knowing their Self!

The Path of Liberation

"Yajnavalkya said: 'The path of liberation is subtle, and hard, and long. I myself am walking in it; nay, I have reached the end. By this path alone the wise, the knowers of Brahman, attain him while living, and achieve final liberation at death." (Brihadaranyaka Upanishad 4:4:8)

Yajnavalkya was obviously no pop-yogi with a yoga studio filled with yoga babes in tank tops and leotards confident that yoga would firm up their buttocks, eliminate cellulite, and give them the kind of body they want (or that others will want). Nor was he a traveling sideshow yogi perpetually on tour convincing people that yoga (his kind, at least) was cheap, easy, fun, and sure to make life a breeze. I know this because of the following statements he has made:

The path of liberation is subtle. Without refinement of mind and the interior faculties of perception, yoga is not going on. Yoga is itself the purification of the mind and heart in order to allow the highest powers of the individual to come into play and transform his life and consciousness. Because this is so, Patanjali puts ten necessary elements for yoga at the top of his list of the eight limbs of yoga:

1. Ahimsa: non-violence, non-injury, harmlessness;
2. Satya: truthfulness, honesty;
3. Asteya: non-stealing, honesty, non-misappropriativeness;
4. Brahmacharya: sexual continence in thought, word and deed as well as control of all the senses;
5. Aparigraha: non-possessiveness, non-greed, non-selfishness, non-acquisitiveness;
6. Shaucha: purity, cleanliness;
7. Santosha: contentment, peacefulness;
8. Tapas: austerity, practical (i.e., result-producing) spiritual discipline;
9. Swadhyaya: introspective self-study, spiritual study;
10. Ishwarapranidhana: offering of one's life or ego to God.

This is a total overhaul of external and internal life—AND IT IS ONLY THE BEGINNING OF YOGA.

The path of liberation is hard. Yes, indeed. When confronted with Patanjali's list there will be a lot of indignation, whining and general complaint. Why? *Because the path of liberation is hard!* Such reaction is proof of that. Only the hardy even really begin the journey, and only the toughest and strongest will end it successfully. This is not a path for the weak and whimsical, and it is definitely not a mere body-splash, a hobby, or a free-time diversion. It is the attainment of Brahman, for God's sake (literally).

The path of liberation is long. It takes lifetimes—many if we dawdle, and not so many if we knuckle down and go for it. And believe me, those pathetic souls that boast of how they are "taking the jet-plane route to God" while looking and living more like a jet crash, do not have a clue. Yes, it is possible to realize God in one birth—*the last birth*. Everybody does. So we need to get busy. There can be no periods of coasting along, deluding ourselves that our liberation is assured and just around the next corner. (Real spiritual life goes in a straight line—there no bends or curves.) Buddha meditated and engaged in intense discipline right up to the moment of his leaving the body, even though he had attained enlightenment decades before. And so did Swami Sivananda. All real yogis do the same.

By this path alone…is Brahman attained. And that attainment is not some swell surprise after death. It takes place right here in this world which is no longer an obstacle to enlightenment. By changing himself the yogi changes the effect the world has on him. What hindered him before now helps him. The once-closed door is now open to him. Death is the final going through that door. For him there will be no return.

No more worlds

"Other worlds there are, joyless, enveloped in darkness. To these worlds, after death, go those who are unwise, who know not the Self." (Brihadaranyaka Upanishad 4:4:10, 11)

Any relative "world" is fundamentally joyless and enveloped in darkness—so the truly wise understand. No world is fit to live in, for they are all realms of death and constant change. There is no peace possible for those who live therein. But those who know the Self have ended that compulsion, for:

"When a man has realized the Self, the pure, the immortal, the blissful, what craving can be left in him that he should take to himself another body, full of suffering, to satisfy it?" (Brihadaranyaka Upanishad 4:4:12)

Desire being the root of rebirth, when it is eliminated rebirth vanishes along with it.

In the body

"He that has once known the glory of the Self within the ephemeral body—that stumbling-block to enlightenment—knows that the Self is one with Brahman, lord and creator of all.'

"Brahman may be realized while yet one dwells in the ephemeral body. To fail to realize him is to live in ignorance, and therefore to be subject to birth and death. The knowers of Brahman are immortal; others, knowing him not, continue in the bonds of grief." (Brihadaranyaka Upanishad 4:4:13-14) The suffering may be very subtle, but it will be there, nonetheless.

Fearless in knowing

"He who with spiritual eye directly perceives the self-effulgent Being, the lord of all that was, is, and shall be—he indeed is without fear, and causes fear in none." (Brihadaranyaka Upanishad 4:4:15)

Even more, he removes fear from others. This is why we experience such great peace and ease in the presence of enlightened beings. Not only have I experienced this many times, I have seen people walk into the presence of a great master and immediately begin shedding tears of relief. In a moment their anxieties and fears were removed.

"He who knows Brahman to be the life of life, the eye of the eye, the ear of the ear, the mind of the mind—he indeed comprehends fully the cause of all causes. By the purified mind alone is Brahman perceived." (Brihadaranyaka Upanishad 4:4:18)

There are no mysteries or puzzles for the knower of Brahman. All is known to him who knows The All.

"In Brahman there is no diversity. He who sees diversity goes from death to death."

(Brihadaranyaka Upanishad 4:4:19)

All our lives are but deaths. When we really enter into the Life that is Brahman then birth and death are finished for us.

"Brahman can be apprehended only as knowledge itself—knowledge that is one with reality, inseparable from it. For he is beyond all proof, beyond all instruments of thought. The eternal Brahman is pure, unborn, subtler than the subtlest, greater than the greatest." (Brihadaranyaka Upanishad 4:4:20)

"Let therefore the wise aspirant, knowing Brahman to be the supreme goal, so shape his life and his conduct that he may attain to him. Let him not seek to know him by arguments, for arguments are idle and vain." (Brihadaranyaka Upanishad 4:4:21)

We need only to reshape our life and go directly to God, not bothering with critics. Just smile, wave, and go on to the Goal.

Know you the journey that I take? Know you the voyage that I make? The joy of it one's heart could break.

No jot of time have I to spare, nor will to loiter anywhere, so eager am I to be there.

For that the way is hard and long, for that gray fears upon it throng, I set my journey to a song,

And it grows wondrous happy so.

Singing I hurry on for oh!

It is to God, to God, I go.

Sister M. Madeleva, C.S.C.

Some Final Words

Since there are three short parts remaining to be considered, I am putting them in this one closing essay.

The Great Unborn

"Verily is Brahman the great unborn that dwells within the lotus of the heart, surrounded by the senses. He is the intellect of the intellect, protector of all, king of all, lord of all. Good works do not make him more, nor do evil works make him less. Lord, king, protector of all, he transcends the three worlds.

"Devotees seek to know him by study, by sacrifice, by continence, by austerity, by detachment. To know him is to become a seer. Desiring to know him, and him alone, monks renounce the world. Realizing the glory of the Self, the sages of old craved not sons nor daughters. "What have we to do with sons and daughters," they asked, "we who have known the Self, we who have achieved the supreme goal of existence?" No longer desiring progeny, nor wealth, nor life in other worlds, they entered upon the path of complete renunciation.

"Craving for progeny leads to craving for wealth, and craving for wealth leads to craving for life in other worlds. Two cravings there are: the craving for a life of pleasure in this world, and the craving for a life of greater pleasure in other worlds.

"The Self is to be described as Not This, Not That. It is incomprehensible, for it cannot be comprehended; undecaying, for it never decays; unattached, for it never attaches itself; unfettered, for it is never bound. He who knows the Self is unaffected, whether by good or by evil. Never do such thoughts come to him as "I have done an evil thing" or "I have done a good thing." Both good and evil he has transcended, and he is therefore troubled no more by what he may or may not have done." (Brihadaranyaka Upanishad 4:4:22)

Verily is Brahman the great unborn that dwells within the lotus of the heart, surrounded by the senses. The ultimate Self of all is Brahman that dwells in each sentient being. It can be said of each of them what Saint Paul said about Jesus: "In him dwelleth all the fullness of the Godhead bodily." (Colossians 2:9) The difference between Jesus (and any Master) and other sentient beings is that he knew the Indweller and they do not. The Self is surrounded by the senses like someone in a theater that has a 360-degree screen, or like someone seated surrounded by video monitors. All of us really are "in the picture," and that is most of our problem.

He is the intellect of the intellect. Every faculty, every quality we possess, is derived from the Self and has its primal archetype in Brahman. This is because everything exists within Brahman as an eternal potential.

Protector of all, king of all, lord of all. This extremely important. The Upanishads continually remind us that Brahman is transcendent and beyond all qualities or conception. Yet here we see that Brahman has an intimate relation with all creation, is in contact with all things, and controls all things. Brahman is also Ishvara, the Lord. So it is an error to try to push Brahman completely out of the picture and exile It to a void that is antithetical to all we presently know or are. Brahman is indeed both This and That. In a short while we will be examining a verse that sums this up quite well.

Good works do not make him more, nor do evil works make him less. Brahman never acts, as both the Upanishads and the Gita insist. So what does this mean? It means that the actions of sentient beings in no way change the Self, nor do they increase or decrease the presence of the Self. However, good actions do help us to perceive the Self as present, and evil actions dim our mental vision and cause us to lose awareness of the Self. Because of that we may think that the Self is affected and drawn closer or pushed away, but we will be wrong. Reality is untouched and unaffected by our delusions and illusions.

The rest of the verse is quite clear, only needing a careful and reflective reading.

The Brahman-knower

"The eternal glory of the knower of Brahman, beginningless and endless, revealed by divine knowledge, is neither increased nor decreased by deeds. Let a man therefore seek to obtain it, since having obtained it he can never be touched by evil. Self-controlled is he who knows the Self, tranquil, poised, free from desire. Absorbed in meditating upon it, he sees it within his own soul, and he sees all beings in it. Evil touches him not, troubles him not, for in the fire of his divine knowledge all evil is burnt away. Freed from evil, freed from desire, freed from doubt, he becomes a knower of Brahman. This, O King, is the truth of Brahman. Do thou attain to it!'

"Janaka said: 'Most revered sir, I offer you the empire of Videha—and myself with it—to be your servant." (Brihadaranyaka Upanishad 4:4:23)

Our gratitude for this wisdom should be as boundless and all-encompassing as was Janaka's. Who can calculate the lives we have passed, struggling to comprehend the truth of things, before at last these great truths have come into the sphere of our life and become known to us? May we now hasten to the realization of Yajnavalkya's final summation:

"Yajnavalkya said: 'The Self, the great unborn, the undecaying, the undying, the immortal, the fearless, is, in very truth, Brahman. He who knows Brahman is without fear. He who knows Brahman becomes Brahman!" (Brihadaranyaka Upanishad 4:4:25)

That and This

The simultaneous immanent and transcendent nature of Brahman (and the Self) is not easy to grasp. But the first half of the following verse is very helpful.

"That is the Full, this is the Full. The Full has come out of the Full. If we take the Full from the Full Only the Full remains.

"Om is the ether-Brahman—the eternal ether. It is the Veda known by the knowers of Brahman. For through it one knows what is to be known." (Brihadaranyaka Upanishad 5:1:1)

The word translated "full" is purna, which means both "full" and "complete." In this verse it means the totality of being: Brahman. So it tells us that the Transcendent (Nirguna Brahman) is the total Reality; but so is the Immanent (Saguna Brahman). The Unmanifest is all that is—and so is the Manifest. The Immanent is an emanation from the Transcendent. If we confine our awareness to the Immanent we will find it to be the Totality of Being. If we turn to the Transcendent and intellectually negate the Immanent, we will perceive that the Transcendent is all. How is this? *Because they are one and the same*. Further, Brahman cannot be labeled or described, so even the words immanent and transcendent cannot be applied to It.

The second verse is extremely significant, telling us that Om is Brahman vibrating eternally in the Ether. That for those who know Brahman, Om is the real Veda, for it reveals all that is to be known: Brahman Itself.

Da! Da! Da!

"Gods, men, and asuras—all three descendants of Prajapati—lived with him for a time as students.

"Then the gods said: 'Teach us, sir!' In reply Prajapati uttered one syllable: 'Da.' Then he said: 'Have you understood?' They answered, 'Yes, we have understood. You said to us, "Damayata—Be self-controlled." 'Yes,' agreed Prajapati, 'you have understood.'

"Then the men said: 'Teach us, sir.' Prajapati uttered the same syllable: 'Da.' Then he said: 'Have you understood?' They answered, 'Yes, we have understood. You said to us, "Datta—Be charitable." 'Yes,' agreed Prajapati, 'you have understood.'

"Then the asuras said: 'Teach us, sir.' Prajapati uttered the same syllable: 'Da.' Then he said: 'Have you understood?' They said, 'Yes, we have understood. You told us "Dayawan—Be compassionate." 'Yes,' agreed Prajapati, 'you have understood.'

"The storm cloud thunders: 'Da! Da! Da!'—'Be self-controlled! Be charitable! Be compassionate!'" (Brihadaranyaka Upanishad 5:2:1-3)

Gods, men, and asuras make up our present human nature. The gods are the parts of us that are superior to the normal human condition. They have arisen as we have begun to evolve to the point where we can take the next step up on the evolutionary ladder. Men are our human traits, and the asuras are the animal traits that we have brought along with us in our evolutionary journey. Consequently the advice to be self-controlled, charitable, and compassionate applies to us. And its following will ensure our continued evolution.

End of Commentary
OM TAT SAT

LIST OF ABBREVIATIONS USED

01. IsU   Ishāvāshya Upanishad
02. KeU   Kena Upanishad
03. KaU   KaTha Upanishad
04. PrU   Prashna Upanishad
05. MuU   Mundaka Upanishad
06. MaU   Māndukya Upanishad
07. TaU   Taittiriya Upanishad
08. AiU   Aitareya Upanishad
09. ShU   Shvetāshvatara Upanishad
10. ChU   Chāndogya Upanishad
11. BrU   Brihadāranyaka Upanishad
12. RV   Rigveda
13. YV   Yajurveda
14. SV   Sāmaveda
15. BS   Brahma Sutra
16. BG   Bhagavad-Gita
17. MB   Mahābhārata
18. BP   Bhāgavata Purāna

ACKNOWLEDGMENTS
References used:

(1) Shri RamaKrishna MaTha Publications on Upanishads by Swamis: Sharvananda, Nikhilananda, Nirmalananda, Madhavananda, Svahananda and Prabhavananda.

Websites:

(2) www.ishwar.com and http://sanatan.intnet.mu/

www.gita-society.com/9Upanishads.html

Free download Upanishads with commentaries:

www.gita-society.com/108Upanishads.pdf

Made in the USA
Monee, IL
06 November 2024

69209579R00059